EARLY CHILDHOOD EDUCATION SERIES

Leslie R. Williams, Editor
Millie Almy, Senior Advisor

ADVISORY BOARD: Barbara T. Bowman, Harriet K. Cuffaro, Stephanie Feeney, Doris Pronin Fromberg, Celia Genishi, Dominic F. Gullo, Alice Sterling Honig, Elizabeth Jones, Gwen Morgan, David Weikart

(Continued)

A CHILD'S PLAY LIFE

An Ethnographic Study

DIANA KELLY-BYRNE

Teachers College, Columbia University
New York and London

Published by Teachers College Press, 1234 Amsterdam Avenue,
New York, NY 10027

Library of Congress Cataloging-in-Publication Data

Kelly-Byrne, Diana.
  A child's play life: an ethnographic study/Diana Kelly-Byrne.
      p. cm.—(Early childhood education series)
  Bibliography: p.
  Includes index.
  ISBN 0-8077-2942-6.—ISBN 0-8077-2941-8 (pbk.)
  1. Play—Case studies.   2. Child development—Case studies.
I. Title. II. Series.
HQ782.K36 1989   89-30665
155.4'18—dc 19   CIP

ISBN 0-8077-2942-6 (cloth)
ISBN 0-8077-2941-8 (paperback)

Manufactured in the United States of America

93 92 91 90 89   1 2 3 4 5 6

For Helen King (pseudonym), whose world is revealed in these pages, and who said she would like to call this book Children's Literature, *because it "means that it has something to do with stories, which is the kinda game we play."*

Contents

Foreword

This foreword is a postscript to ten years of watching Dr. Diana Kelly-Bryne initiate this study, conclude it as a thesis, and ponder over it before bringing it to its present fruition. My part began in 1979 when she sought me out as her dissertation sponsor, after she had already begun this study. Most professors are reluctant to sign on to supervise a study that is already underway; and, even more so, are certainly not at ease with a one-subject dissertation. For my own part, and after some 30 years in play research, I was impressed by her determination to carry this project through and excited at what we might find out if someone "played" with a child, instead of just studying children playing as had been the usual procedure in therapy and research for the past 100 years. It was an amazing idea even if a remarkably simple one. One immediately asked: Why hadn't anyone done this before? What is it about childhood that has militated against such a research approach?

Jean Jacques Rousseau, who is generally accepted as the precursor of all modern child study with his notion that the child is both driven by consuming impulses as well as perfectible if we educate him correctly, would certainly not have had anything to do with such a notion. He saw himself as the first to really take a research interest in the young and wrote in 1778:

> I knew that there never was a man who loved more to watch little children joking and playing together than I, and often I stopped in the street and on walks to watch their cuteness and their little games with an interest I never saw shared by anyone.

But even so, much as he declared he loved children, he preferred to watch them at a distance rather than associate with them. He did not even like talking to them. He said, "I should be more at ease before a monarch of Asia than before a child whom I must make babble" (quoted in Kessen, 1978). And paradoxical as it is that the father of child psychology liked to keep his distance from real children (rather than theoretical children), a strong case can be made that nothing much has changed amongst the philosophers and psychologists of play in the two hundred years since he said this. Their studies are also usually carried out in situations where children are kept at a distance, caged in some way or another by laboratories, classrooms, playgrounds, or playrooms. They seldom deal with the natives in their wild state and never by true participant engagement. Do they also fear that such participation with these Asian monarchs would be intolerable? Trivial? Boring? Puerile? Regressive? Insane? What is it that has kept them all out of direct research participation in the jungles of children's fantasy?

Perhaps it doesn't take long to discover. Already in the first session Kelly-Byrne is describing Helen as haughty, smug, directive, dominating, controlling, demanding, and thoroughly concerned with power. The price of her participation with the child on the child's terms is, in the early stages at least, complete subordination. She is made powerless as a playmate, and they spend all their time engrossed in fantasies of a fictional world in which Helen is the dominant figure who is beautiful, moral, wise, and mature. We learn from her later statements that after three to five hours of each session, Kelly-Byrne, the expert actress in her play of subordination and nonevaluative supportiveness, collapses from fatigue. Clearly Rousseau knew what he was talking about, and even though the children we deal with today are a very cleaned up form of the brutish variety that he had available in his own time, apparently the predicament is the same. Sometimes when we are reading through the explanations of what she has done, we are forced to wonder whether perhaps Kelly-Byrne is also defending herself post hoc against the babbling monarch.

If we ask where this discontinuity between ourselves and children comes from, there are various answers and solutions. Ruth Benedict, in her noted 1938 essay, "Continuity and Discontinuity in Cultural Conditioning," advanced the opinion that the discontinuity was primarily an American problem. Her subsequent apparent advocacy of cultural relativity throughout her own lifetime, however, was generally advanced at the expense of her American examples, and so we have to wonder about her anthropological equity in this matter (Geertz, 1988). Since Aries' 1960 work, *Centuries of Childhood*, most of us have considered that the invention of modern childhood as something separate from adults is a general Western condition beginning somewhere between the sixteenth and eighteenth centuries. For Rousseau the discontinuity began with civilization itself and with the separation of the child and primitive from their trusting and direct relationship with those around them. When people began to live in cities, he opined, they developed that presentation of themselves in everyday life, both in commerce and in every social interaction, that separated them from their original and transparent selves. His theoretical education of Emile, in the book of the same name, in a physical environment with its discipline of natural consequences, was an attempt to defend the child's innocence against such demoralizing sophistications, and to develop in the child, from "nature," that certain conscience that would make the child capable of subsequent submission to the social contract of a communal society. Or at least that is how Ernst Cassirer responds in *The Question of Jean Jacques Rousseau* (1963), which refers to Rousseau's paradox of combining individual freedom in education with totalitarianism in political arrangements.

A simpler if not unrelated view of the reason for our modern separation from the child might lie in our habit of segregating children in schools. It is not an accident perhaps that two thirds of the Aries history of modern childhood is devoted to the segregation of children from the rest of society, first into schools and then into age-graded classrooms. Along with this segregation, he says, there is the introduction of the harsh discipline required to keep the children orderly in such places. Any present discontinuity of adults and children most certainly rests on this three-hundred-year history of the forcible subjugation of children. And that subjugation, in turn, must certainly be seen in the perspective of the forcible subjugation of the insane, the criminal, and the poor that takes place during the same period of time and is a mark, according to Foucault (1965), of the rationalization of modern society, a symptom of the way in which the orderly progress of industrial civilization made sense (or nonsense) out of those various classes of human beings who did not or could not contribute directly to the work life of the evolving national societies (including children and to some extent women). In these terms we do not need any remarkable Freudian theorizing as to why we are strangers to our children, or why they engage in such orgies of power when they get the opportunity as in the present study. The enslaved are reaching for the power that we no longer share with them but once did, at least in the diminished form of the earlier apprenticeship system, where their direct contribution to the sustenance of life was self-evident.

One can argue further that the major modern response to this discontinuity of children and adults has been the practice of a subordinating discipline, which in this century has been given the euphemistic label of "socialization." Socialization is about the ways in which successful parents induce their children into the normative patterns of the larger society. Psychologists with their research descriptions of sex typing, aggression, attachment, prosocial behavior, self, families, peers and siblings, etc., ostensibly yield information about the scientific cause-and-effect relationships within and between these variables. But as they are dealing with specifically cultural rather than universal realities, their work is ultimately a description of how the culture conducts itself and what the culture values in its own behavior and attitudes. It is a local science at best: What is taken to be a research result is eagerly converted into advice for the deficient by a surrounding pack of hungry journalists and writers of books of advice. Any research that states a norm or suggests a superior cognitive or behavioral mechanism, for example, immediately implies the deficiency of those who have not acquired the norm or do not possess the mechanism. We appear to live in a society in which such psychological information receives the reverence once reserved for religion and social status. The point of all of this is that the discontinuity between ourselves and our children is now deeply engrained. The whole force of educated opinion in society is devoted to keeping our children clean, sexless, nondisgusting, nonaggressive, rational, and tidy. In respect to our children, we administer a subtle puritanism, which is none the less real for being disguised in the gawdiness of consumer wrappings.

Our question must be, therefore, where Kelly-Byrne stands in the light of this history of discontinuity that Rousseau so well understood and she apparently seeks to bridge? Rousseau's attempt to rejoin us with our children was, on the one hand, a radical system of education, seldom subsequently copied, and, on the other, a radical political envisagement perhaps emulated in multiple communistic schemes. Kelly-Byrne's solution seems to be more derived from Wordsworth's privatized answers than from Rousseau's public schemes. Wordsworth, reeling from his disappointments in the character and outcomes of the French Revolution, subsequent to Rousseau's death, turned inward to his own childhood as a source of inspiration and, along with William Blake and others, engendered that cult of the childhood that has been the major response in the subsequent two centuries to Rousseau's predicament. What the adult is to draw upon from his own childhood is the "beneficent influence" of its sacral memory and imagination, "from which our minds are nourished and invisibly repaired" (Hartman, 1987, p. xvi). And in Kelly-Byrne's case, this is also perhaps what we are to draw upon from any child we should play with in her manner. She says that children "are capable of teaching adults their system if the adults are open to seeing things from a child's point of view." And if we do "we open ourselves up to a world of wonderful possibilities and the opportunity to recapture something of our own lost power to transform our experience and our lives."

But there is more to the Kelly-Byrne solution than a reiteration of Wordsworth, because she, unlike both he and Rousseau, is actively participating with her child, at least in the temporary and segregated space of the play world. Here she and the child put aside their chains of separation and commingle. However, in the background here and there are hints that make us wonder whether she too, like Wordsworth, is drawing on some important resource from her own childhood. Are these occasions with Helen totally independent lessons for us, or are they also projections of the author's need for some redemption of her own childhood? Ours, after all, is also the therapeutic century, where it is common to think of those who work with children as also working on problems from their own childhood. As Kelly-Byrne says in the text, "We save others to save ourselves." Still, even if this is the case, it is different from that of Wordsworth and Rousseau, who make moral or epistemological uses of the childhood self rather than psychological ones and who have limited concourse with real children. On the other hand, there are grounds, paradoxically enough, for finding the Kelly-Byrne approach to childhood is more like that of Rousseau than that of Wordsworth. Consider, for example, that Rousseau was an advocate of public games and a strong antagonist of private fantasy. For him public games bound the players into a collective consensus. Private fantasy led them into the practice of theatric duplicities, which were again an obstruction to the directness of the childlike soul. He could hardly have countenanced Diana and Helen in their play of multiple voices. In a sense, however, there is no contradiction, because in Rousseau's ultimate social scheme, there would be no need for inauthentic separate selves, and therefore no need for private play (Starobinski, 1988). Moreover, there is no contradiction in this present Kelly-Byrne work, because although the play is given to multiple fantasy transformations (which Rousseau might disapprove), this can only occur because of the deeply genuine nature of the underlying relationship (which he would clearly approve). Kelly-Byrne tells us in no uncertain phenomenonological and ethnographic terms that the relationship as thus described will give us a deeper understanding of play than any other existing methodology in the literature. At least two thirds of her work is given over to defending and explicating the merits of this particular methodology. Intriguingly, Aries spends two thirds of his book showing how children become segregated and Kelly-Byrne spends two thirds of hers showing how she and Helen can be related. She counters the historical unbonding of childhood with the bonding of a superior methodology. While, on the surface, these may be birds of quite a different feather—the public segregation of children versus an intimate relationship between an adult and a child player—in a symbolic sense at least, the latter is meant to be an answer to the former. Kelly-Byrne is quite as earnest as Rousseau about this. They both struggle for transparent relationships and both seek to express themselves in a voice of inner authority.

In sum, it is reasonable to suggest that Kelly-Byrne sees the discontinuity between adult and child as more apparent than real. She has written an article in which she seeks to show that, when you put aside the stereotypes, adult and child players are not as different as they seem. There is secrecy, masking, crudeness, and intimacy in both cases (1984). I would like to suggest, however, that her present book does not gain its power from any new revelation of that kind. Its chief value, I believe, lies in its suggestion of new roads into the discontinuity itself, not into its demolition. What has happened in recent years is not that the discontinuity has gone, as some have suggested (Postman, 1982), only that it has become mollified by the affluent consumer world of gifts, confections, toys, clothes, fantasy worlds, television, and organized recreation for children. But children are still basically outsiders to the sharing of economic powers. As Zelizer (1985) has said: the more useless they have become, the more priceless they have become. They are a popular form of conspicuous consumption; which is to say, children's discontinuity from adults continues in a pervasive and subtle fashion. In these terms, Kelly-Byrne's appeal to make more use of their imagination and to play with them more would hardly change the discontinuity radically, but what it might do is change radically our conception of socialization. The current conception is largely anachronistic. It is concerned with issues that had to be paramount in the control of children in earlier centuries and earlier decades, but now that children have become pampered in their powerlessness, the edge for such concerns has departed, at least in the homes of the affluent. Children of neglect still roam their domains with the dangerous capacities of the dispossessed. What is important about the contemporary pampered, however, is their grasp on the potential future, not their conformity to our own past. In our century, children are still seen as the secular residual legatees of predestination and progress. They still carry both our hope for the future and our relative immortality within it. And here the cultivation of their imagination is central. That children are attached, toilet trained, sexually modest, relatively nonaggressive, and sex-typically flexible gains us no future. It gives us only obedient and docile citizens. The changing future in a world of galloping information, incredible diplomatic problems, and a series of populations to be contained not by force but by the imaginative scenarios and opportunities will be provided by those of imaginative and novelistic leadership. The guarantee for this future is a socialization of generations of children into their own imaginativeness, not into the disciplined behavior of the parents' own idealized past. From birth onward the central topic for such a future would be children's playfulness and their inventiveness. The mundane competences like reading, writing, and arithmetic would be merely some of the agencies to such an education, not a central focus as they mostly are today and have been for centuries. In such an envisageable polity, this work of Kelly-Byrne's might be that of a pioneer in the development of the imaginative young.

Brian Sutton-Smith
Professor of Education
University of Pennsylvania

REFERENCES

Aries, P. (1962). *Centuries of childhood*. New York: Alfred A. Knopf. (Original work published in 1960)

Benedict, R. (1938). Continuity and discontinuity in cultural conditioning. *Psychiatry, 1*, 161–167.

Cassirer, E. (1963). *The question of Jean Jacques Rousseau*. Bloomington: Indian University Press. (Original work published in 1954)

Foucault, M. (1965). *Madness and civilization*. New York: Random House. (Original work published in 1961)

Geertz, C. (1988). *Works and lives*. Stanford: Stanford University Press.

Hartman, G. H. (1987). *The unremarkable Wordsworth*. Minneapolis. The University of Minnesota.

Kelly-Byrne, D. (1984). Continuity and discontinuity in play: The adult-child connection. In B. Sutton-Smith & D. Kelly-Byrne (Eds.), *The masks of play*. New York: Leisure Press.

Kessen, W. (1978). Rousseau's children. *Daedalus, 107*(3), 155–166.

Postman, Neil. (1982). *The disappearance of childhood*. New York: Dell.

Starobinski, J. (1988). *Jean Jacques Rousseau, transparency and obstruction*. Chicago: University of Chicago Press. (Original work published in 1971)

Zelizer, V. (1985). *Pricing the priceless child*. New York: Basic Books.

Preface

A Child's Play Life: An Ethnographic Study is the story of a seven-year-old girl, whom I call Helen, and her play life with an adult, me. Initially, we met in the roles of child and baby-sitter and soon grew to establish a relationship in which we played together. We did this on fourteen occasions for several hours at a time over the course of a year. This was an unusual relationship because adults in our culture do not usually play with young children in any systematic way for lengthy periods. Further, those who study children's play have also generally not sought to understand the behavior by playing with a child. Although some child therapists may play and encourage children to play for diagnostic and therapeutic purposes, they have not gone beyond this to describe the character and nuances of children's play.

However, believing that play is a relational phenomenon and can best be understood by observing and studying the relationship through which it finds expression, I decided to plan and execute a study that focused on the play life of a seven-year-old. I was especially interested in discovering how play occurred and was given expression in the home. Thus my study was to be in contrast to those of most researchers, who observe children's play in school settings. On beginning, I was eager to observe Helen's play relationships with her toys and peers; however, I soon discovered that Helen wished to play with me. It was her price for the privilege I had of being privy to her play life in the home. Consequently, I became Helen's chief play partner during the occasions on which we met. In these circumstances, I was able to observe, record, and understand a great deal about the way play expressed itself in Helen's life. I learned about the many faces of play and its uses, forms, stages, themes, and concerns, as this little girl expressed them.

This book has three major parts. The first part provides information of an introductory nature and acts as a backdrop for the story of the unfolding of the relationship between the child and the adult. The chapters focus on child play studies that have been done within the mainstream of research; on the methods and procedures used for executing the study, gathering data, and ordering it; and on Helen, her parents, and myself as the researcher.

The second part is a storied account of the course of the relationship between Helen and me. It includes a textured recounting of what happened between the child and the adult during each of our meetings over the course of almost a year and is told from the adult's point of view. As such, it is a first-person account but one in which the child is kept in focus and where it is believed that her world is to be respected at all times; one that is to be entered into and participated in—never patronized. In addition, following the description of each play session is a commentary aimed at drawing the reader's attention to significant points of a theoretical nature that are embedded in the narrative details of the shared relationship and the behaviors within it. Attention is also drawn to two developing strands of significance in the study: (1) the development of Helen's world and her relationship to me and (2) the development of the research journey and the ways in which play functions in this case.

The third and final part discusses the import of the study for play research and theory and attempts to locate the case in a wider context. Accordingly, it considers the implications of this study for working with children as informants and how prevailing conceptions of children's play and child/adult interaction patterns should be modified.

This book will be of great interest to those who wish to understand what some children do when they are allowed to play largely on their own terms. It will also appeal to those seeking to understand something of the hazardous nature of establishing relationships with children for the purposes of research and to those who sense some of the trials and joys of working closely with them. It also informs the reader of a child's world of wishes—of fantasy play and the uses of television, play, and lore in gaining such private ends.

Like several other books that record detailed accounts of various aspects of the lives of particular children, this is a highly contextualized account. It seeks to capture the unique way in which a brilliant little girl dealt with her hopes and fears, her dreams and impulses as she drew on many details of her life and experience in forging a relationship with an adult play partner. Nevertheless, it could also be about many children of a similar age and background whom I have known over the past ten years in my work as a teacher, researcher, and parent.

Acknowledgments

I am deeply indebted to the little girl whom I call Helen, who taught me much about the play life of a seven-year-old. To her parents, without whose understanding and generosity this work could not have been done, I also wish to express my thanks.

There are several who served as advisers to this study. During its early stages I appreciated the encouragement and counsel of Barbara Kirshenblatt-Gimblett, Gerald Prince, Bambi Schiefflin, and Shirley Brice Heath. Ray Birdwhistell constantly challenged my conceptions of research, data, and interpretation and alerted me to the implications of working as a member of a dyadic research relationship, especially the notion of researcher reflexivity. In addition, his as well as Dell Hymes's scholarly concerns with and support of ethnography influenced my understanding of work in this tradition. In fact, this study bears the marks of the decade (1978–1987) I spent at the University of Pennsylvania in Philadelphia, during which time I had the opportunity to work with many fine colleagues and learn their multidisciplinary approaches to scholarship.

Once the study was completed and available in manuscript form, several of my doctoral students at the University of Pennsylvania generously provided useful comments and critiques. To them I am grateful.

Hattie Kalish, a social worker in Philadelphia, also read the manuscript and made several helpful comments. I thank her for always supporting and encouraging my efforts. Kenneth Burke also read parts of the narrative of Helen's play and was excited by the work. I benefited from his reading of these texts.

There are two people who stand behind this book in separate but extraordinarily influential ways. They are Brian Sutton-Smith and Kenneth Byrne. Throughout the venture they showed great personal faith in and support of my work. With both, I have had the privilege of endless conversations about all aspects of this work. Under Brian Sutton-Smith's tutelage I have learned a great deal about play, developmental psychology, and other scholarly matters that are close to the heart of this book. Kenneth Byrne, a clinical psychologist, has been a constant presence during the undertaking and completion of this venture. Indeed, much that appears in this book was first introduced for my consideration in conversations with him. In addition, I deeply appreciate the ways in which he has facilitated and supported my work over the years. His friendship and love have been a significant force in my journey of seeing this book move from its inception to its conclusion.

I wish to express my thanks to Sarah Biondello for her thoughtful reading of the manuscript; to Sue Liddicoat and Susan Keniston for their sensitive and careful editing; and to Cathy McClure for seeing this work through to completion.

I thank Sharma De Abrew for her conscientious and careful preparation and typing of the manuscript.

Finally, I would like to thank Megan for her patience during many stages of this venture and Douglas and Annaleen for their support and love.

A
CHILD'S
PLAY LIFE

An Ethnographic Study

Part I
SETTING THE STAGE

My primary reason for undertaking the study on which this book is based was to explore an individual child's play behavior under conditions and with a type and age of child that I felt had been neglected in prior research. This neglect in research design was ironic to me because the conditions that had been lacking appeared to be the very ones that would be especially facilitative to the phenomenon under study—play. It seemed to me that, if play emerged as a property of a relationship between participants, then it would be fruitful to observe the kind of relationship that emerged between playmates when they related to each other in a familiar environment and on an established and ongoing basis.

Although there is no shortage of books about play, to my knowledge there has never before been a study done of the internal play life of a normal child. Further, with the exception of a few published accounts of play therapy (e.g., Axline, 1964; Baruch, 1964), there is no research work that is based on actually playing with a child over an extended period of time. Having perused the literature and also done a prior study (Kelly, 1977) that looked at the play of preschoolers and kindergartners, I was struck by several observations. First, there was great emphasis in the literature on ages 3 through 5 as being the golden years of make-believe play. Second, most of the research concentrated on the acquisition of play and on its manipulation and use for various valued ends. Third, the play that I observed

in the nursery and primary schools was subject to numerous constraints that were part of the life of those institutions. Finally, I
noted that this play was most often of a very public nature. Since I
felt sure that seven-year-olds and others even older used make-
believe, I wondered why their play had been neglected. I wondered
about the nature of what would emerge if we concentrated on a
broad and detailed or "thick" description (see p. 13) of a child's play,
rather than narrowly looking for the child's competence or lack of it
in relation to particular aspects of play. I was also struck by the
thought that what children did on the playground under the supervision of adults might be quite different from what they did in the
privacy of their hideouts, wherever these might be.

Thus, in planning a study of a seven-year-old's play life as it unfolded in the private sphere of the home over the course of about a
year, I hoped to begin to redress some of these gaps in the literature.
This was one of my starting points. The chapters in Part I present
information to help the reader understand how I structured this
study. As such, they comprise the introductory part of the story of
the play relationship between Helen and me.

Chapter 1 briefly considers the play literature so that the reader
may get a sense of how the present study takes its place in relation
to other work in the area of children's play. Chapter 2 focuses on
how and why the research was planned and executed the way it was
and on additional theoretical influences on my understanding of the
play relationship. Chapter 3 concludes this part with portraits of the
key characters in this study: the child Helen, her parents, and the researcher.

1 Play: A Scholarly Matter

Although the phenomenon of play has long been associated with children and today is looked upon benignly by most of us, over the past 100 years it has also provoked a growing body of serious scholarship. Persuaded by various beliefs about the value of play, several prominent adults and institutions concerned with children have taken up its cause and a growing industry has evolved in the service of adults encouraging children's play for a variety of positive ends.

However, children's play as organized, described, and valued by most adults, whether in everyday or scholarly settings, is different from the play that most children engage in when left to their own devices, time, and purposes. It has been argued elsewhere that the portrait of mainstream play drawn by adults tends to be idealized—that is, the qualities that pervade the portraits tend to be nostalgic, sanitized, and functional in nature—and, further, that those who have been privy to the play of children when it has been unsupervised by vigilant adults may paint a different picture (Kelly-Byrne, 1985; Sutton-Smith & Kelly-Byrne, 1984b).

This duality in description suggests that adults' relationships with the behavior of play, whether children's or their own, is at best ambivalent. This equivocation is certainly not new. The work of Spariosu (1982) shows how, from the time of the Greeks, Western society has struggled over how to conceptualize and value play. Throughout history there have been changing fashions in the definitions of play, which in turn have colored our adult conceptualizations (see Sutton-Smith, 1986). In addition to the historical confusion and ambivalence about how to view play, Schwartzman (1978), writing from the perspective of an anthropological researcher, suggests that most definitions of play that have been accumulated over the past centuries have often been "speculative attempts by investigators to arbitrarily define the nature of play, with little attempt made to collect information or data on the subject" (p. 7). She adds that, when data have been gathered, classifications have

3

often been formulated by researchers eager to impose some sense of order on these materials. In the process, however, they have done little more than formulate a classification scheme of dubious value.

My own review of the literature corroborated Schwartzman's (1978) views. I concluded that most of the studies of play, although informative on other scores, rarely yielded much information about the behavior itself, as manifested in the lives of individuals or groups of children in everyday settings. In contrast, most attempted to search for factual and objective information about the behavior as though it were an artifact of the natural world, such as an atom is, rather than of the social world of human and animal creatures.

Although it is important to understand why most of the literature on play to date has contained such abstract, unrecognizable, and idealized descriptions of children's play, it is not possible to present a detailed discussion of the matter here. Suffice it to note that play has been construed differently at various times in history and that Spariosu (1982) has suggested that one explanation for these historical changes is that each theory arises as a way of supporting the hegemony of the currently ruling group.

Accordingly, play was construed as a Dionysian, irrational, and anarchic manifestation of power by Heraclitus and Homer. Later, Plato and his student, Aristotle, subordinated play to Reason and initiated the epistemological split between Poetry and Myth, which included play, on the one hand, and Science and Philosophy, seen to be serious and nonplayful, on the other. What is noteworthy about this construal of play for the present case is that with these two thinkers, we find a polarization of play into good and bad play. The former was seen to be play modeled after Science and Philosophy with their attributed characteristics of purity, reason, and logic. In contrast, the latter was indited as play modeled after Myth and Poetry, which were seen as mere imitations or simulations of Truth exemplified by Science and Philosophy. These philosophical distinctions have maintained a stronghold on conceptions of play throughout the ages and today can be found in the distinctions we make between play that is considered functional and socializing (good play) and play that is seen as irksome (bad play) by adults, whether in public settings or the home.

Researchers, too, have been influenced by these polarized construals and in the main have concentrated their efforts on "good" play. This is largely true of the research by psychologists as well as anthropologists and educators. However, contrasting views are available in the accounts of folklorists (see Knapp & Knapp, 1976; Opie & Opie, 1959; Sluckin, 1981; Sutton-Smith, 1981a).

The dominance of philosophy, logic, and science over art, literature, and play as fundamental modes of knowing affected not only the subject matter and nature of scholarly pursuit but also the methods and standards for research and discovery. Consequently, the natural or physical science model of research and its underlying epistemology have prevailed in psychology, under whose aegis most work in the area of children's play has been done. In this model universality, precision, and certainty are of paramount importance, as is belief in the ideal of objective knowledge, which points to a single reality. Matters of subjectivism, relativism, and ambiguity are treated suspiciously in favor of objective and verifiable scientific proof, which is seen as constituting true and infallible knowledge.

This ideal model has its roots in early Greek conceptions of knowledge and, as has been noted, has dominated philosophy for centuries. It is important to understand this model and its influence on Western thought and scholarship not only because it has governed so much of the study of and theorizing about play until relatively recently, but also because its concerns and thrusts are so different from the model that underlies the conceptualization, concerns, and execution of the present study.

The following sketch of major historical approaches to the study of play will reveal the influence of the early Greek conceptions of knowledge and truth, as just interpreted.

HISTORICAL APPROACHES

Although there are many ways of classifying information and no one watertight system, when considering some of the shifting emphases in play research over the past century, the following picture may be drawn (Sutton-Smith, 1983). Given the hegemony of psychology in the field, it is little wonder that five approaches may be identified as holding sway.

The psychoanalytic/psychodynamic approach includes such famous scholars as Axline, Erikson, Freud, Isaacs, Klein, Lowenfield, Sullivan, and Winnicott. The 1930s through the 1950s were the prime years of this approach. Emphasis is on play as a subjective phenomenon where healing takes place through expression and release of emotions. Questions of interest centered on the character of projection in fantasy play, the role of aggression in play, the mastery of anxiety through play, and the ways in which play could be used as a disgnostic and therapeutic tool.

The correlational approach is associated with theorists such as Ames, Buhler, Griffiths, Jersild, Parten, and Valentine. More recently, Johnson, Rubin, and Stern have done work using a correlational approach and are representative of the surge of researchers doing correlation studies in the 1970s. Much of this work focused on inventorying indices such as developmental stages, sex, intelligence, race, and language and correlating them with play. Major emphases in the 1970s included infant play, family and peer play, sex typing, exploration in play, and socioeconomic and language differences. Observational studies were conducted with the aim of correlating play and these other factors.

The pragmatic approach includes a somewhat miscellaneous group of researchers and play advocates, some of whom are Hartley, Frank, and Goldensen, who worked in nursery schools; Johnson and Lee, who were associated with the early playground movement; educators like Pestalozzi, Froebel, and Montessori, who were advocates rather than researchers; and others who have written about how to play with your children, as well as children's dramatic play and their toys and playground apparatus. All this work was intended to be pragmatic in the sense of being educationally useful and in the spirit of good or socializing play.

The Piagetian and related cognitive approaches are seen by many to be the "real newcomer in this century of play studies" (Sutton-Smith, 1983, p. 14). Piaget is considered the father of this approach and until the 1960s was its sole representative. However, during that decade and the next, there was a flood of studies using a cognitive approach to the study of play. They focused on the structure of play and the various cognitive and characterological skills, operations, and functions implied in different aspects of children's play. Emphases have included the study of make-believe, symbolic play, decentration, role reversibility, and creative play. Besides Piaget, among the many well-known contributors to these areas of play research are, more recently, Dansky, D'Elkonin, Fein, Golomb, Lieberman, Pulanski, and, in a related sense, Vygotsky. Most of these researchers have seen play as a way of expanding and consolidating cognition.

The experimental approach has attracted scholars such as Berlyne, Hutt, Klinger, Rubin, Saltz, and Vandenberg. Much of their work derives from a behavioristic or learning-theory orientation. Topics of interest have included arousal, curiosity, stimulus deprivation, reinforcement, problem solving, and sociodramatic play.

None of these approaches concentrates on children's play for its own sake; rather, all conceptualize play as a functional activity that plays a positive part in the growth and socialization of children. Another way to classify many of these studies is to see them as a series of direct or indirect attempts to deal with play as a manifestation of physiology, biology, or neurology. For example, leading theories have attempted to characterize play as a kind of energy, whether it be superfluous, surplus, instinctive, homeostatic, or aroused (Buhler, 1930, 1935; Groos, 1901; Spencer, 1873). Other scholars have pictured play as a biological mechanism in the struggle for survival. As such it has been conceived as functioning as a kind of atavism, race memory, preparatory activity, or abreaction (Erikson, 1940; Freud, 1976; Groos, 1901; Hall, 1917). Yet others have treated play as a neurological manifestation and seen it as functioning to maintain equilibrium and consolidate information (Piaget, 1952). In a different but related vein, attention is given to environmental principles of stimulus arrangement, such as novelty and conflict, and these are seen as instigators of play. Such theories turn to neurological states as explanations of what happens in these circumstances (Berlyne, 1960; Hutt, 1979; Shultz, 1979).

In all of these instances, because of the overwhelming tendency in Western culture to idealize play in positive and functional terms, it has been confused with the analytic and synthetic functions of intelligence, that is, with exploration, construction, practice activity, creativity, imaginative activities, and daydreams. As argued elsewhere (Sutton-Smith & Kelly-Byrne, 1984b), play need be none of these, although each of these may be carried out in a playful manner. Such confusion has made it possible for researchers to ignore the nature and shape of children's play in and of itself, as it occurs in the everyday lives of children.

Finally, a review of the literature also alerts one to the prevailing individualism within psychology, which has led researchers to search for predispositions within the individual that would account for the play phenomenon. Thus, even in more modern surveys there is reference to play in terms of intrinsic motives within the individual, or the individual's focus on instrumental activities, or the individual's control of the situation, as if these qualities of experience are in fact detachable from their contexts and are the reasons for play's existence (Rubin, Fein & Vandenberg, 1983). This type of separation of play from its milieu has constantly led psychologists away from detailed and "thick" descriptions of the phenomenon, without which we cannot discover the worth of these or any other features of the play situation. Interestingly, the same psychologists who are becoming aware of the importance of context have tried to define such environments for play as those that have toys or peers, allow choices, are nonintrusive, and are available to those whose other needs are sated (see treatment of these in Mussen, 1983). Thus, once again, single aspects of a cluster of features have been abstracted and treated as discrete entities, with little comprehension of the view that play, along with all other meaning systems, is a social phenomenon and as such is part of a network of relationships. For example, it is not improbable that the motives for play discussed earlier are directly responsive to the contexts for play just mentioned and are not independent of each other.

In summary, locating play in the world of natural science and subjecting it to the belief systems, values, and scientific procedures that attend scholarship and research in that domain, has guaranteed us abstract, confused, reified, and generalized accounts of the phenomenon. Although the research has suggested some of the functional and structural aspects of the behavior, it has done little to give us a sense of how play manifests itself in the lives of children in everyday settings, or of the complex ways in which children manage it for their own ends, irrespective of functionality or dysfunctionality in adult terms.

RECENT ALTERNATIVE APPROACHES

In contrast to the literature of mainstream psychology is a body of work that has perceived play rather differently. Gaining import in the last 10 years or so, it has been influenced by an interpretive science model for understanding the meaning of human conduct. The model has drawn scholars from fields such as anthropology, folklore, education, social psychology, sociology, sociolinguistics, communications, and history. Works exemplifying this vein of work include, but are not limited to, books by Babcock (1978), Bateson (1972), Cheska (1981), Fagen (1980), Garvey (1977), Goffman (1974), Herron and Sutton-Smith (1971), Lancy and Tindale (1976), Loy (1982), Manning (1983), Schwartzman (1978, 1980), and Sutton-Smith and Kelly-Byrne (1984a).

In contrast to a natural science model of behavior, the interpretive science model posits an interest in persons as agents (not objects), in intentional acts (not simply the behavior), and in understanding the human world (rather than predicting and controlling events). A human is defined as a self-interpreting being who acts on the basis of his or her own perceptions of the world. Thus, what the social scientist using an interpretive science model offers is insight into possible interpretations of "second-order" constructs of behavior. Second-order constructs or meanings refer to the thoughts constructed by social scientists that are founded upon observed members' methods for making sense of situations and events. Thus, the constructs used by the social scientists are, so to speak, constructs of constructs made by the actors on the social scene. Understanding is thus a major goal of the interpretive science approach.

This model of knowledge comes from philosophical anthropology, an interdisciplinary field that combines the study of humans with philosophical reflections on the nature of its findings. Emphasis is on the process of knowing, rather than on the knowledge itself. In this field, physics and mathematics do not represent the ideal of exact formal knowledge; instead, particularity, plurality, and complexity constitute the norm. There are other differences, too. For example, the belief in objective knowledge pointing to a single reality "out there" is replaced by belief in a community of shared practices and meanings that guide dialogue and negotiation aimed at consensus. Further, rather than the objective/subjective duality posited by natural science, interpretive science talks of intersubjectivity.

Intersubjectivity refers to understanding that is held equally by members of a cultural group, which human actors bring to various situations when acting in the everyday world. These understandings are based on common assumptions regarding the nature of the world and our position as actors in it. These common assumptions are what Schutz (1976) calls "the stock of knowledge at hand." They are part of a tradition brought to bear on everyday situations for engaging in procedures of interpretation, communication, and expression.

Moreover, the ideals of the disembodied, logical subject and the distant, detached, atemporal observer are abandoned as mythical inventions. Just as the subject is taken to be an active construer of meanings, so, too, the observer is seen to stand inside the circle of meaning making. The context of discovery is thus just as important as the context of verification; reality is taken to be construed; and theoretical beliefs or presuppositions are seen to underlie all observation.

In noting such differences between the two models of knowledge, it is not difficult to see that the interpretive science model varies from its predecessor ontologically, epistemologically, and logically. The differences are important because they account for significant changes in the way behavior such as play is treated in recent scholarship and because they are fundamental to the conceptualization of humans and of meaning that I have used in framing my study of Helen's play.

A SIGNIFICANT DEVELOPMENT: PLAY AS COMMUNICATION

Just as there are several views of play existing within the field of psychology as a part of the natural science model of meaning, there are several theories that are used by those working within an interpretive science paradigm. A communications theory of play is one such example.

The discovery that play is a form of communication has constituted a quantum leap forward in the progress of play research. It was Bateson (1955, 1956, 1972; Bateson & Ruesch, 1951) who suggested that play was a paradoxical form of communication. He argued that play is a socially situated act that is characterized by the production and exchange of paradoxical statements about persons, objects, activities, and situations, and the various relationships involving these. Bateson (1955; Bateson & Ruesch, 1951) argued that play framing is accomplished by specific interpretive acts such as the exchange of cues, messages, or signals, which he describes as being metacommunicative in function. Metacommunication is "communication about communication" (Bateson & Ruesch, 1951, p. 209) or a "script" about how acts or events are to be taken (see Wittgenstein, 1958). Bateson distinguished two sorts of play frames, namely, "exchanged cues and propositions about codification" on the one hand and about the "relationship between communicators" on the other (Bateson & Ruesch, 1951, p. 209). Thus, not only do frames codify play among other kinds of events (e.g., everyday acts such as caretaking duties), but they also reveal an attitude toward the play.

In referring explicitly to the statement, "This is play," Bateson (1955) says that, in an expanded form, the message is something to the effect that "these actions in which we now engage do not denote what these actions for which they stand would denote. . . . The playful nip denotes the bite but it does not denote what would be denoted by the bite" (p. 41). Because of the reflexiveness of the message, a circular type of paradox is generated. The frame of the message that "this is play" paradoxically validates and invalidates itself. The message or frame subsumes the whole process, indicating that the behavior engaged in by the players is at once real and not real. Bateson suggested that play occurs only among organisms capable of metacommunication and thus of differentiating between varying logical types of messages.

As I have argued elsewhere (Sutton-Smith & Kelly-Byrne, 1984a), it seems that because Bateson was eager to show that relationships framed as play take on a logical character and therefore generate paradoxes of membership, he was intent on perceiving play as an evolutionary step in metacommunication. Consequently, he saw children's play as a process of learning about metacommunication. This perception has been taken up by post–Batesonian researchers such as Garvey (1977) and Schwartzman (1978) and more recently by Giffin (1984). This body of highly suggestive and valuable work has concentrated on how children organize and communicate about make-believe; on how the play is framed or signaled; and on how it is generated, maintained, and disbanded. Garvey found that a great deal of speech was devoted to setting up, clarifying, and negotiating play, and this led her to conclude that the "saying is the playing" (Garvey & Berndt, 1977, p. 9). Both Garvey (1977) and Schwartzman (1978) talk about the importance of power and control in children's play, and Schwartzman expands Garvey's work by paying attention to the meaning of the texts created in play.

There are many important ways in which the present study is different from those of Garvey and Schwartzman and others working in a similar vein. However, it is similar to these in that it is post–Batesonian and starts from a view of play as a socially situated form of paradoxical communication. With a view to pointing to some of the similarities and differences, it would be useful to report briefly on Schwartzman's (1973) study of preschool children in a day-care center classroom.

Following Bateson (1955, 1956) in executing her study, Schwartzman (1973) adopted a view of play as communication. After Geertz (1972) and Ehrmann (1968), she argued that children's pretend play could be analyzed "as a text in which players act as both subjects and the objects of their jointly created play event" (p. 232). She argued that as subjects of their own play they are able to interpret and comment on their relationships to one another in the particular contexts in which they live, as the objects of their play. She writes that, in brief, the purpose of her study was to "describe play texts in context and the context in play texts" (p. 236). Schwartzman emphasizes the social context of play, suggesting that this information can be gathered by the use of participant observation executed in a "natural" (as opposed to experimental) setting (see Garvey, 1977). She adds that this contextual information is crucial in interpreting play texts, and she reveals a new dimension that she calls "the sideways perspective" (p. 237) of the child at play. Following Geertz (1972), not only does she add this new element but takes it a step further by suggesting that it functions to make play itself a text or "story that the players tell themselves about themselves" (p. 237).

Her primary concern, however, like Garvey's (1977) seems to be to sort out the play in terms of the variety of play statements or types of play communication used by the children to initiate, sustain, and conclude play in a specific social context. Emphasis is on the technicalities of setting up and sustaining the event. When interpreting the play events in their respective social contexts, Schwartzman (1978) suggests that the play was very much about dominance and manipulation, that it was "both a reflection and interpretation of these concerns" (p. 243). She also suggests that relationships of varying types ("genres" or "play styles," as she calls them) were used in play by the children to interpret and comment on their experiencing of their own relationships to each other (p. 245).

Schwartzman's (1978) study keeps close to the Batesonian model of the reciprocity and interconnection of structure and content, where each is a comment on the other. Her interpretation of the hierarchical relationships set up in the play illustrates the weaving of the children's social histories with the texts of their play and the relationship of both elements to the wider sociocultural context of the place of children and their hierarchical ranking in a variety of institutions such as the family and school.

What Schwartzman's (1978) study seems to ignore is that Bateson (1972) also drew attention to the dynamics of play by suggesting that "the psychological validity of the paradoxical frame depends on . . . the continual operation of the primary process part of the mind" (p. 184). However, because of his own emphasis on the logical structure of play and his evolutionary bias, it seems that in Schwartzman's work as well as that of others, it is the structural emphases that have tended to gain prominence.

The present study supports the spirit and epistemology that scaffolded Schwartzman's work but departs from it in many important respects. Primarily, it seeks to include the dynamics of play in considering its meaning. Other points of comparison and contrast will emerge as further details of this study are revealed.

2 Observing and Interpreting Play

Although issues of methodology are often decided upon prior to entering the fieldwork situation and thus, in conventional accounts of children's play, are not generally taken to be part of the meaning of the event under consideration, in this case I take them to be inextricably linked to the import of the study. This is because of my belief that methodology and epistemology—or scientific practice and the belief about knowledge—are two sides of the same coin. They are motivated by and contingent upon one another. Thus, my beliefs about how knowledge is constructed and about how to think about the phenomenon of play, thoroughly affected the ways in which I set about designing and executing this study.

The design (a longitudinal case study) and research style (a descriptive account based on participant observation) reflect an ethnographic approach that provides a more direct sense of comprehending people and events than is provided by casual and often unexamined classifications. The position taken in designing this study is that one cannot make general assumptions about the role of play but that one has to find out what play means in the particular cases at hand. Thus, this premise has its basis in the interpretive science model discussed in Chapter 1.

One of the assumptions of an ethnographic account is that an event or utterance cannot be understood without considering its significance to those who are involved in it. Such a study therefore inquires into the worlds of the participants with the intent of gaining some knowledge about the texture of their lives and worlds. As Hymes (1980) comments, "Whenever meaning having to do with resonance and consequence is successfully conveyed, one suspects a process of inquiry that was collaborative" (p. 84). In a similar vein, when Geertz (1972, p. 6) described an ethnographic account as a "thick description" of something, he meant that such a description gave a detailed account of the event or series of events from the standpoints of all participants.

Thus, participant observation provides the opportunity for entering into a mutual relation of interaction and adaptation between ethnographer and informants—a relationship that will change both.

Changes in the relationship result from undertaking to represent participants in their own terms, which requires a commitment to get close to them, to form a relationship with them, and to engage in face-to-face interaction. "Face-to-faceness," writes Lofland (1971), "has the irreplaceable character of . . . immediacy that furnishes the fullest possibility of truly entering the mind and definition of the other" (p. 2).

Studying people in this manner is of necessity a process of discovery. Since a major part of the event is provided by the participants in their own terms, it is counterproductive to impose on them preconceived schemes of what they are about. Generalizations are finally made on what the participants actually do. It is therefore necessary to assume a flexible approach to dealing with a reality that is changing and dynamic. This way of working contributes to as well as takes in the world in which it operates, as the story of Helen and myself illustrates. The descriptions arising out of participant observation are considered to be intersubjective accounts of the realities constructed by the participants.

RESEARCH PROCEDURES

Data Sources and Collection

Data were collected from my interactions with one child over the course of a year, during fourteen visits to her home. Visits varied in duration but on average lasted two to three hours, with some as long as five hours.

From the outset, field notes, written immediately after each session, were made of relevant features pertaining to social context. Such information included details on circumstances in which meetings were initiated, on beginnings, on behavior prior to play, on play behavior, on behavior after play, on relevant family interactions, and on endings. In addition, a log was kept of all telephone calls between the informant, her family, and me; of written communication between the parties; of visits to places outside the home with the informant or for the purpose of visiting her; of conversations with the child's parents, teachers, and friends; and of books read, television programs watched, and games played. This information was considered to have possible bearing on the study and its interpretation.

Audiotaping procedures were used to obtain a relatively accurate record of language in the relationship; however, this procedure was not introduced until the second session. Many of the details of the first and second sessions were recorded using shorthand whenever possible and at length immediately after leaving the house. Training of one's memory for the recording of all kinds of observed, felt, and heard detail is crucial when undertaking such research.

The decision not to use the recorder on the initial visit was for Helen's comfort. I felt that it was necessary to establish some rapport with her first and then introduce the recorder as casually as possible. In fact, I initially introduced the recorder as part of a fictive world that the child had already begun to construct. The opportunity to do so was serendipitous and could not be ignored. Consequently, she accepted the machine as part of her play world with enthusiasm.

However, the presence of such a machine in a social situation does affect the character of the speech forms produced. This is not to imply that the speech produced is in any way unnatural, but rather that "people speak in specific places, on specific occasions, about specific topics, to specific others" (Wolfson, 1979, p. 200), rather than in a social or situational void. Specific conditions such as these affect the speech forms people use and must be taken into account if we wish to have a realistic sense of the range and functions of the forms we wish to study (Wolfson, 1979).

Data in the present study suggest not only that the child is aware of the recorder but, in fact, that she frames its role in several ways. On occasions the machine is treated as an object to be ordered about and manipulated, as when, by my suggestion, it becomes to the child a "secret slave"; on others the recorder is given the role of an audience to her enacted stories; and on yet other occasions, tape recording itself becomes the sole object of her activity. She is wary of it at times, comfortable with it as often as not, but is clearly conscious of its presence.

What I taped were Helen's interactions with me and, on occasion, with her friends. Taping was usually confined to her play areas: her bedroom and bathroom. In general, the recordings were of conversations we had in preparation for the make-believe stories we staged, the performance of these, and the child's evaluations and celebrations of these during and after the performances. Each session yielded about 80 to 120 minutes of recorded material, although on most occasions the time we spent together was much longer (two to five hours). A total of thirty hours of these interactions was recorded, and an additional hour and a half was videotaped.

The conversations I had with Helen's parents were not audiotaped. I interviewed them casually about Helen's reading interests and patterns, television viewing, play behavior, relationships with peers and schoolteachers, and school experience. These conversations, in addition to the times I spent chatting with them over meals or coffee, were recorded only after leaving their home—the "research site." This was the case because, as Hymes (1980) writes, "In adopting an ethnographic approach one works in situations which require the trust of others, accommodation to their activities and participation in ways that often preclude writing or recording at the time" (p. 74). In such circumstances, he suggests that, in a bid for depth and the validity that this effort brings, certain kinds of reliability are sacrificed.

Transcription

After each session, the audiotapes were listened to, transcribed, annotated, and typed. Because the recordings were of the actual play activities, such as planning and enactment, all the material on each tape was transcribed. Standard spelling was used, even in instances of sound play, although in such instances, attempts were made to represent stress patterns, rhythms, and other textural features. Given the conversational and dramatic, scriptlike nature of the speech performance, the data were organized sequentially into dialogues. This sequencing, however, does not imply an assumption that everything that was said was always contingent upon and relevant to what preceded it. At times, however, speech was linked forward and backward to other passages and could be seen to reflect expectations for turn-taking by the different characters involved in the play enactments. Effort was made, however, not to impose such contingency links on the data, despite its spatial organization, and to keep the emphasis on the child, rather than the adult, as initiator and controller of the interactions. It is Helen's utterance that is taken to be the reference point, although I, as recipient of child-directed social behavior, am considered to be an important concern.

The quality of my recording of the nonverbal context of behavior was reduced by the physical constraints of note taking, especially since I was acting both as researcher and as participant in the play enactments initiated by the child. Therefore, although some gestures and other nonverbal behavior accompanying the verbal exchanges were described and included in the tape transcripts, verbal behavior became the center of attention and the nonverbal context was presented as an aid to interpreting it. While this was necessary under the circumstances, I am of course aware of the fact that, in some instances, nonverbal gestures themselves constituted important parts of the ideas and messages conveyed in the interactions, and that verbal means were often used conjointly with nonverbal means to convey the child's meanings.

All tapes were listened to a second time with an outsider. This was done to provide a reliability check and involved much more than a simple test of the accuracy of a given transcript. It became a means of extending and enriching the ethnographic and linguistic material originally obtained. Through discussion of the audiotaped material, we learned much about the evolving nature of the relationship between the child and me, as revealed in the content of our dialogue, the types of linguistic forms we used, and the voice quality and rhythms we used.

Much of this material could not have been obtained without these discussions with an outside listener. What they revealed so clearly was that verbal exchanges are composed not just of linguistic forms but of content and mood as well. Simply to deal with the text as a linguistic structure rather than a translinguistic one is to fail to grasp the meaning of the event for both the individual and society, and to ignore the fact that human communication patterns entail much more than verbal facility and are embedded in more than linguistic forms.

PRESENTATION OF THE DATA

Inclusion of Personal Details

Research involving extensive observation of individuals in their homes poses an obvious threat to privacy. The problem is exacerbated by the use of recording methods such as audio- and videotaping, which are used to gain detailed records of behavior. In the light of these considerations, in this study, the family and I signed a written agreement that allowed me to use the information I gathered for elucidating the aims of the study and for scholarly purposes, but guaranteed their rights to privacy and confidentiality. To this end, all names of places and participants and some minor details have been altered to preserve anonymity. In addition, personal information about the child, her family, and other participants is used only insofar as it illustrates the play texts, the relationships between participants, and the major propositions supported by the case at hand. Where its immediate relevance to the texts could not be demonstrated, any personal material, although taken into account in interpreting the data, was excluded from the descriptions presented.

Nature of the Data

The data are made up of a series of texts and their interpretations. I have not attempted to capture reality and store it, in order to retrieve and instantly replay it for whatever purpose. Rather, my data are made up of many codes, of many structures for which I have to account. On the one hand, I have to account for the actual process of human construction which has produced the text. On the other, I have to account for the event of interpreting or understanding the text.

Ordering of the Data

The data are presented as a verbal description, based on accounts contained in detailed notes, on the annotated transcripts, and on abstract categories derived from both the notes and transcripts. The description is influenced by the particular theoretical lenses used, which are described in the next section and discussed further in Chapter 9.

The data are organized in narrative terms, as a story to be told about what happened on each of the occasions on which Helen and I met. This storytelling approach to the actual events is meant to show, in the absence of film, something of the texture and proportion of this child and her play world, while in interaction with me. In addition, it charts the evolving relationship.

While a narrative depicting a temporarily ordered sequence of events is not the only form of organization possible, it is the form I have chosen for recounting a lived experience. I believe that this is the best way of presenting social science material about how human beings relate to each other because that is the dominant way in which human beings perceive their own state of affairs. Thus, by reconstituting the data in a story format, I believe that I am most clearly paralleling the way in which human beings assemble their own meanings in their own lives.

While social science has traditionally had a distrust of narrative or fiction, this is no longer the case (Hymes, 1981). It is increasingly realized that there is a close relationship between the character of fiction and the social construction of reality. We do not get an "objective" record simply by ignoring the nature of human "subjective" realities. If humans are storytelling creatures, then our social science had best mirror the nature of their stories. Not only is much of what we know based on personal accounts, but narrative is an influential form of knowing and a primary form of making connections. As Bateson (1979) writes, "Thinking in terms of stories must be shared by all mind or minds" (p. 13).

SOME INFLUENTIAL THEORETICAL LENSES

All of my interpretations of the data in this study are influenced by a symbolic interactionist paradigm of human behavior, which holds that human beings in interaction are engaged in a process of mutually defining their social worlds as they proceed. Thus, in analyzing my data, I have used several "terministic screens" (Burke, 1966) drawn from a number of interrelated perspectives such as phenomenology, ethnomethodology, dramatism, sociolinguistics, and communications theory. The theorists whose work has been of prime importance are Alfred Schutz (1964, 1976), Gregory Bateson (1956, 1972, 1979), Kenneth Burke (1941, 1966, 1969a, 1969b), Erving Goffman (1959, 1961, 1967, 1974, 1981), Dell Hymes (1964, 1974a, 1974b, 1975, 1981), and Brian Sutton-Smith (1971, 1974, 1976, 1979).

In addition, I have also used some psychoanalytic theories as interpretive lenses. These formulations have been regarded as comprising an etic system and thus seem to have been ignored by symbolic interactionist analyses, with the result that we have been alerted to the social aspects of behavior to the detriment of individual symbolic material. This may be explained by the monism traditionally embedded in the symbolic interactionist position, that the influence of the social world and the socialization of the individual outweigh the idiosyncratic tendencies of the individual. In interpreting my data, however, I have operated under the belief that, although the dynamics of the inner person are never objectively seen, they are always implied in social interaction and must be explained. Thus, although the major focus for presenting the data and for its intersubjective interpretation throughout this book shows the influence of Schutz and Goffman, more inferential paradigms such as those of Bateson, Burke, and Freud have also been used where it seems their insights would contribute to the understanding of the events presented.

In particular, Burke's theory of the symbolic action of literature as a kind of persuasion or rhetoric has been a primary influence in my interpreting these data. Burke has written many works, but those that have been most influential here are his *A Grammar of Motives* (1969a), *A Rhetoric of Motives* (1969b), and *Language as Symbolic Action* (1966). Although Burke largely restricts himself to literary symbolism, there seems no inherent reason why his intentions should not also apply to play and to its narratives and dramas. For instance, in my study, play can be seen as an attempt by the player to persuade herself or the other about certain meanings (rhetoric); it can be seen as a structure that sets up expectancies and dramatic excitement in the participants (grammar); and it can be seen as a kind of action through which the participants reveal their feelings and natures (symbolism).

This triad of concerns—rhetoric, grammar, and symbolism—has always been central to Burke's theory of symbolic action or "dramatism," as it is also called. Particularly, however, Burke argues that the rhetorical aspects of symbolic action have a priority in human affairs. We use symbols to persuade, to convince, to establish identities, to make identifications, and so on. [As most of the work of Goffman, in particular, in many ways extends this aspect of Burke into public behavior, it becomes a particularly appropriate source of semantics for the realm of play, which exists in between the realms of literature and public behavior.]

Thus, drawing upon Burke, I found it useful (1) to think of the ways in which the participants were persuading each other to do things and believe things (their rhetoric), (2) to try to understand the dramatic plot of the events they created (their structure), and (3) to attempt to know what was personally at stake for both of them (their symbolism).

In addition to this triad, Burke (1966) also uses various literary figures of speech as if they were paradigms for the ways we symbolize and behave. Thus, metaphor is for him at the basis of all thought. It helps us to see one thing in terms of another. In Burke's view of reality, if we are fluid enough in our thought, we will use many metaphors, knowing that life is a multiplicity of perspectives. Typically, however, we tend to be gripped by particular metaphors that confine us within the understanding at which we arrive. He calls this a "terministic screen" or a "metaphoric key."

Being possessed by a metaphoric key would also be expected to have much to do with the personal symbolism through which the individual wishes to find expression. Like Freud, Burke (1966) feels that personal motives cannot be ignored in the analysis of symbolic action. However, unlike Freud, he does not take symbolic action to be merely a defense against underlying motives or as merely a vehicle for serving personal motives. Rather, he sees it as part of the rhetorical character of social life, as well as the content of real performer-audience dramatic excitement. Indeed, Burke's view is both a "performance" (Bauman, 1975) theory as well as a symbolic one, in which symbols are forms of action and also kinds of emancipation.

For Burke (1968, 1969a), reality is the way in which all these ingredients—rhetoric, grammar, and symbolism—balance one another, according to the basic principle that none is more essential than any other except in the circumstances of some particular case. He speaks of such balancing in terms of "ratios of importance," "dramatic equations," or as the "proportionalizing of strategies." He suggests that Freud, as a consequence of his focus on symbolism as essential, has precommitted himself to one ultimate reality, rather than seeing that reality is never so simply possessed.

Finally, in Burke's (1966) theory of symbolic action, a symbol is always the means for interpreting a situation. It allows us to recognize and accept some inner or outer state of affairs we might otherwise ignore or repress. As such it is a composite of an emotional attitude (symbolism), a human relationship (rhetoric), and technique (grammar).

In discussing rhetoric I have been much influenced by the works of Erving Goffman, who was a leading thinker in interpreting the rhetoric of everyday life in face-to-face interactions of the kind that are being dealt with here. The accounts herein borrow heavily from his works, especially *The Presentation of the Self in Everyday Life* (1959), *Encounters* (1961), *Behavior in Public Places* (1963), *Interaction Ritual* (1967), and *Frame Analysis* (1974). What he showed so clearly throughout all these works was how we each seek to persuade others as well as ourselves of the interpretations we wish to have made of everyday situations.

In discussing structure I have followed those innumerable literary and anthropological thinkers who have analyzed literary works or human events in terms of their plots, their conflicts, and their rise and fall of dramatic tension. In particular, I have drawn on Brian Sutton-Smith's work, "The Dialectics of Play" (1978), in which he interprets play structures as being situation-specific syntheses and reconciliations of the oppositions to be found in everyday life.

On the level of symbolism, my debt is an older one. Beginning with Freud there has developed a vigorous tradition of play interpretation by psychoanalysts. In the modern era the most famous and most quotable interpreter must surely be Erik Erikson, who has written in great depth on the subject in works such as *Childhood and Society* (1963) and *Toys and Reasons* (1977). His notions of play as self-healing and as a kind of childhood planning are well known, and when he says, "With advancing age prolonged conversation would take the place of play" (1963, p. 205), he precisely anticipates the course of the present study. Perhaps more generally pertinent to the present work, however, is *Playing and Reality* by D. W. Winnicott (1971). Winnicott's sense of play as a special space, as a medium in which many things can come to fruition which are not possible in the everyday world, is very descriptive of the present study. Play is, as he called it, "an intermediate zone" between the self and the outside world. What one expects from psychoanalysts, however, is that in play one will find a symbolism and a working through of everyday concerns. That expectation is fully justified in the present work, in which the child's fundamental conflicts about herself in relation to the various worlds and relationships she inhabits are symbolized and transformed in the dramas of that intermediate zone.

In Chapter 9 I present a further discussion of play theories as they relate specifically to the interpretation of the play relationships discussed in Part II.

3 Portraits of the Participants

Having decided to undertake a study of the play of a child in the six-to-nine-year-old age range in the home and neighborhood environments, I needed to locate a family who would be willing to have me visit their home and its surroundings on a regular basis over the course of about a year to observe the play of their child of that age. Finding such a situation was not easy; however, in time I came across a couple I will call the Kings, who were looking for a baby-sitter for their child of almost seven and were comfortable about allowing me to make a case study of the play of their child. The parents were both social scientists and knew what a study like the one I proposed would entail.

THE CHILD

Helen, the child, is a white, mainstream middle-class female who was six years and eleven months at the time of our initial encounter. On that occasion she was filled with thoughts of being seven and was eagerly anticipating her birthday, which followed in a week.

Helen was told that I was a university student who would baby-sit her on several occasions and during the course of this might also ask her questions about her play and stories because of an interest I had in studying this topic. Being looked after by students was a familiar occurrence in Helen's life. Although she was initially made aware of my research interests, it seemed that she saw my role in the home as primarily that of caretaker. Throughout the study it became apparent that she wished to maintain this care-taking role on my **part** and tended mostly to ignore references that I made to writing a book about her play.

Helen comes from a bilingual home and is herself bilingual. At the time of the study she was an only child.

Prior to meeting my informant, the factors that governed my decision regarding her suitability were age, her socioeconomic back-

23

ground, and a situation that allowed me access to the child in the home. The baby-sitting arrangement was attractive because it facilitated such access and was an arrangement of mutual convenience for the family and me. It also turned out that Helen enjoyed our times together and, other than dealing with the difficulties of intermittent separations and the eventual ending of the relationship, seemed to benefit by the play times she and I shared. Thus, in many important ways the child was chosen on the grounds of convenience to the parties involved, and the relationship as initially negotiated was one of reciprocity.

My first meeting with Helen confirmed her suitability. She was a child in whose life fiction and play seemed to assume an important role; hence I made a commitment to continue working with her. During the time of my study, I spent about eighty hours getting to know and understand much about Helen.

It was her large and wistful blue eyes that first struck me upon seeing her. They were the same eyes that often trailed me into the distance when I bade her goodbye before what seemed to her an interminably long parting. They marked the privacy and silence of her public demeanor, for, as a child who was often among adults in every-day situations, Helen was noticeably reserved in the presence of strangers and disinterested in relating to adults in whom she had little investment. It is worth noting that a recently published book on the seven-year-old corroborates this picture of Helen's generally with-drawn public demeanor (Ames & Haber, 1985).

In contrast, as a participant in her own worlds she was active, lively, and both initiating and controlling of much of the course of events. This was especially true of her in the fantasy and play worlds of the present study. In addition, it was evident in her play with some of her peers. She was always eager to play with me, the investigator, as well as with those "chosen" friends who were also her school pals. She found engaging in fantasy and in the creation of impossible worlds highly exciting. During our play periods she was alive and passionate and I found her behavior to range from being active, domineering, and superior to being malleable, warm, extremely uninhibited, nonsensical, and babyish.

Her highly verbal, intensely dramatic, fun-loving and passionate character emerged when Helen felt sufficiently safe and relaxed to let down her guard, which hung upon those wistful blue eyes. Accordingly, I also found that the child was intent upon keeping her special friends, exclusive and away from the scrutiny of others. For instance, she often sought to keep secret from her parents the nature of these relationships by denying that we played and by locking the bedroom door on what might be an intrusion from the outside world. The occasional neighborhood child who wandered into the backyard during the course of a game was asked to leave. The privacy of meaningful relationships was important to Helen. Not only did she work to keep these and her manner of relating within them private, but her public face was markedly different from her private and more vivacious one. Observations of this child in public would fail to reveal much about who she was in other situations where she felt a sense of comfort and control.

Helen attended a small private day school which catered largely to children of middle- to upper-middle-class parents who valued education. In school, she was regarded by teachers as an outstanding student who was a highly competent reader. Some described her as "imaginative and literary minded." This view corroborated Helen's own pride in herself as being an avid and advanced reader. On several occasions she told me that reading books was her favorite "sport," whereas she hated "real gym and sports." Although she appeared to read widely and was quick to display a knowledge of history, science, and current affairs in particular, her most favored and consistent diet was fiction, particularly myths, high fantasy, and science fiction. When asked about her reading interests, Helen said, "I like fiction books with plenty of magic and adventure. Also a few realistic fiction books, mainly Judy Blume." She added that she liked folk tales and myths. Her favorite authors were C. S. Lewis (the Narnia series), Frank Baum (the Oz books), J. R. Tolkien (*The Hobbit*) and Lloyd Alexander (*The Book of Three*). As a much younger child she had been fascinated by J. M. Barrie's *Peter Pan* and on occasion still talked of it.

Her television viewing was monitored. She was allowed to watch shows for a selected period of time each week, and there were a few programs that she religiously watched. For instance, at a younger age she had enjoyed "Sesame Street" and "The Muppets." During the course of my visits to her, she eagerly watched "Wonder Woman," "Battlestar Gallactica" and "Mork and Mindy." I also noticed that she liked watching holiday specials like Halloween shows and extravaganzas with dancing girls, floats, and a carnivalesque spirit. Helen mentioned that many of her school friends watched the same shows but tended to spend more time than she did watching television. On occasion, she voiced a somewhat censorious attitude to television watching by saying that "too much television watching spoiled your mind." However, she defended herself by saying that when she watched television, she did not just sit there but was thinking about how she could use all "the stuff" and "make it into a big play or story with her imagination." As the description of her play will attest, in her play with her peers and me she did indeed draw on various television images and scripts, as well as several plot elements derived from her reading. But these were always transformed by her own needs and agenda.

Over the course of the year of the study, Helen expressed an interest in going to college to pursue a range of careers. These included being a poet, a scientist, a folklorist, and an actress; on later visits to her, she seemed intent on becoming a psychiatrist because "friends always expected her to solve their problems," she said.

Among her peers, I observed her to wax and wane in her popularity. She was described by one of her friends to be "a neat kid" and one she liked. However, Helen herself suggested that there were several of her peers who were mean to her and disliked her.

In all, she was on the one hand an unusual little girl, given her precocity; yet, on the other, she showed a range of behaviors and interests that seem "normal" for a child of her age and sociocultural and familial background. The details of the portrait suggest that Helen is typical of many firstborn, often gifted and bookish children of mainstream nuclear families. The gradual growth of the middle class and its values in our society in the past several hundred years and the thrust toward early literary socialization have meant that more and more children have spent time in solitary activity, either in the presence of adults or with objects such as books or toys, in front of television screens or alone in their bedrooms. A convincing case has recently been made for the solitariness of today's children's play lives and for the increasing subjectiveness of much of this activity (Sutton-Smith, 1985). In short, what all this might suggest in terms of the present case is that, although there is much that is uniquely wonderful about Helen and the way she set about making a relationship with me as we jointly constructed her play worlds, nevertheless, she is not unlike several other bookish children we may encounter in the literature (Butler, 1979; Crago & Crago, 1983; Scollon & Scollon, 1981; White, 1954) or in the everyday world.

THE CHILD'S PARENTS

When this study was proposed, the Kings were happy for me to proceed with it under the condition that they would be guaranteed anonymity. As such, not only have all the names of the participants been changed but specific details pertaining to their personal lives have been approximated wherever possible and sometimes even withheld.

Thus, although there may be instances where the reader may desire more information about the Kings, the lack of it is a means of protecting the family. The details that follow are accurate but of a general nature.

Don and Pamela King are both college educated, highly independent individuals, each of whom aggressively pursues a career. They are both social scientists, are bilingual, and have traveled and lived in different places in the world. Pamela King is of American birth and her husband is of Middle Eastern origin.

The Kings encouraged Helen's participation in as many aspects of knowledge gaining as possible and greatly valued both this quality as well as education. An eagerness to learn, industriousness, discipline, puritanism, and independence were encouraged and prized by the family.

Although the Kings were keenly interested in Helen's well-being, spent time encouraging her interests, and shared time with her, their extremely busy professional lives led them to spend much time away from her. She had been looked after by baby-sitters from a very early age. Being grown up, mature, adult, and responsible were important and desired qualities her parents looked for in Helen in relating to her.

Pamela and Don were a constant and important backdrop to the study. Although they did not figure in the play as active participants, they were a very significant part of Helen's life and inevitably affected the play material. Further, their attitudes toward the study and toward me constantly affected the course of the relationship that Helen shared with me. However, details of the ways in which they affected Helen's and my behavior have been largely withheld in accordance with our agreement regarding privacy. On the whole they were very supportive of a situation that could at times have been experienced as an intrusion into their lives, and without their support the study would not have occurred. I am extremely grateful for their openness of spirit on this score.

THE RESEARCHER

An unusual feature of this book is that I played the double role of researcher and participant in the study and also am an active construer of the interpretations presented herein. Data more commonly are presented solely as they pertain to the informants. However, in the view of interpretive science, researchers and writers are not neutral beings and in these roles bring several aspects of their biographies to bear on the decisions they make and the behavior in which they engage as they observe, select, and document any set of events. Indeed, for some time now, anthropologists have commented that the researcher is a factor in the inquiry, for better or worse (Nash & Wintrob, 1972; Ruby, 1982). Hymes (1980) suggests that, on the one hand, this is for the better, because some researchers are more skilled than others in getting at the desired knowledge. On the other hand, it is for the worse because of an acknowledged partiality. However, this dilemma cannot be avoided and the only way to deal with it is to recognize it and allow for it in the interpretation. The following is the information that I feel with hindsight affected my role as well as those of my informants in the study.

There is no doubt that there is a degree of serendipity in discovering good informants; in finding families generous enough to permit an outsider access to their homes and lives for the purpose of investigating questions of scholarly interest. My meeting the Kings was most fortunate. I was introduced to them by a friend who had once been a student of Don King's and had also done some baby-sitting for Helen. My friend knew that I was looking for a child and family with whom I could work, and she also happened to discover that the Kings were in need of a baby-sitter during the afternoons and evenings. This friend told the Kings of my work and interest in observing a child's play in the home and inquired whether they were interested in striking some mutually satisfying deal. The Kings were open to the idea; in fact, Don King called me to set up our first meeting. I persuaded him that it would be better to discuss the matter on the telephone. If they were agreeable, I would make my first visit to them one in which I could meet Helen and that I also could take to be the official beginning of the study. In this way I could make the relationship with the Kings reflexive from the outset. Don King was quite happy for me to do all this, and we arranged a date the following week when I could meet and spend time with Helen. The details of this first meeting are included in Part II.

Before arranging this study, I had taught for a couple of years in high school, had taught university and college students for four years, and had worked on several research projects with children ranging in age from three to fourteen years, both in Australia and London. Thus, I was no neophyte when it came to dealing successfully with children from varying age levels and backgrounds. Therefore, although I did not know how Helen would respond to me, and knew that at first she would most certainly hold all the cards, I had some confidence that I approached her with a range of tested instincts and hunches in hand. As the story will illustrate, this experience as a teacher and researcher facilitated my ability to understand the ways that children think and some of the archaic and obscure language they use—in particular the language of their fantasies, in which the actors are supermen, wonder women, and monsters and the settings are freezing-cold planets, Olympus, and dark holes.

Further—and most important—I knew how to play. I come from a family where paradox, exaggeration, and irreverence are valued; where pranks, jokes, and histrionic behavior are thought to be humorous and are encouraged. I have had a great deal of practice in entering situations that call for role flexibility. My presentation of self in this fieldwork situation benefited from this pattern of family interaction. My familiarity with a great deal of children's literature and my experience as a teacher of children's drama also allowed me to recognize and enter easily the many fictional worlds that Helen created.

I felt comfortable with children. I felt free to move from the position of power and control that I had as an adult in the everyday world of caretaking, to one where I was regressed in play and often directed by the child's whims and dictates. The only stricture that I placed on Helen was that she could in no way physically hurt me. My ability to play and be empathic to her fantasy worlds at some level accounted for Helen's increasing interest in and enchantment with me, her adult playmate. It is relevant to what occurred in this study that I brought to our interactions patterns of relating that were familiar to Helen and that, in addition, I valued the cultural forms of play, story, and drama and the childlike precocity that Helen brought to the situation.

Although those biographical factors positively affected the relationship that was forged between us and the wealth of play that occurred, there were other factors that negatively affected the dynamics of the relationship between Helen and me. I was an Australian national and new to the American culture. Although I had traveled extensively and lived abroad for lengthy periods of time, in doing this research I encountered a clash between my sense of appropriate presentation of self and that adhered to by the sociocultural group to which the Kings belonged. My presentation of self was as a Ph.D. student. My appearance was relatively youthful and my manner indirect and understated. I took the use of indirection to reflect modesty, politeness, and discretion. In contrast, the Kings were highly direct and forthright about themselves, their opinions, and their achievements. The Kings, who took my presentation of self literally, often rushed to inform me about matters about which they felt I was ignorant or unsure. In turn, I experienced this behavior on their part as insensitive and rude. This misreading of cultural positions ricocheted off the relationship between Helen and me from time to time by lessening my desire to see the Kings. I felt I needed to recover from a way of relating that I sometimes found abrasive. At first, my foreign status prevented me from understanding many aspects of the family's behavior as being conventional within their cultural context.

Further, in my role as baby-sitter, which was the role that the family and I decided I would play in entering the Kings' home, I was often treated as a subordinate and one who was in the family's service, although I requested that no money be exchanged for the service. However, having grown up in a home where there were several servants who had worked for the family and were carefully regarded as hierarchically separate from the family, I found it difficult to accept this role of baby-sitter and one who was instructed on how to care for this child. Although I did not anticipate such difficulty, I felt immense relief when I was able to renegotiate my relationship with the family after the first three months so that I no longer played the role of a baby-sitter but was one who came to visit Helen and play with her.

My attempts to personalize the relationship I had with Helen, which meshed with her efforts to draw me into her world, were, I believe, unwitting bids to be more than a domestic, which the notion of baby-sitter held from me. Such examples illustrate the fact that one cannot escape from the effects of one's own cultural experience and the multiple communities to which one belongs, which dictate all kinds of reactions in various situations. I believe that, as teachers, researchers, or members of various helping professions, when we deal with children and their families, we never act as neutral beings but as informed professionals who nevertheless run the risk that our biases, needs, and vulnerabilities will blind us or color our vision.

In relation to Helen, I soon came to understand that she saw me as an adult who was different from others she had met. This was important in legitimating my role as a researcher to the child. Helen knew that I was an outsider to the culture, but she also knew and was enthralled by the knowledge that I was particularly interested in children's books, play, and stories. She was especially impressed by my ability to play. She was personally motivated to facilitate my agenda of discovering as much as possible about "children's stories," as she often put it, in exchange for having an adult who would play with her exclusively in ways she initiated. As Pelto and Pelto (1978) write, "Success in the art of fieldwork depends, to a considerable extent, on establishing a very special role that legitimizes a kind of information gathering behavior that was not part of social expectations within the community." They point out that, although the researcher may identify with local inhabitants, "the role of gatherer of information, persistent questioner and stranger from another culture is always part of one's social identity" (p. 182).

I believe that, throughout our relationship, Helen saw my foreign status, most evident in the way I spoke, as something different and complementary to her fantasy worlds, which, after all, had little to do with her everyday life. For my part, I attempted to achieve both the role of friend and confidante, in much the same way a trusted family friend or teacher, with whom a child may have a special relationship, might do. In addition, however, I was the adult inquirer who stood apart in order to gather as much information as possible and lived a life that Helen saw as interfering with her wish to have me play with her constantly. Indeed, it was not always easy to keep the roles of friend and researcher apart. At times, their blurring led to difficulties for both the Kings and me, as the story reveals.

My patterns of social interaction; my professional training as a teacher of language and literature and as an educational researcher who espoused an interdisciplinary approach to understanding the worlds of childhood; and my personal dynamics, although thoroughly individual, may also be located and understood within larger cultural patterns and group allegiances. The same is true for the child. It is my hope that the portraits presented in this chapter will enable the reader to recognize each of the actors and compare my findings with those of other pertinent cases in this culture.

Part II
STORY OF THE RELATIONSHIP

In this second part of the book you will read the story of the play relationship between Helen and Diana, as told by me. It is a story told on several levels. First there are the stories made up by Helen for the purpose of our playing together, which are a central part of this relationship. Then there is the narrative description of the way Helen arranged the relationship, through tests and initiations, in order to introduce me gradually into a closer relationship with herself. Our total relationship has a beginning, a middle, and a final phase. Finally this is all told to the reader within my reported account of the sessions. Many other stories of this sequence are possible. There is never only one perspective or only one true story. The interpretations made of these three accounts in this section of the book comprise yet another story.

It became clear early in the piece that my preference for telling the story of our relationship was to envisage it as something constructed by the participants. In interpreting what has happened I have found it necessary to distinguish between the relationships Helen and I constructed in the *everyday realm*, where we dealt with each other as public persons; in the *play realm*, within which we shared fantasies, narratives, and dramas; and the *intimate realm*, within which we related to each other as private persons. This kind of approach, which focuses on the way human beings construct their social meanings together, is called a *phenomenological approach*. It is usually

a part of that kind of philosophizing which argues that in understanding human events we should first try to discover what the
meaning of those events is to those who participate in them (Schutz,
1964). Although this would seem at least an intelligent starting point
for any human inquiry, it has been largely neglected in the study of
children, and in particular in the study of their play.

This is not to suggest that it is easy to do. There is much reason
to believe that the invention of the kind of childhood that we know
in modern civilization has much to do with our own needs for adult
self-control. In some senses we appear to have an investment in not
knowing too well what children really mean and how they really feel.
Perhaps it is not surprising, then, that no one had done extensive
and systematic "participatory" studies with children before, even
though such studies are accepted practice in anthropology. It probably takes a special skill to participate with children in their doings for
any length of time when it is the children who, by and large, are allowed to suggest the direction of events rather than the adults. As
you shall see, the present study was not accomplished without considerable fatigue for me, the investigator, as I sought to make the everyday, playful, and intimate communications between myself and
the child the center of the inquiry. Given that the inquiry had this
"intersubjective" character, it also followed that we had to be concerned not only with what the child brought to the situation, but
also with what I brought. We had to seek to understand how my
personal needs in their own subtle ways might be guiding the ways
Helen and I played together.

The readers must judge for themselves whether the story as I
tell it has the ring of authenticity. Whether it does or not, my present point is that the focus of this work is in the first place upon my
description of the evolving relationship within the everyday, play,
and intimate realms, where Helen and her world are always kept in
sharp focus. It is a story about what happened in the narrative that
we created for ourselves.

To help the reader, I would like to describe what will be revealed
as the major thrust of the relationship constructed by the child in
these fourteen sessions. Although this only became clear to me after
much laborious analysis, it is pointless to put the reader through the
same process. Thus, as I see it, this child's major theme (or "metaphoric key," as Burke (1966) would term it) was to articulate a
system of dimensions through which she sought to establish power
in the everyday, play, and intimate realms. A diagram of its elements
is shown in the Figure. Some of these elements are introduced in the

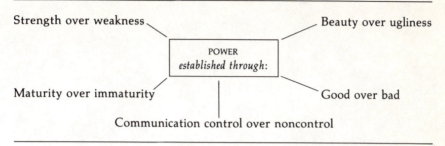

Dimensions through which Helen sought to establish power

narrative of the first session (see Chapter 4). They are then reiterated, developed, and added to throughout the course of the relationship.

As a final note, it is worth saying that relationships are complex and unpredictable and begin from the moment of meeting. At the beginning and many times thereafter, certain cues and propositions are tacitly exchanged. These become the bases for a series of events that shape the course of the relationship. In addition, although Helen's and my initial purposes in coming together were different, the relationship was nevertheless reciprocal. Even though careful observation of Helen was my primary purpose, there is little doubt that she watched me for her own and rather different purposes.

As true stories sometimes do, the story of Helen and me may bring the shock of encounter for some readers. It may also further understanding of the difficulty and reward of studying play in a way in which the gamut of behaviors, strategies, rhetoric, symbols, moods, and phases occurring in the life of play partners may be acknowledged. In addition, it stands to remind the reader of the varied course of any human relationship in which people risk encountering one another.

Readers may find that at some points in the narrative the descriptions of the play and the extracted transcripts from the recordings are somewhat long and tedious and have their moments of unintelligibility and incoherence. However, such difficulties are an integral part of the experience of understanding something of what it is like to play with a child on her own terms. As an adult, I often experienced a similar difficulty in understanding the child's play and dealing with its protean character, while I was in the midst of playing with her. It was no easy task, but it provided me with an opportunity to study and understand the phenomenon of play in a way that I had not been able to by reading prior accounts.

4 *The Beginning Phase*

Beginnings are beset with many fears and hopes, which coexist in our minds. The less we know about the situation to be entered upon, the freer we are to invest it with good or bad qualities, with wishes as well as anxieties. This was true for me, and I presume for Helen, as we turned our attention to our first meeting. As you will discover, my anxieties were not without ground. Although I was an adult, I was a stranger who needed to be accepted by the child and family if my hopes for initiating a research project in this home were to be realized. From the moment we all met, our respective relationships were set in motion, as the details that follow suggest.

SESSION 1, SEPTEMBER 19
The Preliminary Tests

It was 5:00 of a summer's evening when I first met Helen. After she opened the front door to me, she rushed behind her mother, a tall, dark, attractive woman who smiled as she gestured for me to come in. Being intensely aware of Helen, who was, in contrast to her mother, blue eyed, pale, and wan looking, I managed in the midst of these initial moments to greet the child, saying "Hi! I'm Diana." What I heard in response from Helen was a comment that struck me as somewhat uncharacteristic of children one does not know. Under her breath, she said, "Um! Another Wonder Woman." Such evaluations are usually part of an inner response to a situation and are rarely voiced so candidly during introductions in face-to-face encounters. Nevertheless, as I was to discover, it was a comment that linked the child and her world by allusion to me, the stranger and new baby-sitter. It was also a cue for what was to come, although at the time I did not recognize it as such.

This direct encounter was then displaced by Pamela, who briefly explained her plans for the evening, showed me around the house, and told me about caretaking details pertaining to Helen. She also suggested that the child be taken to Gino's (a fast-food restaurant) for dinner and added that her husband and she planned to be back about eight o'clock. Then, indicating that she was in a hurry, she left, leaving Helen and me standing in the living room. While her mother had been speaking to me, Helen had remained silent but had continued to watch me carefully. As soon as her mother left, Helen sat down on the sofa and gestured to me to join her.

She initiated the next question, asking me whether I had read the Bible. When I replied that I had read a great deal of it, Helen said that she had read the entire Old Testament. Offering to read me some of it, she duly turned to a passage from the Psalms and read it accurately although somewhat stiltedly and with not much sense to it. She then arbitrarily stopped at a certain point and looked at me as if for approval. I complimented her efforts and inquired whether she knew many of the stories in the Bible. Helen replied that she did.[1]

Helen then laid the Bible down and initiated another conversation. She asked me what we should do, and I asked her whether she would like me to read her a story. She replied proudly that she could read herself. With the reading activity thus rejected and the child's own competence in the area underlined, I asked the child what she would prefer to do instead. She answered, rather haughtily, "Don't you think we'd better get to know each other first?"

When I agreed with her suggestion, she set up a further condition: "Okay. But then you have to come to my room." This may be regarded as yet another element in Helen's bid to control the encounter successfully. Given my motivation to succeed with her, I agreed to move to the bedroom. As we walked up the stairs and stood on the threshold to Helen's bedroom, she stopped short. Turning to me, she announced an interdiction: "I tell no one my dreams, secrets, secret language, or about my superheroes, so don't ask me about them." As she said

---

[1]Helen's question about the Bible and subsequent behavior demonstrating her reading prowess suggested a particular presentation of self. Although the presentation was implied and therefore indirect, in Goffman's (1959) terms it was "frontstage" behavior; that is, it was an act by which the child wished to regulate and shape the encounter by presenting herself in a particular and favorable light. The self presented was that of a competent, well-read, literate, and superior figure.

this, I could not help noticing the backstage scene: The surface of the door to Helen's room and part of a bedroom wall were filled with posters of Wonder Woman as well as other allusions to the world of superheroes.

Supporting the child's right to reveal only what she wished, I said that that was fine and asked about what we would do instead. She assured me that we would find something to do. Once we were in the room, Helen asked me whether I could fly and showed me how. I accepted the challenge and said that I thought I could. With Helen urging me to fly, I followed her in a flying movement; that is, I put my arms out sideways like an airplane and moved across the room. She continued flying, to the accompaniment of whizzing noises, and then interrogated me once more. She asked me whether I knew who she was. As I shook my head in puzzlement, she said that she was "Beauty the Butterfly" and then "Golden Bird the Raven Helper." When I commented that they were all good at flying, she rather emphatically and smugly commented, "Of course they are, since they are superheroes." At this point she introduced me to the flying superheroes and challenged me to imitate them, which I did. In mirroring her behavior, I "consensually validated" her fantasy realm.

Next she introduced me to another feature from her fantasy world by asking me somewhat challengingly whether I had been to a secret place where they spoke secret languages. She told me about her own land and language, but the words she used were a play of nonsense syllables. When I said that I did not know her land or language but knew another secret language, Helen displayed great interest in it and wished to hear it as well as be taught it. After I had taught her a secret language that I myself had used as a child, we used it to talk with each other for a while.

A little later, Helen turned again to mentioning her secret land, emphasizing that she knew this place very well. My inquiry as to how she knew this place so well resulted in a rather elaborate answer in narrative form: "I know this land, Balalulaland, where they speak secret languages very well. I was there as a baby. I grew into a very powerful princess with magical powers. I was invulnerable, the most beautiful girl. I could conquer everything. My father the king was dead, killed by enemies . . . Swabs. It was always war there, and we had to make it peace—be nice to everyone, care about people, like I did. Not like Michael, who doesn't." When I asked who Michael was, she said that he was a boy in her school whom she hated, and who was a tease and also hated her. By way of noting a contrast, she added rather quietly, "I like teenagers like you."[2] Although I was far from being a teenager, Helen's view of university students was that they were older teenagers, an image no doubt corroborated by my being casually dressed in blue jeans and wearing long hair.

After this, I suggested that we have dinner, to which Helen agreed, saying, "Come on, let's go. I'll show you where it is." As we walked a few blocks to Gino's restaurant, we chatted about her friend Michael and other children in her school who were mean to her. On entering Gino's her talkative manner subsided. After we had ordered our food and sat down to it, she informed me that she did not wish to talk while eating. We ate quickly and in silence.[3]

On returning home Helen ran upstairs, asking that I follow her. When we reached her bedroom, she collected some miniature animals off her bookshelf and suggested that we play with them. The animals were a squirrel, dog, pig, dinosaur, cow, and a few others. She set them up in two groups and quickly designated some to be robbers intent on stealing the treasure and jewels, and the others as "good guys." She was very directive in this game, asking me to animate the "bad guys" while she animated the "good guys." She suggested that we would "do a story with them. Come on, how will it go?" she asked, eager for me to outline a plot. I, however, kept avoiding her question and looked at her for suggestions because I wished the direction of this play to be developed by the child. In this, I was cueing her about my nondirectiveness and tendency to allow her agenda to hold sway.

Finally, Helen began to play out a story involving the two opposing groups. She used a statement and counterstatement routine in which

---

[2] The sharing of this fantasy autobiography seemed to signal that Helen had reached a level of safety with me, after which she relaxed into desultory, formless functioning. For example, she began to play with nonsense words that trailed off into tunes, asked that I tap dance with her, lassoed imaginary figures in the air, and requested that I follow her into the bathroom, so we could continue talking while she toileted.

[3] This activity seemed to be "time out" if you will, a period during which the child may not have wished to have our prior relatedness interrupted. It seemed as though she was minimizing her contact with me as baby-sitter, who, as an adult, was now a more public figure. It was only after returning to the house that Helen resumed her animated chatter and activity. This pattern of being quiet in public situations became evident in several other sessions and may be a feature of her public front, where she is much more the kind of child who is seen and not heard (see Ames & Haber, 1985, for a view of the taciturn seven-year-old).

she directed me to play the role of the antagonist. She would often laugh at each of our responses, adding, "It's so funny" in a somewhat caricatured voice. Her parents returned while we were playing, but, on hearing them approaching her room, she asked that they not come in until we had finished our game. At the end she said, "I like you. You are a good actor and player," and then reverted to using the secret language we had played at earlier in the evening. She was eager that I evaluate her performance at storying and also wished me to share my thoughts about the moral dimensions of her story. I declined answering either query, in accordance with my own motives which were that the child's agenda should not be explicitly evaluated by me.

Following this we went downstairs. As we did so she continued laughingly to talk in our secret language, this time in her parents' company. They seemed amused at her behavior and commented on it to each other in a foreign tongue that I did not understand. Her father said to me, "She's hyper. We'll have to quiet her down." I said that I thought she would soon calm down and gathered my belongings to leave. At this point Helen, who had been circling around the room said, "Pie pove pyou. Pum pagain poon." Laughingly, I said, "Pie pill" and left. It was 9:30 P.M.

Commentary

This first session is filled with much that is of interest regarding Helen's world and the ways in which she manages her relationship with me as the adult researcher/baby-sitter. Much that occurs in this crucial session sets the scene for what is to come in future meetings. It is a good example of the principle that the first few minutes of a meeting can reveal much about the issues that will be later developed, if we are able to recognize and clearly perceive what is going on between the parties involved.

Contained in this first encounter are the announcements of many themes with which Helen will concern herself throughout our play relationship. As discussed in Chapter 2, Burke (1965, 1966) uses the term *metaphoric key* to describe these motivating concerns. Helen's metaphoric key included a concern with power, beauty, morality, wisdom, maturity, and the control of communication. By virtue of my name at least, Helen associated me with one of her heroines and sources of identification (Diana, the Wonder Woman of television and cartoon fame). Thus, the child's opening statement, "Um! another Wonder Woman" was not only an evaluation of a stranger and an early orientation to the child's world, but also a symbolic statement vis-à-vis herself.

Helen's heroine, Wonder Woman, was also her own symbol of power, associated with beauty, morality, and wisdom; and it is striking how she expressed her interest in these qualities and their opposites at the very beginning.

By placing these motivating concerns constituting Helen's metaphoric key at the center of the interpretations in this study, we can see that these concerns are a statement simultaneously of the focal point of the child's psychology, of her social management techniques, and of her dramatic elaborations. For example, Helen's rhetoric, as Burke (1969b) calls it, or her management of the social situation, was predominantly concerned with power and dominance, with controlling both the situation and the adult through her own presentation of self as competent. The large number of rhetorical questions that she asked me appear to have been her attempt at mobilizing the activity between us as well as directly seeking permission to focus attention on sharing information about herself with me. Helen's strategies were crucial to her psychological purpose: to move me from a more public domain into her more private world.

The child's bid for control of what was going on was further focused by the conditions she laid down for the ritual of getting to know one another. First she designated a separate location for the process. Thus, in addition to setting the stage for a particular kind of managerial yet loose relatedness between us, she used the location of that activity to differentiate between that which was outside and that which was inside. The nature of this new domain and the quality of relatedness Helen desired were soon revealed by her fantasy behavior.

The new location, the bedroom, was to become the setting for the next phase of our interactions. As a symbol, it suggests privacy and autonomy for children and thus is an environment that can become charged with personal meaning and symbolism.

As researcher and co-participant I complied with the child's suggestions, and the resulting interaction depended as much on this compliance as upon the child. As researcher I was also managing the situation to meet my own ends. My "script" dictated that I should be as supportive, nondirective and accommodating of the child as possible and allow her to structure the occasion overtly. Thus I was facilitating a situation in which my informant would feel free to relate to me and share her multiple worlds. My assumption was that, if I were as accepting as possible of the child and allowed her to initiate behavior, then I had a better chance of engaging her interest and becoming more than an outsider or stranger.

As we have seen, the rhetoric never stops but is a constant part of the social process, the whole of which is always sustained by personal and motivated involvement (see Adler, 1956). Helen's behavior on the threshold to her bedroom once again alerted me to her rhetoric, but its focus had shifted to a new realm—the *play realm* that she and I, her adult co-participant, would enter. Her barring of certain areas of experience from our conversations (no dreams, secrets, secret languages, or super-heroes) was a metacommunication about the order of events in which she was soon to engage. The posters and other visual "scenery" rein-forced her assertions about the structure of her private world and further illustrated her metaphoric key. This is not unusual: The posses-sions we cherish often signify what we are about and what sort of interactions might develop (Csikszentmihayli, 1980). Helen's behavior at her bedroom door is also entirely consistent with her own grammar or plot for the occasion. In fact, the entire scene reveals Helen in the process of staging her own drama, one where her interactions with me would unfold in a narrative way.

Helen's interdiction about secret languages served two functions. First, it became part of a series of *tests* that the child gave to me regarding my suitability as a partner in her world. In terms of her own ritualistic plot for the occasion, they became rites of initiation. There is a natural progression unfolding here: Having already oriented me, her co-participant, to another frame of activity (play) and marked it by its location (her bedroom), Helen further underlined the import of this behavior by a series of staged tests. Van Gennep (cited in Douglas, 1966) shows how a threshold symbolizes the beginning of a new status, and Douglas adds that no experience is too lowly to be taken up in ritual and given a lofty meaning. What was at stake for Helen was initiating me into her inner world, an action that to her was worthy of ritual.

Helen's interdiction, by drawing attention to what was *not* to tran-spire in the new frame, began to define the activity that *was* to be engaged in within the room. It thus was a cue to me she was not going to be dealing with the meaning of secrets and superheroes in a basic referential sense, but that she was going to deal with them in a playful one (see Bateson, 1972). As such, it was a frame for telling me how to "read" what was to come, how to understand the paradoxical nature of the behavior shortly to be engaged in. What Helen was going to reveal, she suggested, were not *really* her dreams, secrets, and so on, but rather a *play* on these phenomena. The play would be of the order of Bateson's (1956) "nip" rather than "bite," as discussed in Chapter 1. Her subsequent play behavior in the bedroom exemplified the paradoxical nature of her interdiction.

Once in the bedroom, Helen broke through into dramatic performance, including flying, whizzing, using secret languages, creating secret lands, and talking nonsense. All of these activities were arousing and part of the grammar of her behavior in the new play realm. Here too, she asked me questions in a bid to engage me in her private world as well as to test my suitability as a play partner. Her questions in this realm (such as, "Can you fly?" "Can you speak secret languages?"), unlike those in the everyday realm, were explorative rather than rhetorical. They reflected Helen's interest in discovering whether her potential play partner could fable as she could. By encouraging me to mimic her physical activity, she was exemplifying a type of initiation that often occurs in very young children's play. In such instances they imitate each other and in so doing both test and validate their suitability for acceptance by the partner.

In sharing this activity we both had entered a very different realm from that of the everyday. We had moved into the play realm—the realm of fantasy, play, drama, and story. The paradox contained in her notion of "playing at dreams" created an "intermediate zone" (Winnicott, 1971) for mutual risk in regression. Such zones of play behavior are reassuring and generate trust, acceptance, and intimacy.

Given that Helen conducts the investigator through a number of zones within her play realms—flight, secret languages, Balalulaland, and nonsense—each one presumably more deeply seated in the child's fantasy life than the last, it is difficult at this stage to talk of the structure of the fantasy. It is the sequence of play or genres that is more remarkable in this first session. However, Balalulaland, briefly sketched with its baby, princess, magic, dead king, Swabs, and war, held considerable promise for future elaborations of complex narrative structure, and this is what indeed occurred in later sessions.

Personal Symbolism

Helen's narrative proved to be a fantasy autobiography, a fictional representation of her private self as princess and as a super and wondrous being. Her telling of the tale also marked a deeper sharing of herself with me. The self presented in this story was another of the faces of her competent, controlling self of the everyday realm. The various selves revealed through her behavior in the three realms may be considered as laminations of her composite, everyday self. They were felt to be no less real than the everyday self.

Although the story symbolized the more private dream self, it was clearly marked as being of another place and time; it was of the realm of faraway, magic, mystery, princesses, and Swabs, in which there is no mother and the father is dead. However, as in fairy tales, there were few details of scene or time (Luthi, 1976). Instead, we have a cast of characters, a series of actions, and a clear purpose or cause to which the princess must attend. She must bring peace and destroy evil, and her agency for this is magic.

The narrative also provided a means by which Helen was able to share an important piece of information with me. Her sentence comparing me to Michael, by introducing a new element into the telling, marked another juncture. It created a point of transition and reorientation that the child required, both to bring me back to her everyday world and to communicate her evaluation of me. This evaluation had resulted from what we had shared in the play realm; however, it pertained as well to the everyday and intimate realms. Finally satisfied that I had allowed her to reveal herself as multiply constituted, Helen was able to take stock of what had transpired so far and announce her liking for me. This was a gesture of sharing and trust and also an intimation of wishing to continue the relationship. This lent closure to her fantasy narrative as well as to that part of our encounter.

The desultory, formless activity that followed plunged Helen back into her play realm, spotlighting her play self. All her activity at this point may be seen to have rested on a set of shared assumptions about play, on our mutual motivation for and joint attention to it, and on our co-construction of meaning about play, fantasy, and relatedness. There had been a stepwise progression whereby the child had moved through a period of negotiation and from there into play, for a further deepening of intimacy and testing the waters for "regressive" or at least festive behaviors.

On looking back at the staging and action so far, the narrative nature of the total occasion, and not just the play occasion, becomes clear. That is, the whole evening had the character of a narrative plot, with its early character elaborations (as Bible reader and dominant person), its complications and interdictions (bedrooms, negated dreams and superheroes), its many tests (secret languages and lands, as well as flying actions), its internal plot (kings, princesses, and Swabs), and its final resolution through a declaration of love.

It was on my initiative that we moved back into the everyday and more public realm for a meal. Once more, Helen resumed her competent, all-knowing, initiative-taking, public self. Her behavior during the restaurant scene emphasizes her exclusive demand for privacy in public. By insisting on the manner of relatedness between us as being one of closeness, Helen was unwilling even to engage in social small talk. This may also have been a move to safeguard fantasy in public.

On entering her bedroom for a second time, the two of us once more moved into the play realm. Helen's fantasy game became focused on her preoccupation with the themes of good and bad. Her earlier allusions to Michael, as well as to other children in her school and to the Swabs, were all concerned with badness as opposed to her own implied goodness and victimized state. It was also once more in the play realm that Helen momentarily but in earnest asked me the real question, signaling that she expected me to participate fully in the activity and provide information. She momentarily relinquished control, asking me to evaluate her performance at the storying activity and share my thoughts about the story's moral dimensions. However, as I declined to do so, the child's concerns and personal style led her to continue to direct and manage her own game. Helen's occasional caricatured evaluation of her own behavior may be due to concern and accompanying anxiety about the symbolic actions she was representing through the game. Such an assessment was in contrast to her more forthright and certain evaluation of me as being a good actor and player. It also underlined the value Helen placed on behavior in the play realm and the kind of relatedness she wished for us to share.

Her interactions with her parents at the end of the evening again displayed her bid for privacy, for circumscribing and guarding her relationship with her new playmate. She excluded them from this fantasy world and in so doing demonstrated a spirit of collusion and exclusiveness between the two of us. Such exclusive sharing is characteristic of intimacy. Ironically, her parents' use of a foreign tongue, which worked to exclude me from some of their talk, was mirrored by the child as she used a secret language developed in the earlier play to create a boundary between her parents and us and maintain a spirit of privacy and exclusiveness. Together, we had laid a groundwork of shared meanings on which our future relationship depended.

Our last secret-language exchange encapsulated the spirit of our prior sharing. It contained a sense of power and collusion against the public world (her parents, in this instance), as well as a spirit of play and intimacy, between the child and me, her play partner. It was a gesture that controlled the immediate situation through the agency of language and play and fulfilled her purpose, which was to keep the investigator to herself in her private world. In turn, I, the adult, had accepted the child's purposes and meshed them with my own.

Conclusion

In considering the management of everyday circumstances, I have made the point that the participants in a situation must define it for each other. I have shown how Helen and I did this via our use of metacommunicative signals such as initiations, orientations, evaluations, temporal and spatial arrangements, front- and backstage behavior, and so on. I have shown how the everyday world is constructed by the joint action of the participants. However, the management of the situation is also very much affected by the personal character of each of the participants. Helen's and my situation is one involving a dominant child and a compliant adult, which is most unusual. Because of the compliance of the adult, the management of this sequence was particularly rapid. The theoretical point is that encounters are never just encounters; there are particular kinds of people involved whose actions and motives need to be considered. Helen was clearly reversing her typical childlike compliance and powerlessness with parents, in her relationship with me. She played a power role in the everyday and also adopted a power content in the play realm. She was dominant in this relationship, though she was subordinate in her other ones. In Session 1, the nearer we were to the everyday realm the more she played the superior role. However, as we moved into the play realm, she began to relax her vigilance on her transformations; and finally, in the intimate realm, she showed greater flexibility in being carefree and regressed.

Although this pattern, as we shall see, undergoes modification in the advancing relationship, it is clear that power (good, beauty, maturity, wisdom, and communication) is the common item across all realms. From its actual use to its magical use, from its restrictive use to its beneficial use, Helen's is thoroughly concerned with power. This meaning is central to all realms and unites us in a performance in which rhetoric, structure, and symbolization have to do with power. In subsequent chapters we will see how these preliminary patterns of our relationship deepen and become clearer in their character.

SESSION 2, OCTOBER 20
"I've Missed You"

A month later I met with Helen again, once more to baby-sit her. At the front door to her house, she greeted me, accompanied by a caterpillar on a stick. It was 4:00 P.M. Helen smiled shyly as her mother said "hello" and explained what needed attention while she was gone. She and Don, who had already left, would not be back until fairly late, she said. As Pamela gathered her belongings and left, Helen said, "My new pet. Just found today," as she thrust the stick at me so that I could examine the green creature. As I admired it, she sought my advice about where she could house it. When I suggested an empty shoe box, she excitedly said, "Come on, up to my room!" She took me to a corner of her room, where she had already arranged such a box as a house for her pet. "See," she said, "here's what I have for it." Helen then laid the creature in its box, surrounded by a few green leaves. "I think I'll let him sleep," she said. This newly found pet was attended to at various times and remained a concern during the evening.

I then said to her, "What have you been up to since I was last here?" She replied, "Waiting for you," quickly adding, "I've missed you. Where have you been?" "I've had lots of work to do," I said. "What work?" she inquired. "Oh, just work for the university," I replied. After a brief pause she said, "Have you baby-sat anyone else?" I replied that I had only done so for my nieces, besides her. She then became curious about these children, and asked me about their names and ages and what I did with them. On telling her that I played with them, she asked, "What do you play with them?" "Different games," I replied. "Do you play superheroes with them?" she asked. When I reassured her that I did not, she said "You only play those games with me, then," adding inquiringly, "Right?" I said, "Of course."

Helen then got up from her bed where we had both been seated and walked about her room in contemplation. She began asking me what I wanted to do next. Being careful not to initiate the next activity, I kept saying that I did not much mind and turned the same question to her. After several unsuccessful attempts to elicit an answer from me, Helen went to the shelf on which her miniature animals sat. She threw a few onto the floor, saying they were mine, and then collected another handful, which she also scattered on the floor but with no comment. These were the same animals she had introduced into our play toward the end of the first meeting. On finally settling herself on the floor beside me she said, "Let's play that game."

Although she had placed a handful of characters in my charge, Helen played at being director and animator of most of the activities that followed. Once involved in the game, she played most of the roles herself. The characters comprised three "bad guys," one of whom was a large, evil dinosaur who could not fly, five "good guys," and three other animals—a small dinosaur with a clay ring around its tail, indicating that it could fly and was also to be a spy; a large squirrel whose tail was made exaggeratedly large by a clay cloak that Helen added; and its ally, another dinosaur who could fly and also had a clay ring around its tail. The squirrel and the second dinosaur were cast as powerful superhero types with whom Helen allied herself. In addition to these creatures, the child also used a plastic disc-like object with a string attached to it, which she swung around in the air. She enjoyed the sounds this disc made as it cut through the air, and she used it to capture the evil doers. She cast it as an all-powerful, flying, magic, supertool, a half-animate object that swooped down on the bad guy and often would engage in very sophisticated dialogues with the captives.

The basic plot of this enactment involved a struggle between good and bad guys, where the powerful superhero squirrel and its allies sought out and captured the large dinosaur, who was cast in the role of the "evil, killing, robbing, bad guy." It was important that the superhero not divulge its identity to the victims. Helen, who enacted the squirrel's superhero role, claimed certain attributes for herself, namely that she could fly and possessed wisdom, knowledge, and "justice." In this role, she delivered a sermonlike speech on love, suggesting the bad guys needed to know love and give up their hateful ways or forever be banished and killed. It was I who animated the bad guys, who were finally captured and tortured. The conflict reached some resolution only after the bad guys promised to be good.

At this point, I, in my role as baby-sitter, suggested that we should break for dinner. To this Helen replied, "Okay"; then, in an announcer-like voice, she added, "And this is the end of the chapter." It was this that alerted me to the way in which she so clearly marked her narrative segments, and I commented that it was a pity that we had not been able to record the chapter so that we could perhaps continue the story at another time. Helen was taken by this idea and lamented not having "one of those machines that records things," as she put it. Not wanting to miss the opportunity to tape her enactments, I told her that I had a tape recorder in my car and offered to bring it inside if she wished. Helen's response to this was, "Beautiful, but we'll have to start at Chapter Three."

Helen accompanied me to my car, and got the recorder and brought it inside. Earlier in our storying activity, the idea of secrets and slaves had been introduced by Helen, so I suggested that we could use the machine as our "secret slave, who recorded every word we uttered." On hearing my idea, Helen laughed and said, "Great idea!" We took the recorder into the kitchen, where we sat it on the table and played with it as I prepared our dinner. We recorded different noises that each of us made. They sounded like distressed cries, noises of crying at birth, clicks, flying, and humming.

Dinner was eaten fairly quickly. Helen was in a hurry to move upstairs, this time to her parents' bedroom, where the television set sat. She was eager to watch an episode of her favorite show, "Wonder Woman," and wanted me to see it, too. On our way to this room, she collected her night clothes from her own room. Once we were in front of the television set, she became very absorbed in watching, relating to me very little, even though we sat together on the bed. She was thoroughly intrigued by an entertainment show that preceded "Wonder Woman," in which several young women dressed in nightclub attire danced and sang somewhat provocatively. During "Wonder Woman," she openly admired her heroine and her feats, although seemingly to herself. It was only as the drama became more intense and there was a great deal of suspense that she edged her way to me and curled up close.

Helen's parents returned while we were still watching television. As they came upstairs toward the room, she called out to them, asking that they leave us alone. She said, "We'll come down soon. Don't come here, it's too exciting now." After the film, she changed for bed and asked that I tuck her in. She said, "When you go down, you can tell my parents to come up." I did as she suggested, and as I pulled the covers over her, she asked, "Did you like 'Wonder Woman'?" When I said that I did, she told me that it was on every week and that I, too, should watch it. I said that I would. She then added, "Don't forget, we have to start at Chapter Three for the tape recording. . . . Er, no. Let's start at the very very beginning, with the birth of the squirrel and the superheroes. You can come tomorrow."

I assured her that it all sounded fine but added that I could not come the next day but would do so very soon. Then having said goodnight to Helen, I went downstairs to see her parents. As it was late and I was eager to get going, I gave the Kings a brief summary of the time I had spent with Helen, in which they continued to be interested. They inquired whether I could look after Helen again later that week, to which I agreed. I walked outside to my car as a nearby clock struck 9:00 P.M.

Commentary

What was of prime importance to the participants on this occasion was a reestablishment of contact. Given that a great deal of consensual sharing had been experienced and a positive relationship of trust and affection had been initiated at the first meeting, it was necessary for both the child and me to concern ourselves with reaffirming and picking up the threads of what existed between us. In contrast to Session 1, Helen's initial negotiations during this session were far more open and straightforward. For example, whereas the first session involved some eight kinds of preparatory episodes prior to the beginning of dramatic play (first orientation, Bible reading, rejection of story reading, invitation to room, interdictions, invitation to fly, discussion of superheroes, and use of secret languages), on this occasion there was only the episode of the worm in the box prior to the exchange of personal details about being a baby-sitter for other children. One might say that the first session had to provide for its own preliminaries to play, whereas on this second occasion the first session itself had already accomplished that task. In the first session there were no personal revelations until after the dramatic play of Balalulaland. (I don't like Michael. I like you.) In this session there were such friendship revelations even prior to play. The dramatic play in this session occupied a much longer period of time than in the first and included play planning, with the discussion of the tape recorder. This session also finished with a longer period of affectionate relating while watching television together.

Taken one episode at a time, in sequence, my interpretation is as follows: First, Helen chose to reestablish contact from the very beginning, which she did by calling my attention to the caterpillar. At first it was the gesture of thrusting the stick out that served to achieve her purpose, as she competed with her mother for my attention early in the encounter. It was only after her mother had left the scene that Helen once again seemed free to structure her own relationship with me.

Helen used her newly found pet to introduce a discourse topic for the purposes of reestablishing contact, securing my interest in her, and inviting me to her bedroom. Moreover, this gesture itself proved to be designed to invite me into her play world, and Burke (1969a, 1969b) would argue that this was her intention from the beginning. In his terms, her strategy for moving me from the foyer to her bedroom was to use a "scenic" question (Where could we protect the caterpillar?) to lead me to her room, where a different order of behavior from that of the everyday domain would transpire. This question was rhetorical too in that Helen already had an answer to her problem. It was not real information that she was seeking but a means of engaging my interest and carrying out her own purposes.

Helen's room, moreover, was seen as a protective sphere, as opposed to the more public everyday domains, and her relationship with the caterpillar was portrayed as one of caretaking and protection. Management and dominance are aspects of a mothering character as Helen portrays it in this case. She has reversed her own dependent relationship with her mother (or with me) by becoming the mother for the caterpillar. Clearly those who protect worms are not themselves the least powerful. This was one more expression of the way in which she dealt with power throughout this series.

This initial sequence of behavior, which began in the foyer and soon moved to the bedroom, marked the first juncture in the session. It was initiated by the child and carefully focused and bounded by the activity around the caterpillar. It was closed by Helen's decision to let the creature sleep—an act of protection toward a weaker creature. A version of this theme was first sounded in the fantasy autobiography of Session 1, where her role as a powerful princess was to protect the good and avenge the wronged or victim of evil, her dead father. In the second session, however, the power or protection had passed from fantasy to everyday life.

The next sequence of behavior, which marked the opening of the second juncture, was initiated by me. It was my turn, it seemed, to check out my relationship with Helen, on the one hand, and, on the other, to initiate a topic for conversation. My somewhat broad question ("What have you been up to since I was last here?") resulted in a very specific and personal response from Helen. She acknowledged her warm feelings for me when she said she had missed me. Other responses included statements of affection and testing of a very personal nature. The rhetoric she used sprang from the personal sphere as she sought to persuade me that she needed me. It was not put indirectly, as in the interdictions of the prior session. She inquired about other competitors for my attention and emphasized her need to be central and special to me. She sought reaffirmation of the intimate nature of our ludic (or playful, from *ludens*, to play) sharing, as opposed to my ludic activities with other children. It was as if she were showing me, through the caterpillar, that she now needed my attention and care. Helen's responses revealed more openness, vulnerability, and intimacy in this session. Not only were they in contrast to her behavior in Session 1, but they also validated the claim I made about the intimacy that was sought and established at the end of that encounter. Power and affection previously dealt with through play were being addressed more directly. This second phase of behavior ended with Helen having made her feelings and anxieties explicit and my reassuring her. This created a shared affective frame of reference from which both participants could proceed.

The third juncture in the session dealt with Helen's attempt to shift our interactions from those of the everyday world to those of the play world. Although it was she who initiated this phase of behavior, she did so by inviting me to suggest the type of activity in which we could engage. This was in contrast to her behavior in Session 1, where I was predominantly a bystander to a range of expressive acts she initiated without consulting me. This change may be attributed to the intimacy of the first session. Perhaps it could be argued that the ludic sharing of the first session had made the child more flexible, open, and willing to yield some of her dominance.

As on the first occasion, however, my own nondirective agenda resulted in Helen suggesting her own scheme for action. Her use of the same animals and the same game seemed to reflect her attempts to recreate safely the intimate realm we had previously shared. The identity of items here was an invitation to reconstruct our prior interaction. Implicit in this may also have been an evaluation of the time we shared together as being good or pertinent to our purposes and therefore a reliable "stock of knowledge at hand" (Schutz, 1967).

On the other hand, Helen's gesture of casting the animals on the floor may have reflected her frustration at my silence and refusal to take the lead in structuring the play domain. In any case, this gesture marked the onset of a new phase of behavior and a movement out of the everyday realm.

The fourth juncture was marked by our activity within the play realm. Having assumed leadership of the game, Helen remained dominant in this realm. She was both director and animator of the play activities. There were several key features of the created fantasy plot. The enactment on this occasion concerned the capture of evil beings and the secrecy of the superhero's identity. Psychologically we may interpret the secrecy as important because the "play" identity must not be known to the parents, whose role had been usurped in this sphere in order for Helen herself to outdo evil and bring love and protection to the good and weak. Through the agency of language (a sermon) she equated wisdom, knowledge, justice, and fantasy or magic with power. She used language with illocutionary force to achieve power. These qualities, which she elaborated in this symbolic action, represented facets of her metaphoric key that had already been introduced in Session 1.

In the play realm, I was once more lowly and degraded in the fantasy enactment, as in Session 1. This is in contrast to the more equal and positive role that I had just been accorded in the everyday realm. Nevertheless, within the play realm, I was no longer a bystander but much more a participant. Some increased teaching and acceptance by Helen are demonstrated here.

Although the drama was developed as a dialogue by both of us, Helen still placed herself in a position of control. The plot concerned the theme of a struggle between the forces of good and bad; the characters were protean types and, within this fantasy universe, she presented herself as a superhero. This figure turned out to be a multiple hero in that it seemed to be made up of multiple laminations of the self; that is, it was both the child and the squirrel (another small creature who was accorded great power by virtue of being a super being). As an inanimate object it was a tool among others for advancing and controlling the story line and action. This symbol, although not very different in power from the fantasy self presented in her fictitious autobiography of Session 1, better served this fictive domain, inhabited as it was by animals. There were no human characters per se in this text, although the animals were surely anthropomorphic. Finally, the struggle was won by the representatives of good, while the bad forces were converted to espousing love.

A transition from the fourth to the fifth juncture was initiated by me, as I was anxious to get on with some of the business in the everyday world and suggested that we break for dinner. Helen accepted this termination, suggesting that a considerable degree of consensus and cooperation were operating. It also suggests that Helen accepted my adulthood at this point, in contrast to Session 1, where she seemed intent on being domineering and controlling of my actions, even in the everyday realm.

Before we finally terminated the story and our activity in this realm, however, Helen supplemented it through acting out her concern with creating a more definite sense of closure in this realm. Her announcement "And this is the end of the chapter," indicated her strong sense of the structure of the activity in which we had just been engaging. She used a shift in register and adopted a more formal tone to make her announcement. In addition, her use of this terminal marker indicated that the genre she believed she was using for her fantasy making was that of the story.

This comment not only marked the end of the fourth juncture but provided a link to some crucial business in the fifth sequence of activity, by prompting my comment about recording our efforts. My strategies for introducing the tape recorder into our interactions were influenced by and drew on the child's own metaphoric key. As a subterfuge for attaining my ends, I suggested that the instrument could be a part of the fantasy domain and even gave the machine the role of being our "secret slave who records every word we utter." I thus drew on notions of collusion, dominance, and power, all of which had been introduced by Helen in our earlier sharing activity. This was a fortuitous contribution on my part and was comparable to my efforts at introducing the secret language in Session 1. To Helen, it was further proof that I valued fabling and could contribute to it.

This fifth sequence of activity thus consisted of an interweaving of everyday concerns, such as preparing dinner, with those that related to the child's fantasy concerns, such as exploring the tape recorder. For example, Helen recorded her own sounds and cries of distress while I cooked, thus playing at being a regressed baby. This was significant in that I was not then her play companion (except for minimal participation in experimenting with the tape recorder) but an adult in the everyday realm who was nevertheless privy to her regressions. This, too, corroborated Helen's increased flexibility in relating to me in the everyday realm and was a further sign of the growing intimacy between us. Our conversation during this juncture was primarily focused on how to weave this new element, the tape recorder, into our fictive universe. Dinner assumed a secondary and fairly perfunctory role. This machine was to become an important character in the private domains of the play world.

The sixth juncture was marked by a new topic of interest and scene of activity, that is, by the child's interest in watching her favorite television program, "Wonder Woman." Although conversation was minimal during the next hour, engaging in this scene of joint attention was important. This program and its heroine were a symbolic token of power, beauty, goodness, and wisdom; hence, Helen's sharing of this program with me was also a gesture of sharing her "key" or symbolic woman. It spotlighted what had so far been backstage behavior and only expressed indirectly, that is, that this Wonder Woman stood in an antithetical relationship to the child, Helen of the everyday world, and also to the worm and to the distressed regressive baby of the crying episode during dinner. For Helen, Wonder Woman was a symbol of what was possible through the symbolic actions of play, dramatization, and storytelling.

Our shared experience during this sixth juncture was also striking because it introduced a new expressive frame for sharing: television. During this activity Helen maintained her new relationship as a child in relation to me, an adult. Her gesture of edging closer to me and curling up was one of intimacy and an acknowledgment of her own vulnerability. This stood in sharp contrast to her key symbol: Wonder Woman. Helen further marked this activity as intimate and as belonging to us alone by keeping her parents out of it, just a she had done in Session 1. She excluded them from the play sphere. Their departure and return marked the beginning and ending of her friendship with me on this occasion. She had created an intimate realm that she shared with me but which stood in opposition to her parents and authorities and, in this instance, to representatives of the public, everyday world.

The seventh juncture was marked by our sharing after the conclusion of the television program. It acted not only to conclude the session and reiterate the important concerns of the evening but also as a forerunner or bridge to the next encounter. Her rhetoric in the bedroom underlined our growing friendship. I had become not only a co-player and equal but also a trusted adult to whom Helen could relate. Her final comments on doing chapter three next time displayed her use of rhetoric pertaining to plans for the next occasion, as she sought to persuade me to come back to share in her play world. I finally left with the promise that our next meeting would involve a new beginning to the drama.

Conclusion

In conclusion, this session may be seen as building on the first. Important transformations in behavior were evidenced here, in contrast to those evidenced in Session 1. For example, although this session was also concerned with shaping our relationship, it was less so than the first. In addition, the staging here was far less concerned with power and dominance in the everyday realm. Further, the child's feelings for me were far more direct and expressed early on in the session. Intimacy was acknowledged much more quickly in this session, as Helen and I moved faster into shared plots. The point here is that staging behaviors are necessary and sufficient to accomplish the purposes of the public world, but, although necessary, are insufficient for the intimate world. Given that it is this latter world that Helen most wished to share with me, she was able to move more directly from the rhetoric of the public world to that of the intimate world, as a result of our behavior in Session 1. A quick reestablishment of this world was preliminary to the new developments in the second session and necessary for its advancement.

Several other points are important. From these two sessions it begins to appear as if showing flexibility was easier for Helen in the everyday world than in the play world. Although she showed some of the latter by giving me a participatory role in play, this degree of flexibility pales in significance when compared with her increased differentiation in the everyday world. Thus, her initial dominance in Session 1 can be compared with her openness to suggestions, her regressive behavior with the tape recorder, and her sharing and cuddling behavior during the television program in this session.

In these two sessions, then, the domain of play, which is so often treated as an area of flexibility, creativity, and potentiation in the play literature (Lieberman, 1977; Singer, 1973; Sutton-Smith, 1975) seems, relative to Helen's other behavior, to have been rather rigid, at least as far as power relationships are concerned.

It is also clear from this session that I had taken on a very special twofold role, first as caretaker, friend, and protector in the everyday realm and second as a relatively passive and supportive companion in the play realm. This is an unusual role. Mothers are usually mothers and children are children, and we may suppose that this was the case between Helen and her own mother. Children usually reverse that situation only in their own secret play spheres. In this case I had shown the ability to play both mother and child roles, displaying that I contained both powerfulness (adulthood) and powerlessness (childishness, nonsense, passivity) and thus could mediate between the two aspects. This ability led, I suppose, to the astonishing rate of progress that subsequently ensued within this relationship.

SESSION 3: OCTOBER 23
"Five or Four Chapters"

It was three days later that I visited Helen for a third time. When I arrived, at about 5:00 P.M., Helen crept up on me, flung a rope around me, and, laughing, led me out to the backyard rather than into the house as usual. Although somewhat startled, I quickly recovered and joined in her playful act of leading me out as prisoner. On the way outside, Helen said, "We're going to a secret place." I pretended to look suspiciously at her but said nothing. On reaching the backyard, Helen let go of the rope and began to talk to me about "Wonder Woman," the television show. She asked whether I had liked watching the show with her on the last occasion. "It's my favorite show," she said, adding that, although she did not watch much television, she never missed this show. She began to talk about the details of the plot in the last episode but then stopped abruptly and said, "Let's play, okay?" I agreed, and Helen set up a game where she cast me as Wonder Woman among other superheroes such as Batman. She said, "You'll be a good Wonder Woman 'cause you look like her. I mean in real life." "Do I?" I asked, looking puzzled, and she added, "Yeah. You know, like Linda, the one who lives in New York. Not Diana, in the show, but the one who acts

Wonder Woman." I nodded my head, indicating that I knew what she meant. Helen then said that she herself had all the power the super-heroes had, and even more, and therefore was the most powerful of them all.

I was cast in a room with an "evil robber," as Helen described this other character. "Like robbers, he will find ways of breaking out and you will have to fight him," she said. She added that she, in her super-super role, would always appear at the right moment to save me and "'Victor' the robber." Here, too, she posited a situation of conflict which she then elaborated and finally resolved with the capture and surrender of the robber. Helen used magic sticks (twigs picked from the yard) to strike ferociously at the air and seemed pleased by the noise this generated. She also played with a long piece of rope, her lasso, which she had previously thrown over me and later used for capturing the robber.

After this episode ended, we spent the next half hour playing at another "adventure," as Helen called these imaginary enactments. While the first had been largely influenced by the last episode of "Wonder Woman," the second was drawn from a variety of myths. Helen played Aphrodite, Goddess of Wisdom, and I was the pilot who flew her on a trip to the Garden of Eden. Once we arrived at this place, she alighted from her airplane and held several conversations in an undertone with imaginary groups in the garden. After these conversations, she would sometimes inform me of the next step in the plan. It was almost as though these groups were being consulted for pieces of secret information. Her reportings and communications were often elliptical and parataxic. For example, Helen would say something jumbled and barely audible and then say to me, "Come on, do it." Often I had little idea of what "doing it" meant. If I interpreted her direction in a way contrary to her omniscient, tacit inner plot, she said, rather shortly, "No dummy, not that. We've finished that part. Now we're doing something else." Often my actions were redirected by her to fit in with her inner narrative scheme. At times I was so frustrated by this behavior that I had to interrupt the game to tell her that I did not know what she wished me to do unless she told me clearly. She seemed to ignore this and continue in her own style, as before.

Having spent some time conferring and darting about the Garden of Eden, Helen suggested that we had to cross the river of Ice, get past Pluto, and kill the seal men who were guarding the maidens whom she wished to free. Of course we got over these obstacles, with the aid of her superior power, although the course was rife with danger. Finally, when we got to the seal men, we had to stage a battle against them.

This was a very active fight in which she wished me to join. Eventually, we lassoed the seal men and freed the maidens one by one. We were then ready to board our "secret plane" and travel back to Earth.

During our return flight, a little boy from next door appeared on the scene. Helen promptly ordered him off, saying, "Would you mind leaving? We are in the middle of a secret adventure." At this juncture, two stray dogs entered the yard, too. She informed me that they were Pluto's dogs and incorporated them into the fantasy: "This is Pluto's last attempt to frighten us." At the end of this fantasy game, Helen turned to me and said, "This is the best adventure I've had. I loved it." We then walked to the step of the back door, where we sat for a while.

A few minutes later, Helen's father came out to call us to join the family at dinner. Helen was asked to help with setting the table, which she did somewhat reluctantly. During the meal, the family spoke in both English and their other language. I felt rather left out from time to time and felt that this second language was used for intimate conversation among the family members as well as for controlling Helen's behavior. I felt as though the child's relationship with me was both modified and controlled by her parents' presence. In this situation, Helen was a child among three adults and may have experienced her relationship with me as being in some ways changed. However, the meal was over fairly quickly, and Helen's parents left soon afterward. Prior to leaving, Pamela said, "She can wash her hair before going to bed. Just see that she doesn't forget to. We should be back about 9:30 P.M., and Helen should be in bed by then." Pamela and Don then left.

Helen and I went upstairs. On our way up, she said, "Let's make the stories for your secret tape." On entering her room, she promptly went to her shelf and threw the miniature animals onto the floor. She joined me on the floor and said, "Okay, let's do it from the beginning. We'll do it from the birth." She then giggled as she asked me if the machine was on. I told her that we could start whenever she was ready, so, after some whispering, she signaled with her head that she was set to begin. What followed was an elaborate enactment of the story we had been playing on the prior occasions.

Helen began her story enactment by setting the scene through the use of sounds. She made crying noises representing a baby being born, which were immediately followed by the dialogue of a mother tending her babies. Helen manipulated several miniature animals according to the sounds and dialogue. The cast comprised good and bad prototypes, with the good hero Supersquirrel and the evil antagonist being a large dinosaur. Each had a mother and several allies. Helen carried 95 percent of the dialogue on this occasion. Although I was supposedly in charge of the bad guys, when it came to enacting their roles, Helen took over. Similarly, at certain points she assigned me the role of the mother of Supersquirrel (via a whispered direction), but when I failed to play this role according to her inner script she immediately took over this role, too.[4]

Helen's themes concerned good and bad; making friends; the discovery of flying, which equaled power; secret identities; and the victory of good over bad. The actions displayed a growth dimension (baby to child) and a moral dimension (doing good, making friends, defeating evil, and punishing wrongdoers). The plot cycled through a dialectic of positive and negative features. Helen tended to alternate positive scenes involving the life of the good guys with negative scenes involving the bad. For example, she first presented a scene of a caretaker attending the good guys as babies. They were gently tended and discovered the positive power of flying. This was followed by a scene depicting a mother attending the bad guys. They were rougher and louder and were rebuked accordingly, in direct contrast to the earlier scene. The third scene concerned the good child's discovery of her flying power and her deliberations about whether this power should be used for good or evil purposes. She (Supersquirrel) finally decided to use it for good and celebrated this decision. In contrast, the bad child (dinosaur) bemoaned her lack of flying powers and acknowledged jealousy of the good guys' power. Her caretaker urged her to do bad. The story ends with the good guys killing the bad guys, in the name of God, and triumphing over evil. This ultimate victory of good over evil was celebrated by all the good guys, with Supersquirrel being the heroine.

Interspersed with these sets of actions were two episodes of behavior that relate to the child's everyday, nonplay world. However, they also have bearing on what Helen was preoccupied with in this story. These are questions of her own identity and her struggle with her badness or aggression. The first of these episodes occurred within the play. As Supersquirrel, Helen kept her identity away from her enemies. She attempted to define who she was by suggesting what she was not. This is illustrated in the following transcript of a dialogue where Helen plays several roles. Note that C denotes child (Helen) as speaker, while A denotes Adult.

---

[4]Although it is unlikely that one of her peers would allow her so much autonomy in the story performance realm, I was content to let her agenda hold sway. It was the child's world I was interested in understanding, not mine.

C: Do you not know, what, who are you?
C: You are the child.
C: I shall still kill you.
C: Yes, but you're not a child.
C: Oh! Excuse me. I always thought of myself as a child. I'm always in the university and I'm not a teenager.
C: Neither am I a teenager. *Neither* am I a child. And I'm not a baby (*softly*).
A: What are you?
C: I cannot tell you. That is my secret.

Although on the one hand this seems to be a discussion with the bad guys where Helen takes all the roles, indicating the changes via shifts in her voice, on the other, it seems to be a voiced inner discussion she has with herself. It is taken up at different points later on in the same story. For example,

C: And I am very patient as not a god, and not a child, and not a teenager. (*Whispers to herself*)
C: (*In a different voice*) What are you again, I ask? What is your name?
C: What, you may ask, but I don't know. (*Whispers as if to herself*)

The second episode occurred at a point of juncture and served as a bridge between the everyday and the story realm. We had come out of the game to answer a ringing telephone. On the way back to the bedroom, Helen suddenly grabbed my hands and began tying them together. She said, "I hate it when my Momma pretends to be angry at me—don't you?" I replied that it usually felt horrible when people were angry at you. Then, putting on a voice, she said, "You're my slave, and I'm going to tie you up forever. If you ever get loose I'll kill you . . . and I mean it." With her last sentence, we returned to the room. After this, we went back into the story, as though there had neither been an interruption, nor the little episode about the slave, the hand tying, and her mother's anger.[5] Later on in the game, Helen tied up the evil dinosaur and treated him as her slave. She hurt him and he momentarily retaliated and fought back, in addition to continuing his evil killing.

---

[5]Perhaps during that brief moment, the child, caught and preoccupied with being the victim of her mother's anger, reversed the situation so that she could be the controlling, powerful, victimizing adult in relation to me, the real adult, whom she subordinated.

She enjoyed playing the role of the provocative evil guy. Finally, as the good heroine, she hit and killed him, gaining victory over evil.

After the story was finally brought to a conclusion by Helen (she partook in a celebration as part of the performance and then stepped into the narrator's role to announce the end), I attempted leaving the recorder on to catch the child's responses to her efforts. Once again, she became acutely aware of the machine and its role and attempted to turn it off. After I persuaded her that the recorder would simply take down our plans, she agreed to leave it on and then proceeded to initiate a discussion herself. Her tone and manner were public and self-conscious, suggesting an element of performance.

C: How was that story? Do you think it was good?
A: Yeah. I thought it was very good. Is there anything you liked especially about it?
C: Well . . . I especially liked the superheroes.
A: Yes. . . . Do you think other people might like it?
C: Oh . . . I should think so.
A: Did you think there was anything particularly bad about it?
C: Yes. The bad guys were too bad, I think.
A: Mm.
C: Well, actually, they all died.
A: They all died, the bad ones?
C: Yes . . .
A: Is that good?
C: Yes. Of course it is.
A: And what about the good?
C: That's the best part. They all lived.
A: Do you think we should give it a title?
C: Well . . . "The Chapters," because there are a lot of chapters. How many do you think?
A: Four.
C: What? Oh, four. "The Chapters" . . . "Five or Four Chapters." How is that?
A: That sounds like a good title . . .
C: What'll we do for our next story? Oh well . . . I don't . . . We'll check up next time on the other side.

After this, she wished to listen to parts of the tape and commented on it as she did so. She was in the role of audience to and evaluator of the performance as captured on the tape. Her formal evaluation alluded to the story in general and highlighted her struggle over the power of aggressive or evil forces and clarified her investment. Her conflict, however, was finally resolved for her by the resounding triumph of good. While listening to the tape of the performance, she also laughed at certain melodramatic parts, thought the sound effects were terrific, and commented on her voice. She became quite excited by some of the more boisterous parts and joined in, mouthing the words. She began to roll around on the floor in laughter, and push me down with her. She thought the idea of the chapters was a good one, felt the whole performance was exciting, and wished to make more stories for my "secret tape."

While we were in the bathroom and Helen was washing her hair, she was also concerned about her own voice and did not like the fact that it sounded "childish" on the tape. She wished to know why that was the case and whether she could improve it. We then talked about the distinction between her real voice and her many play voices. She concluded the conversation by suggesting that she preferred my voice.

I then helped her dry her hair and braided it, in keeping with her parents' wishes. She admired her braids in a mirror and sought my approval of her. I told her that they suited her and then suggested that she get to bed. On settling into bed, she mentioned that she had some good ideas for our next story and could hardly wait until my next visit. Promising her that I would be back soon, I wished her good night and walked downstairs. It was 9:05 P.M.

While sitting in the living room waiting for the Kings to return, I began to go over the day's events in my mind and turned to recording much of it in my diary, as was my custom after a visit to Helen. At about 10:00 P.M. the Kings walked in, very apologetic for the lateness of the hour and eager to pay me for my caretaking services. I declined, however, and reassured them that I was happy with the reciprocal nature of the arrangement as it stood. We parted on friendly terms.

Commentary

It is striking that, upon my arrival for our third session, Helen immediately oriented me to her play world. There were no preliminary negotiations on either Helen's part or mine. With Helen's gesture of stealthily creeping up on me and imprisoning me, I was immediately assimilated. This play gesture was her access ritual, and it was possible because an intimate and shared relationship already existed between us. Helen's comment, "We're going to a secret place," and my mock suspicion in response to this, were our rhetoric in the play realm. The end of this first episode was signaled by Helen's letting go of the rope on our reaching the backyard. This indicates that we must modify the notion that management or exploration always precedes play. Among friends, play gestures can provide the initial connection. The conversation about the television program, "Wonder Woman," marked a juncture, shifting our interactions from the play realm into that of the everyday.

The structure of the second play episode was based on the latest episode of "Wonder Woman." As a bridge, it served to orient me to the story world we would soon enter and to strengthen and confirm Helen's metaphoric key. For example, Helen made several connections between her heroine and me; between the reality of the play realm and that of the everyday. She argued implicitly that not only was her heroine on television, but, in addition, Diana, her play partner, resembled her. She finally added that Wonder Woman was indeed the most powerful of superheroes and then, as if having legitimized her metaphor, moved back into narrative plotting.

Although I had been granted this elevated and positive role, it was only a propagandist act. Helen, in this play episode, used not only the agency of language but also several physical actions—such as lassoing the robber, creating magical effects by striking the air with twigs, and moving around the yard in pursuit of the robber—to generate meaning within the play realm. With the defeat of the robber (evil) by Wonder Woman and her helper (forces of good), this second play episode was brought to a close.

The third play episode drew its rhetoric, symbolism, and structure from a variety of myths. Here the child was the central character, and, although I was on her side and an active participant in the play realm, I was nevertheless assigned an ancillary role. Helen's tendency to keep me uninformed, to negate my behavior, and to confuse me was part of asserting her power over the situation. It was reminiscent of her bossy style in Session 1. This was her rhetoric within the story realm, and it was different from the rhetoric she used to evaluate her story later on and to converse in the everyday realm. In both of the latter areas, she had become more flexible.

As has often been claimed by play therapists, for Helen, as for most children, this fantasy realm was her arena for real autonomy, where she felt less inclined either to explain her behavior or to surrender her authority (see Erikson, 1963). The story rhetoric here consisted of many actions used to overcome obstacles and evil forces. All this was accomplished with the aid of superior powers or magical agencies. Meaning was created by verbal, paralinguistic, and physical behavior. Acts, agents, and agency were elaborated in play, although space and time were minimally sketched and mythic. These features are consonant with other children's stories and artwork at this age, as well as with fantasies in folk and fairy tales.

During this third play episode, there was an interlude during which Helen attended to claims from the everyday world. On the one hand, she rejected the little boy from next door, displaying a generally bossy temperament even with her peers; on the other hand, she incorporated the dogs into her story world. The ease with which she oscillated between the everyday and play realms was striking. The play episode was ended by Helen's final evaluation of the story realm: "This is the best adventure I've had. I loved it." This comment marked another juncture in the occasion and was also a transition by which she returned to the everyday realm.

The fourth episode during the evening was having dinner. For our purposes, what is noteworthy about this was Helen's parents' use of two languages, by which they seemed to exercise control over me. One was the language of the home and family; the other pertained to the outside world. Helen's use of secret languages as well as her view that language is an agency of power and control may have some roots in such a family dynamic.

The fifth episode took place in Helen's bedroom. The conversation on the stairs signaled Helen's agenda for what was to transpire there. It was an orientation to the play realm that we would once more enter and was elaborated upon by her behavior on entering the room. Her gesture of throwing the animals on the floor, as well as her comment, "Okay, let's do it from the beginning. We'll do it from the birth," were a preface to the story that would shortly be played.

Before launching into the play realm, however, Helen turned her attention not only to managing me but to managing the recorder, too. This marked the sixth episode in the session. Her giggling, whispering, and nonverbal signaling indicated she was ready and also suggested a new self-consciousness to her play, which added a novel lamination to her enterprises beyond anything revealed in Sessions 1 and 2. The act of recording was paralleled by a change in the meaning of what was going on. The presence of the tape recorder began to influence the nature of Helen's performance and added a significant element to her behavior. The play text to be produced was to be a performance for the machine. Not only was the machine to record the performance, but it was to be an audience and an implied evaluator of the played-out story. Its introduction made inevitable a paradigm of tale enacting in which there was a new distance between author and product, albeit inconsistent; hence, spontaneity was mediated indirectly, although falteringly.

Nevertheless, the new agent was incorporated as a part of the secret, intimate world of which she and I were members. The taping itself was to be a part of our collusive activity.

The seventh episode brought us to the actual performance of the story for the tape recorder. The new activity was clearly marked by Helen, who alerted me and the audience that the story performance was beginning. My next response personified the recorder becoming a story realm character; it was to be our slave and record all we said. This performance was then interrupted by Helen, who once again became aware of its evaluative and perhaps authoritarian aspects and at first wished to place it further away from her and then turn it off. When I persuaded her to leave it on, she protested that she was not yet ready and then dictated my next response to me in a whisper. The line she offered me ("I'm sure this will be a great story") was evaluative in nature and part of the rhetoric for persuading the audience of the quality of the story to follow. She then moved directly into presenting her story.

The play she enacted was essentially the same one we had done on the previous two occasions. In recreating our earlier play activity for the tape recorder, she was offering a story that had been tried, tested, and evaluated as successful. It was a story of the birth and growth of good and evil creatures, and of their subsequent conflict with each other, with the good guys emerging victorious.

Despite the similarities, however, there were significant differences in this third taped version. It was much more heavily auditory in quality and thus clearly responsive to the tape recorder. Helen used additional and more elaborate sound effects for establishing her meaning. The story was longer and had a more conscious and marked sense of structure. In fact, Helen used several opening and terminal markers to lend the story cohesion; beginnings and endings were sounded, chapter headings were signaled, and prefatory summarizing and explanatory comments were made about the action. For example, to open the first chapter, she said, "And now we start our story; now to the enemies we go," and accompanied this with terrible, gruff noises. Later she announced, "Chapter Three. Now we go to the chapter of the child's life." Often a different focus of attention was signaled with a noise, for example, grunts to signal bad guys. Further examples of her narrative explanations and instructions include "And now, we shall meet each other," "The chapter of friendship," "Let us start the discussion," "Back at the man's land," and "That is the end of the one whole story and another chapter." These comments were said with a voice and pacing that were distinctly different from her voice and pacing as she assumed different roles in the action. All were metacommunicative strategies for rendering her story enactment accessible to her perceived audience.

As mentioned earlier, the performance had an elliptical quality to it. It was made of minimal images and had a schematic structure akin to dreams. It was highly changeable, and the drama moved forward through the dialectic interplay of the characters and forces in conflict. The plot behaviors cycled through arousal, climax, and resolution and centered around acts such as birth, eating, play, and battle. All these tended to be brought to their conclusion and stood in contrast to the prior staging behaviors. Within this performance, staging was already set and context was taken for granted.

In terms of structure, what is striking is the polarization of roles. There are clusters of positive and negative roles, played in this performance almost exclusively by Helen. Although I was cast in a maternal role and later in the role of an evil slave and dinosaur, these roles lasted very briefly, primarily because I seemed insufficiently involved and active and because Helen disliked some of my responses. She took to playing all the roles in the drama: good and evil, child and parent, and subordinate and authority figures. These were pitted against each other and resulted in a final synthesis where the good child overcame evil, by dint of being powerful and by being identified with the morality and authority of parental figures. The actions concerned the gradual evolution of these powers and manifested a synthesis of them in some victorious and celebratory form. Space and time were mythic, and the agencies used were those of language and magic.

The central rhetorical principle was also that of dominance, which was exerted through sermonizing about love, wisdom, and justice; through logical explanations about growing up; through making choices between good and bad; through the process of making friends; and through discussing how to use power profitably. These were the techniques Helen used to illuminate her central character dimensions and manage her symbolic actions in both the everyday and play realms.

Conclusion

I can summarize by saying that dominance was both the dramatic content of Helen's play as well as the rhetorical technique that she used for controlling what was going on, though I should note that it has been necessary to analyze her texts and her play structure to come to this conclusion. It would not have been sufficient to concentrate only on the context, that is, upon the way in which she managed the situation.

Dominance and power were also what she was most concerned about coming to terms with in her personal life. As she stated herself, she was having difficulty in dealing with her mother's anger (as do many small girls), and in the course of this and other sessions she often managed to make me angry by frustrating me with inscrutable directions. But within this text she resolved her own reciprocal anger toward her mother, by siding with those creatures who were good and whose mothers, in consequence, taught them how to grow up (to fly). Then justified by her power, she killed off the bad guys, an action she relished. There was some mild guilt to all this for her, insofar as she expressed her feelings that the evil of the bad guys might have been exaggerated.

The reasons for naming power as her primary metaphoric key have become clearer than ever before. There is a confluence of evidence on the dramatic level that she was engaged in a struggle of good over evil, and of life (for the good) over death (for the bad); and on the rhetorical level with controlling both her dramatic characters and me. On the psychological level, meanwhile, she was engaged in a struggle to control and manage her own frustration and rage through intellectual and verbal means. Power is a psychological need, a technique of management and a form of dramatic expression and the means whereby goodness can exercise evil at the same time as it exorcises it.

All this activity is powerful evidence that play of this kind is a struggle to deal with the conflicts of experience in terms of a variety of disguises that will protect the child from the dangers perceived in that experience and yet also permit an intensely motivated assertion of one's own power to make sense of and synthesize the experience and to overcome the dangers.

SESSION 4: OCTOBER 30
"The Rule Is to Keep You in the Dark"

A week later I met Helen for a fourth time. On this occasion, at about 6:00 P.M. I picked her up from a neighboring house where she had spent time after school. As soon as I rang the neighbor's doorbell, the child rushed to the door and on seeing me smiled quietly but said nothing. She ran back inside to gather her coat and bag and then returned to the door. She and I walked quietly back to her house. Helen said very little on the way.

On reaching her house and going inside, Helen announced that she was hungry. When I offered to get her some dinner, she said that she wished to prepare it herself. She informed me that we would have hard-boiled eggs followed by ice cream, which she loved. As I was not ready to eat just then, I said that I would have some yogurt instead. She insisted on getting this for me. All this was attended to fairly quickly and without fuss. As we were nearing the end of our meal, Helen told me that she could't wait to go upstairs to "do the tape recordings." On finishing our business in the kitchen, this is just what we did.

As soon as we went upstairs, Helen took off her sweater and shoes, saying she would be more comfortable without them. While changing, she asked me whether I knew of any other superheroes other than the ones to whom she had introduced me. I mentioned Batman and Tarzan, to which she said, "But there are many others, Spider Man, Ockle Man, Mrs. Marvel. What about them? Do you know about them?" I said that I did not.

Helen then asked if she could listen to the tape from the last session. She became extremely involved in this activity and would from time to time laugh and mouth the words on the tape. After a few minutes she asked me to turn the machine off and said that she wished "to play a different story with different superheroes." I said "Okay" and asked her what she had in mind. As she began to tell me, she noticed that the tape recorder was on and instantly moved to turn it off. I attempted to persuade her that it would be much more useful to leave it running if she wished to build on her plans. Finally she agreed to leave it on. The following transcript from the tape begins in the middle of a period of talk, in which Helen was planning for our story:

C: I was borned and Miss Marvel, Mr. Marvel, so er . . . , so I got the power of all the superheroes.
A: Aha.
C: Remember?
A: Ya.
C: And I have this sword by my side, also.
A: So, when were you born?
C: Yes. I was just . . . I'm now seven years old.
A: And you were born seven years ago.
C: Yes. Of course.
A: Of course.
C: Well, you don't know about me. You plan the *wicked* deeds. Okay?
A: I'm evil.
C: Yes. Of course. I fight you. I'm the strongest girl in the world, and I have the power of every superhero living, and all the gods of 'Greek' and Rome. That means, there's a secret.

A: And where did I come from? How long have I been living?

C: Oh, you're about . . . thirty-two.

A: About thirty-two.

C: And you're a man.

A: And I'm a man? Okay. And how was I born?

C: Oh, forget *that* part.

A: Okay.

C: It's not of, er, any of *our business*.

A: You mean I'm just here?

C: Yeah (*mumbles*). Though it's important to know when I was born.

A: Why?

C: Because of the . . . From whom, from who are my parents. And to know that I'm seven years old.

A: Are you going to tell me who your parents are in the course of the story?

C: No . . . er, no, no.

A: Well, how . . . ? Er, do I need to know who your parents are?

C: Well, no.

A: It's a secret?

C: Yeah.

This planning section consisted of the first seventy-two lines of dialogue and served many purposes. It was the beginning of our story-making activity. It was a preperformance segment during which the central idea or conflict was introduced. In addition, other story components such as character outlines, scenes for the action, and some strategies to be used by characters were set out. More specifically, the discourse in this first section concerned a delineation of both Helen's and my roles and their histories. On the surface, she assigned herself the role of a "seven-year-old plain girl, going to school." However, she turned out to be a superhero, the "strongest girl in the world," who promised to appear and disappear magically. She cast me as a "thirty-two-year-old evil man who turned out to be Satan." My job was to "plan the wicked deeds." Finally, I was reformed and saved by her, "the Princess of Good" and emissary of God.

The first section also served the purpose of a preface. In it, the child attempted to make the point of the story clear, that is, that my job was to fight her and hers to outwit me, although the latter part of the point was only implied by the superior position in which she placed herself. This initial characterization of the story served both to motivate us and to instruct me on what I should anticipate in the performance. When I asked Helen whether she would explain various pieces of the story as it developed, her response to me was, "No, you don't ask me. You just ty to fight me. . . . You can ask me more, who I am, and I'm going to say, 'It's up to you. You didn't hear me and so bye-bye.'" I attempted to gather information, via questions, on plot elaboration and then finally told her directly what I needed to know from her in order to proceed, namely, more information and guidance. However, her response to this was: "The rule is to keep you in the dark."

The child soon became impatient with my questions and said, "Come on now," indicating that she wished to proceed with the actual playing out of the situation. I then made a statement about what I thought my situation was as the story opened, which was intended as a clarification. Helen modified my statement, thus adding further detail about the opening scene. I asked her who her parents were, and she responded as follows:

C: It's a secret.
A: So I have no idea of your existence, even . . .
C: No you don't. (*Whispers*) Come on.
A: I'm just here by myself, giving my evil orders?
C: No, well, you have hired some people, and that's all.
A: And am I on Earth?
C: Yes, *of course* you were.
A: But I could be on another planet?
C: Oh no, you couldn't.
A: Why not?
C: That's not the way superheroism goes.
A: Okay. So I'm this evil creature who has no idea of you.
C: No.
A: You are absolutely invisible.
C: Yeah. You, to you, to you, I seem to just come like clouds out of thin air if they can turn invisible.
A: Right. And I'm supposed to give this terrible evil laugh and summon all my friends.
C: Yeah. But then we go to my part, where I am. And I'm a little girl going to school.
A: Okay, but you'll have to lead me, right? You have to set it up so that I can follow you, otherwise, I won't know.
C: But *you* don't know about me. Of course, you just think that I'm a plain old girl. But when I turn into *the strongest girl in the world*, pow, Wonder Woman . . .
A: Then I'm startled.

C: Yeah, you sure are. You think that I've come out of nowhere and that I'm nothing. And that it's only a make-believe thing.

A: Okay.

C: You never heard of me.

A: No, I ask you . . . But do you tell me?

C: You *don't* ask me. You just try to fight me. You know . . . But you can ask me more who I am and I'm going to say, "It's up to you. You didn't hear me and so bye-bye."

A: And you disappear?

C: Yeah. I just come and I disappear.

A: Okay. Shall we start?

C: Yes.

And so we began, moving into the next phase of our interaction. Helen proceeded to mark formally the opening of the story realm. She said, "And, here is the stor-ee-ee" in a clear, loud, announcing voice. I added, "of?" seeking elaboration of the opening. Following my signal, she said, "The strongest girl in the world . . . fighting the men of Earth, of badness." She then gave me a quite audible stage direction and in so doing set the scene for the listener/audience: "Go back to, become, and start at the bad place where the criminal called Satan is working." After this I had an extended turn at establishing my fictive character and scene of activity. This was followed by Helen once more alerting the audience to a change in scene and character by saying, "And back at the girl's place . . . Well, of course, she's just a plain old it, girl, going to school, in place, working . . ." To this she added, in a stage whisper, "But the real reason is that she feels something tempering [tempting] her . . . The tingle that badness is coming."[6]

The following twenty lines were used to launch the next major action in the story, the appearance of the strongest girl on Earth. It occurred in response to the "plain old girl" sensing "the tingle that badness is coming." She launched this action through explanation and paralinguistic effects such as gesture, pitch, and sounds. In addition, she played the roles of narrator, stage director, and the female plain-old-girl/strongest-girl character. I include the following excerpt to suggest a more precise flavor of what went on. The text begins

---

[6]What Helen did here was use the sophisticated devices of bracketing the story, in order to delineate its setting to the audience, and of asides, used to explain the situation to the audience and give them access to information that she, the narrator, had but was kept from the other central character, Satan.

where Helen is setting the scene at the alternative camp, that of the girl.

C: And back at the girl's place. Well, of course, she's just a plain old it, girl, going to school in, in place, working . . . (*In role*) Oh teacher, I've hurt, my headache feels . . . I'd like to call home, could I? (*In narrator's voice, as an aside*) But the real reason is that she feels, something tempering her. (*Pause; next part said loudly*) The tingle that badness is coming. (*In role*) Oh, thank you. (*As narrator to audience, sotto voce*) But instead she goes into the bathroom and locks it and insures that nobody comes . . . And as she has . . . (*Out-of-performance comment to me*) Where are those sticks? (*As narrator, continuing from where she left off*) Suddenly, Phew! Almighty Isaac! She is turned into the strongest girl on Earth. (*This is accompanied by much swishing around, twisting, and beating the air with sticks, interspersed with some directive whispers to me.*) (*Said in my role but without a change in register*) Mmmm, here, feel it. (*She makes a noise, then as narrator/interpreter*) I think he said . . . (*As director to me, prompting a comment that I am supposed to say to my men*) Tell them that it's coming from here. (*In my role*) Ssh. (*Makes a noise, then, Offstage directorial comment to me*) Let's pretend that something hit you. (*Makes a loud noise*) Phew . . .

A: What was that? . . . Oh, some silly leaf or twig. (*Out-of-role whisper*) Do I see you?

C: (*Audible although out-of-role comment*) No, I'm invisible.

A: (*Out-of-role question*) Do I continue being evil?

C: Nods her head.

A: (*Back in role as Satan*) I wonder who dares to drop something on me? The winds, they roar outside, but how dare they send a leaf in to brush against me, Satan, King of Evil? I am the strongest of the evil powers.

C: (*In role*) But how about of the good?

A: Did I hear something?

C: Of course you did.

From this point on, the child and I sustained a fluent and extended dialogue for about an hour. There were no more specific stage directions, nor did we come out of our roles to inform the listener of what was taking place. Explanations, modifications, or contradictions of information were woven by Helen into responses within the acting out of the story.

The story reached a resolution at the point at which the villain was persuaded to consider being good, but it had a final section or coda that continued for an additional 150 lines of dialogue. What was restated was the outcome of the story, which was the victory of good over evil. This triumph was celebrated in the form of an active physical duel between these conflicting forces, summarizing the import of the story. This activity may also represent a concrete expression of the verbal battle that had taken place so far, resulting in a more powerful realization of victory. Helen insisted on making this duel a lengthy affair, first reassuring me that she would not really hurt me but only do so in play. Once the fight was over, she began to wind the story down and we then moved into the final stage or conclusion of the event. This was marked by a shift in location within the performance: After the fight, she and I went down to Earth, and the following was our final exchange:

A: And you have been the victor.

C: And now we go down. Down.

A: The sword is moving.

C: No, it isn't. Oh yeah, I made it move upward. So now we have to go down to Earth.

A: And now am I your slave?

C: No. Only helper. You have to do good.

A: So shall we then leave this kingdom, and shall I follow you out to the world?

C: Yes.

A: Okay. Bye-bye my friends. I shall come back. (*Much moving around and whispering; a door closes behind them as they leave.*)

C: Bye all. (*She walks down the stairs.*)

C: And so, if we find the way, er . . . Why don't I teach you a little bit of something called magic, though it's not really magic? It's good. (*She makes a gesture indicating a magical transformation.*) Now you see, I'm in another place and I do not want to change. But, have you decided to make up your mind? Look out there. (*We peer into the beyond.*) Don't you see all the good people and what they do?

A: There sure are many of them.

C: Yes. There are a lot in the world. I'll change those to feet (*makes magical noise indicating that she is changing my wings into feet*), and those away into hair (*makes same magical noise over my head and horns*).

A: What am I now?

C: A person just like everybody else.

A: And you mean you're going to send me out into the world to be good?

C: Well, no. You can stay here for a while.

A: Okay. Thank you Princess.

C: Of Good.

A: For giving me this chance. (*More whispers, spelling out the next move*)

C: (*In a more audible whisper*) I'm gonna end it now.

C: And now, now, no lying as you have done before, haven't you?

A: I will try not to lie, Princess.

C: But a white lie you can do. You know what a white lie is?

A: No.

C: A white lie is when, um, you don't want to hurt somebody's feelings, so you say a lie.

A: Okay. Will you help me to learn some white lies?

C: No. You can just make it up, them up.

A: Okay.

C: But to hurt somebody's feelings or if you don't want to tell the truth, really, really. And it's too hard to tell the truth . . . And never tell that you were once a devil, or nobody will like you.

A: Okay, I'll try not to. Thank you Princess of Good.

C: And I shall make you good. (*She makes a twirling swishing noise as she prepares to exit.*)

C: Good-bye. (*whizzing noises*)

A: Bye-bye.[7]

As soon as we had finished, she turned the recorder off and said, "This is the best fun ever." She laughed as she recalled parts of the action and some of the lines in the improvisation. She also began to relive some of the actions and noises from the fight. As she listened to a replay of the recording, she became excited and laughed a great deal.

These actions may be seen as interstitial to the everyday and play realms. They faced both inward to the play realm and outward to the everyday and celebrated the excitement and close sharing that had occurred during the evening. The listening became a reward as well as a recapitulation of the play that had gone before, and was thus part of the general postperformance euphoria.

---

[7]In this final section or coda, Helen played an adult, authoritative, or parental role, while I played the role of an alter ego to the child. In psychological terms, I represented evil, one extreme of the polarity with which she was struggling, as opposed to her personification of self as the Princess of Good. Helen's moral sense of that which is permissible in the everyday world of doing good was clearly stated.

Helen then turned from this to a different expressive realm: the world of television, changing into her nightclothes before leaving for her parents' bedroom to watch a special Halloween show. She became quite involved in the program. Her parents returned during the show, and, although she wished me to stay and watch it with her, I had to leave fairly promptly. I said goodbye to her upstairs and made my way out alone. The time was 8:50 P.M.

Commentary

Helen's quiet and taciturn behavior while away from her own home was evident at the beginning of this session. This was in sharp contrast to her active, dominant behavior on reaching her own kitchen. Her behavior in the everyday realm of our relationship was especially noteworthy, as it displayed a quality not evidenced before. Although dominant, the role she took on this occasion was that of cook or nurturer in relation to me, the adult, as opposed to the controlling dominance of the everyday realm she had showed in Session 1. Such a transformation in behavior alerted me to the two faces of domination as expressed by Helen so far: bossy and controlling on the one hand and protective and nurturant on the other. In addition, it suggested a new flexibility in her behavior in the everyday realm. It may be claimed that the trust and intimacy that were shared through our activity in the play and intimate realms, together with the flexibility that I had modeled in all three realms, enabled Helen to risk flexibility in her own behavior.

While in the everyday realm of meal preparation and sharing, Helen inserted a comment that served to shift the focus of attention from this realm to the play realm. Her eagerness to go upstairs to "do tape recordings" signaled a point of transition in the encounter. It conveyed positive anticipation and was most likely based on the successful tape-recording activity of Session 3.

Helen's bedroom provided the scene for several actions that led up to the story performance and its recording. For example, her display of information about the several superheroes with whom she was familiar and her wish to listen to the recording or our prior activity were all a warm-up to the storying, playing, and dramatizing in which we would soon engage (see Schechner, 1977).

Some of the effects of the tape recorder were clearly discernible in this session. For example, in listening to the tape, both Helen and I became an audience to our prior performance. Helen as audience both mimicked her own performance and also demonstrated a deep involvement in it. Further, her reluctance to allow me to record her talk in these warm-up phases suggested that she made a distinction between preparatory activity and the "real" action, which in her mind was the only part worth taping.

The tape recorder had also introduced a strong evaluative component into Helen's behavior in the play realm. For her, the recorder played many roles. It was part of the performance scene but also an intruder. As a scribe and evaluator it was to be colluded against, hence her out-of-performance whispers in case the machine should record flaws or plans, thereby detracting from the finished and surviving structure.

Helen never completely abandoned this suspicious perception of the machine, and in many encounters I struggled to introduce the machine at times other than "performance" time. It seems that the tape recorder might have been a threat to Helen. It might, after all, have prevented her from controlling the play, since her plans and negotiations were recorded. The recording was to be reserved for playful action, not direction. In play, one's secrets were presumably protected by their pretense, but in planning they were not. In planning, one's everyday desires would be exposed. In play, by the nature of the reaction, they were disguised.

The planning section, then, was most clearly accentuated for the first time in this session by the use of the tape recorder. This listening or audience device, which created the chance for both a review and preview of material, led to an amplification of Helen's role as director, both before the performance and during it. In addition, for the first time, I drew attention to the role of the machine in assisting such an endeavor and named this activity as *planning*. I suggested, too, that planning was a prerequisite to the performance. Consequently, our effort on this occasion was far more a team one, where we played collaboratively, in contrast to the more fragmented or solo performances of earlier sessions. For instance, in Session 1, there was the merest hint of a plan when Helen first introduced the animal game. By this session, however, she gave an outline suggesting that the game consisted of opposing forces (good and evil) and that good sought to capture evil. Again, during the first two play episodes in Session 3, Helen had outlined only brief schemes for the action to follow. In the first, the television program, "Wonder Woman," which we had watched together in Session 2, provided a shared source of information that served as a blueprint for our action. In the second episode, however, the lack of planning resulted in a far less collaborative venture and one where I was continuously at sea.

The first tape-recorded performance in Session 3, which took place after dinner, was of a well-known and tried story, so that minimal cues about the performance were necessary. Even here, however, Helen found it necessary to stall the performance temporarily, in order to modify or elaborate the next series of actions through "off-stage" whispers. This was a persistent feature of her style for managing and creating these fictive worlds.

The planning phase consisted of metacommunicative activity that informed the play performance to follow. Our conversation during this phase was focused on providing each other with a preview of the plot. Several dramatic elements were first sounded here and became a persuasion for me to participate in the "drama." These included the scene (conflict between good and bad), the action (overcoming evil and converting it to good), the agents (Satan and the Princess of Good), the agency (verbal, magical, and physical actions empowered by the rules of make-believe), and the motive (to contest her powerless, plain, evil self, and to surprise me, the evil adult, with her power and position of control). However, Helen refused to deal with my desire for further information, which she regarded as undermining her goal, which was to be all-powerful and outwit me. Her strategy for achieving this was to be in sole control of information in this fictive sphere. In addition, guarding vital pieces of information guaranteed excitement in the game.

To be in control while I was out of control appeared crucial to Helen's strategy for organizing the story performance and giving it its momentum. In addition, such a tactic created a reversal of the power from the everyday realm, because Helen became the figure in charge (the adult, parent, or authority) and I became the anxious and questioning child. I disliked being in the dark and hoped that my persistent questions would elicit some detail. My own anxiety and frustration on this score were evident in my responses throughout this text and others.

In addition to previewing the grammar or plot of the story to follow, the planning phase was also one of negotiation between the participants. As metacommunicative information was exchanged, markers such as "okay," "remember," and "of course" were used to seek consensus on an idea; to allude to, reinforce, and share information; and to request or concede permission to proceed.

The next juncture moved us into the performance of the story. This was a scene of action, with minimum attention to individualized portrayal of scene and character. The tendency of the portrayals was again toward being extreme and in sharp contrast to one another. The characters were emblematic and of a mythic order, for example, the evil Satan and the emissary of God, the Princess of Good. In the course of the action, these polarities were constantly counterposed. Although appearance and inner feelings were not portrayed at any length, they became outwardly visible as relationships were revealed in action and symbols.

In performance, Helen's rhetoric included bracketing the story (explained earlier) and shape shifting, which involved giving her character the power to transform herself into several guises. She used these to outwit her opponent, to elaborate the game and prevent early closure, to keep her identity hidden, and grant herself autonomy and control of the plot and participants, in keeping with her motives. As Burke (1969a) would suggest, these narrative devices were part of her grammar. They allowed her to exercise her power and were related to other areas operating in her text.

Helen's distinctive agency in the performance was a verbal one. She used a conversational style of language to tell a story or make a point through an improvised, enacted debate between the participants.

The respective roles played by Helen and me showed some new dimensions. Both characters in the play had become full-blown entities, rather than only manipulators of toy objects, as had been the case before. Thus our actions confronted the motivational issues in this drama more directly and intensely. Further, for the first time, Helen took the role of a less powerful character (a plain old girl), which indicated a slight relaxing of her need for power. I became a strong antagonist in the play and one who had active control over her own role rather than merely playing an auxiliary or assigned role. In addition, although my role was reminiscent of the earlier prehistoric evil dinosaur (see Session 3), on this occasion, I was saved rather than destroyed. It occurred through my transformation so that I might join the ranks of the good. Finally, through my role, Helen more clearly conjoined the qualities of maleness and evilness. Satan was her symbol for suggesting such a view and was crucial for developing the moral dimension in the text she and I created together.

In this story, Helen's concern with power and morality continued. In this session, though, she added a third concern, beauty, which subsequently continued to be of importance to her. Beauty became an important quality of the desired self and was implied and stood in contradistinction to the qualities symbolized by "plain old girl." In play, she was to be grown-up, powerful, good, and beautiful, a far cry from her perception of her everyday childhood status.

Helen's symbolic concerns were clearly reiterated in the conclusion to the story performance. In fact, she sought to strengthen her position and the attitudes embodied in the symbols by aligning herself with God, the ultimate source of power and model of perfection. This was part of her rhetoric for persuading both her audience and herself of her authenticity in the midst of her own ambivalence. For example, she allowed some leeway to the newly reformed Satan, who had become a human being rather than a devil: White lies were acceptable if accompanied by good reason.

In this session, as in others, it was the child's particular symbolic concerns that propelled and shaped the structure and its outstanding ingredients. The true battle was not the surface encounter between good and evil but the inner one between what she was and what she wished to be. As Burke (1968) sees it, symbolic acts center in initiation, change of identity, rebirth, purification, and other related magical ceremonies (Hyman, 1955).

Conclusion

Session 4 has shown two important things: First, it has served as an example of Burke's (1969a) dramatistic pentad (of agent, agency, act, scene, and time). Second, it has illustrated how some mix of Burke's (1969a) three principles—rhetoric, symbol, and grammar—intertwine to lend shape to the participants' interactions. More particularly, I have noted that, as Helen extended her everyday role and became more protective of me in the kitchen, having hitherto been first dominant (Session 1) and then dependent (Session 2), she was also able both to allow me more power within the drama and to give herself a more ordinary identity, at the same time expanding her own vision of power to include beauty. This was clearly a session revealing considerable growth on a number of dimensions. At the same time, even as I was given more initiating power within the drama, it was in part taken back from me by Helen's increased use of inscrutable language. Still, it can be seen that the everyday and play realms were brought closer together and made less antithetical than was previously the case.

SESSION 5: NOVEMBER 9
"Barking as Talking"

On my next visit with Helen, ten days later, I once again picked her up at a playmate's house. When I arrived at 5:30 P.M., Helen was lying on the floor of the living room, seemingly engaged in a tussle with her friend, to the accompaniment of much laughter. Although Helen saw me, she continued with what she was doing. I chatted with her friend's parents, who remarked on "how well the girls played together." Since the family was getting ready to have dinner in a short while, I suggested that we should leave. I indicated this to Helen, who had in the meantime joined us in the kitchen and seemed eager to go. As we were leaving, the parents informed me that Helen had refused to have anything to eat, insisting on having supper at her house.

On the way to the car, Helen mentioned that she did have a piece of pie at her friend's house but that it was not her favorite kind. When I asked which sort of pie she liked, she said that it was pumpkin pie and added that her mother never made it. I then said that I would make her a pumpkin pie. She seemed pleased and commented that she would share it with her father because her mother was on a diet. She added, "I'm never allowed to have cookies and candy. They're unhealthy for you. But my father and I like them."

On reaching her house, Helen went straight to the kitchen and opened the refrigerator, saying she was hungry and wished to eat. "There's yogurt," she said, looking at me. She had decided to have toast and eggs, which, once again, she was eager to make herself. All this was done with ease and in an orderly way.

While having dinner, Helen told me that she had been playing a game about dogs, cats, and girls with her friend, before I picked her up. This led to a brief conversation about animals. Helen told me that she liked them and wished she could have a pet, but that her mother did not like animals very much. Although I did not realize it at the time, Helen was orienting me to the game we would later elaborate in the play realm.

After dinner, we moved upstairs to Helen's bedroom, where I inquired about the friend with whom she had been playing. Helen said that she did not like the girl much but that her friend's parents were friends of her mother. She then rather quickly said, "Anyway, how about if we play that same game I was playing before?" "You mean now?" I asked. "Yeah. For the tape-recorder," she said. I agreed, and she added. "*You* can choose what I'll be . . . er, I could be a plain old girl or a superhero dog or a cat." "Um, perhaps you could be a dog," I suggested. "Okay. We'll do it how we were captured by some men, you and me, okay?" I agreed. We had now clearly entered the first phase of the play realm, an arena where our talk revolved around planning and elaborating the plot to be shortly acted out using techniques of improvisation.

Between this and the next spate of activity, the phone rang, and she reminded me to answer it. After this brief interruption from the everyday world, we returned to our planning, at which point I once again switched the tape recorder on. Before moving into performance, we continued with our planning talk for about fifty lines, as follows:

C: And what do you want me to be? The beginning or the beginning how it was we were captured?

A: Hm.

C: And . . . er . . . or the other way?

A: What are the choices? In the beginning when we were captured, or what?

C: (*Wishing to turn tape recorder off, whispers*) Turn it off.

A: (*Attempting to persuade her to keep it on, whispers*) But it's our planning. Remember, we did it last time, too? So that if we don't get enough done today we can still turn it back and get the plan.

A: So we have one choice—that's to go right back to the beginning.

C: Well.

A: Or.

C: I don't know. . . . Or in the middle, how when we captured us.

A: When the dog captured us?

C: (*Vehemently*) No!

A: The . . .

C: The bad guys.

A: The bad guys, okay.

C: They're like slaves.

A: So, I'm just an ordinary slave, right?

C: *No!* Girl!

A: I'm a girl. But I'm also a slave.

C: Well . . . It depends if we do it when they're captured or the other.

A: How many characters are there? There's you and me and the bad guys.

C: Yeah, we're the slaves. (*Whispers something inaudibly*)

A: What do you mean?

C: And do you want any, er, robot dogs scratching you?

A: Okay. That might make it interesting.

C: Yeah, but when they scratch you, you better be planned because you will die. It really will hurt.

A: It'll hurt?

C: Yeah.

A: Not really?

C: Yeah, but it'll pretend hurt. . . . But you can't say ow.

A: You can't make any noise?

C: Yeah, but you try to get up and that dog puts you down. And I'm the dog.

A: Okay . . . Okay.

C: So, what should we do?

A: Maybe we'll do it from the beginning.

C: Well, how will the beginning start is the question. So, no—how—the beginning will start?

A: You don't know?

C: No.

A: We can just make it up?

C: Okay, We'll find out.

A: We'll find out.

C: You're just a plain old girl, walking.

A: Okay.

C: Having a good time . . . okay?

A: Right.

C: Now we'll start the story.

Helen's announcement of the beginning of the performance was made in a distinct and rhythmic fashion. She also whispered to me to move from my seated position and enact walking my dog, to depict the opening action. She clearly marked her role by barking at the beginning of the scene.[8]

C: Woof! Woof!

A: (*Whistling*) Hi, doggie.

C: Woof! (*whispered cue about my next line*)

A: Come on dog. Come on for a walk.

C: (*Whispers for me to call her Sandy.*)

A: Come on, Sandy.

C: (*Quick barking*) Woof! Woof! Woof!

A: Be a good boy. What's the matter?

C: (*Much quicker barking continued*)

A: What's the matter? What's exciting you?

C: (*More quick barking*). Woof! Woof! Woof! Woof!

A: Are you sensing some danger?

---

[8]Given that the audience was the tape recorder and thus was akin to a radio audience, it was perfectly appropriate that she used an auditory cue to establish her role as dog. However, she then attempted to extend the use of barking, introducing it as an alternative vocal code for communication. She seemed to be experimenting with ways of getting the story going in dog language. She worked hard at using this system to communicate her meaning but struck difficulty due to its very limited range of expression.

C: (*Nods head, indicating she does*)

A: You are? What's it like?

C: (*Long wailing bark*) Baowww!

A: Are you angry?

C: (*Shakes head in negation*)

A: You're frightened?

C: (*More wailing and yelping, with head going up and down, indicating yes*) Baowww! Ayy! Ayy!

A: You want to be carried?

C: (*Prolonged quick sharp barking*) Aaarf. Arf! Arf! Arf!

A: Tell me what you're sensing, Sandy.

C: Woof! Woof!

A: What's the matter? You think there's some evil around?

C: (*More barking; turns head to look in a certain direction*)

A: Is it coming from that direction?

C: (*Loud barking, indicating that my guess is right; whispers my next line to me: "Say, Is that a man?"*)

A: Is that a man?

C: Woof! Woof! (*Nods head*)

A: And you think he's evil?

C: (*Vigourous barking with head nodding*) Woof! Woof! Woof!

A: Okay. I'll protect you, Sandy.

C: (*Barks out complicated rhythmic message; long whispered passage explaining what's going on, though mostly inaudible on the tape*)

A: Well, Sandy, I know there's evil and I know there's a man and there's some connection between the man and evil.

C: (*Lots of agitated barking and jumping about*) Woof! Woof! Ayy! Ayy! Ayy!

A: You think he's mean and he's going to capture me? What will I do though? I don't think I'm strong enough.

C: Woof! (*Raises paw to forehead, indicating that she has an idea*)

A: You've got an idea? You think you'll bite him?

C: (*Barks and nods head through all this*)

A: Good idea. Good, Sandy. Shall we trick him? Shall I leave it all up to you?

C: Woof! (*Assent*)

A: Okay. I'm in your hands, Sandy. I feel pretty frightened.

C: (*Complicated barking sounds*)

A: You don't want me to be frightened? You want me to trust you?

C: (*Another rhythmic, complicated bark; then whispers because I do not seem to understand her barks*)

A: Oh! You're going to help me.

C: (*More quick barks, shaking head from side to side indicating no*)

A: Oh! You want *me* to help you?

C: Woof!

A: Okay, sure. I'll do anything you like.

There were some clear difficulties developing with Helen's use of barking for communication, which she was addressing through the use of gestures and even whispering. The next dialogue section describes the plot as it was elaborated in performance. The cast of characters consisted of the dog, Sandy, who at times became a robot dog, played by Helen; a plain old girl, played by me; evil men, played by both of us; and a mysterious character who claimed to be the strongest girl in the world and also claimed to be Diana, played by Helen. A link was suggested between the dog, Sandy, and Diana, the mysterious heroine figure. Although I did play the roles of the evil men, the more striking role that Helen forged for me was a plain old girl who was protected and given courage by a superior power because I was very special. Therefore, in this instance, Helen both protected and fought me, although, in contrast to the story of Session 4, my principal role was as that of a good person, who was ordinary, weak, and in need of protection. My role as an evil man was a secondary one, which Helen also briefly shared.

The story, as we have seen, opened with the plain old girl out for a walk with her pet, Sandy. While out, the dog sensed danger and alerted the girl to this by barking out various signals. The danger came in the form of evil men who were out to capture and attack the girl and dog. However, the dog attacked the men ferociously and the first scene ended with Sandy saving the girl by her heroic attack. Helen marked the end of this first scene by saying, "Finished." After this, she whispered the next stage of the play to me and then announced it: "And now, we're on *another* part." She then cued me as to my next line: "And this part has to do with the girl being captured." It is likely that her explicitness had to do with the tape recorder.

This next section of the play is considered the middle one. During the girl's state of capture, Helen alternatively played the role of Sandy as well as the evil men who interrogated Helen. As the men attempted to get rid of the dog, she once again turned into a vicious, attacking creature. The girl warned the men not to make her dog angry if they wished to be spared by her. This theme of making the dog angry was fed me by Helen. During this battle, Sandy suddenly became transformed into a mysterious character who asked the girl what she could do for her and then went on to explain that she had come to "take care of the girl" and asked her to trust her. She explained that Sandy, who was a special dog, almost like a human being, had told her of the girl's plight—hence her arrival. When the plain old girl inquired about who this mystery being was, Helen, in role, said, "Well, you can call me the strongest girl in the world . . . which I am." During this scene, the strongest girl in the world explained why, on the one hand, the men had captured the girl and dog, and why, on the other, she was eager to help the pair.

The following extract from the transcript provides details. It opens with me, as the plain old girl in captivity, asking the mysterious visitor, who had appeared before me in place of Sandy, whether the dog who had suddenly vanished was safe.

A: Do you think he's safe?

C: Yes, he is. Of course he is.

A: So I don't have to worry about him?

C: Yes. Just as you trusted Sandy.

A: Whoever you are, thank you for appearing. But I'm puzzled.

C: Well, you can call me the strongest girl in the world.

A: The strongest girl in the world?

C: Yes . . . Which I am.

A: But how did you appear out of nothing?

C: Well, Sandy told me.

A: Sandy told you.

C: Yes.

A: I don't understand.

C: Sandy is more an important dog than you are an ordinary girl. And I put a radio in her head that makes her tell me.

A: I never knew.

C: So, whenever you have badness, she'll tell me and I'll come. Or, you better say—when she says close your eyes you have to and then I'll appear.

A: And I have to obey Sandy?

C: Yes.

A: And trust her?

C: Yes.

A: She's a very good dog.

C: Yes, I know. She's like a human being, actually.

A: Is she really?

C: Yes.

A: Well, she certainly has protected me.

C: I know. Now, for another thing, where are the men? (*Referring to evil men, who have left the girl alone for a while*)

A: They've only just gone down the street. I think they've just gone down to have a drink, but they said that when they come back, they're going to take Sandy and throw him in the river, but since there's no Sandy I think they might take me and throw me in the river.

C: Oh no, they won't. I'll put something on you. (*Clicking noise with gesture of bestowing something magical on me*) That's a swimming thing to save you, and you'll turn invisible. (*More clicking sounds*)

A: Ah, thank you. You mean I'm even more protected now?

C: Yes. You have a swimmey thing and that makes sound whenever what they do [isn't] good. (*Whispers to me to say the next line*)

A: It makes me safe?

C: Yes.

A: Oh! Wonderful.

C: Because do you know how much Sandy really likes you?

A: No, I don't.

C: She likes you as much as you like her. And that's how much I like you.

A: You mean you like me, too?

C: Yes. That's why I came.

A: What is it about me that you like?

C: Well, first of all, Sandy. Second of all, you didn't do anything bad.

A: No, I don't think I have.

C: That's why. I come to people who don't do bad.

A: Oh. You protect the good?

C: Yes. That's why I'm the strongest girl in the world . . . My parents wanted me to go . . .

A: Go where?

C: Well, they always told me of this mission.

A: Your parents must be extraordinary people.

C: Yes, I know. I won't tell them, won't tell you who they are. But keep all that I tell you a secret.

A: I will. But I mean, you tell me that your parents sent you on a mission. Can you tell me something about these parents?

C: I said I won't tell you. But I know that they're superheroes.

A: Oh—they're superheroes, too?

C: Yes.

A: Well, all I can say, Strongest Girl in the World—May I call you that?

C: Yes, or if you want, Diana.

A: Oh! Okay, Diana. Any minute I fear our enemies are going to come back.

C: Okay. I'll be on guard.

A: And will you take them on when they come back?

C: Yes, I'll even go there.

A: And get them?

C: Yes. And you see this magic glass?

A: Yes.

C: Now, of course, your parents aren't rich, are they?

A: My parents aren't rich?

C: I'm asking, are they?

A: No, they're not.

C: Hm! Fine. For it has to be something with the dog.

A: What do you mean, it has to be something with the dog?

C: If your parents aren't rich, they wouldn't kidnap you.

A: You're right. Perhaps they want my dog?

C: To kill him . . . (*The scene ends with the girl and Diana prepared to meet the men.*)

A: I'm getting a bit nervous. I think I hear some footsteps.

C: Fine. Come on. (*Makes gesture to accompaniment of swishing noise*)

A: (*Noting the effect of her gesture*) I feel different.

C: I know it. I made you not feel scared. Come on.

A: I feel strong.

C: No, you don't. You don't have muscles, but I made you *not* scared.

A: I feel full of courage.

C: That's what I want you to. But don't fight.

A: No, I won't. I'll just trust you.

C: Fine.

At this point in the play, a door-opening noise was heard, signaling the men's entry. In this new scene, the men, having returned, discovered that the dog had disappeared and that they had to contend with a mysterious creature in the room. The men taunted her, and she engaged with them in verbal battle, outwitting their challenges by her ability to change into various animal forms. Finally, the men tired of her and wished to know what they had to do to get rid of her. Strongest Girl, who had not yet identified herself to them, said, "You have to stop being bad. . . . And you have to let go of the dog and the girl, not silly but smart [girl]." She added that, from then on she wanted to fight bad and, since the men were bad, she was fighting them. This, she suggested, was her mission. This fourth section was very extended, but the men finally confessed the details of their interest in the dog, which was due to its specialness. For example, they said, "Okay, if you must know, we captured you because we felt a certain power from this strange dog of yours. . . . We figured that this dog could help us in our missions because he had extra power." Then they agreed to apologize and be nice to the girl and her dog.

The fifth and final scene dealt with the girl and Sandy going free, after which they sat down, tired and worn, to recount their adventures. The play returned to a scene similar to that with which the drama began, namely, one of quiet celebration and bonding between the girl and her pet. It was a time of trust, relaxation, and intimacy which followed a time of activity and climax. The dog, in this scene, was looked after and protected by the girl. This was a reversal of all earlier scenes, where the dog, Sandy, and later the strongest girl, who was allied with the dog, protected the plain old girl.

This story, like that of the fourth session, seemed to have a double ending. Although the story came to a resolution and end, the child seemed to prolong the end, replaying parts of the earlier action. For example, Sandy sensed evil again and saw the men once more, so the tension of the earlier sections of impending threat was recreated and relived. Diana reappeared, scenes of fighting where heads were cut off with swords and blood gushed forth were acted out, and the men were finally killed. The coda ended with the plain old girl being asked to close her eyes once more, during which the superhero figure disappeared and Sandy stood in her stead. The final lines suggested that Diana and Sandy were one:

C: Ayy! Ayy! Ayy!
A: (*As plain old girl*) Oh, Sandy, good . . . Wait for me . . . Come on, little doggie.
C: (*In a very babyish voice*) I'm that girl, I'm that girl, I'm Diana.
A: You're Diana.
C: (*Nods in agreement*)
A: Okay . . . Let's go home. We've had a hard day.
C: (*As dog, whines softly; then, in a loud announcing voice*) And that is the e-end. . . .

The fifth session ended with Helen wanting to listen to the replay of the taped performance. While listening, she walked around the room and changed her clothes in preparation for bed. She would smell her clothes and laugh; then, unasked, she would stop to sit in my lap while she paused to listen further. She thought the performance was "just fine" and thoroughly enjoyed listening to herself barking. Before too long, however, she tired and suggested that it was time to get to bed. She asked that I bring this tape with me when I next visited, so that she could listen to more of it. I then saw her into bed and talked awhile to her about dreams. Helen mentioned that she dreamed about spirits, which frightened her. She told me that she had a notice on her room door that read, "I'm not afraid of anything" so that the spirits would not bother her. I tried to reassure her that real spirits would not bother her and that the spirits she dreamed of were only in her head. She laughed at the idea and turned over as I tucked her in. It was about 9:15 P.M. I then went downstairs, where I worked until her parents returned about an hour later.

When the Kings came home later that evening, I felt a sense of good will from them. They were apologetic about the lateness of the hour and thanked me for sitting. As I left at 10:30 P.M., I felt both exhausted and amazed by the wealth of information I had gathered about Helen's play life. I felt that each of us had by this stage invested the relationship with positive and idealized feelings. The child clearly admired me, and this led to some hero worship. I felt positive about our relationship and a growing fondness for the child. I also found the play life rich and amusing and secretly delighted in many of her scripts and antics. I felt that being privy to this child's play world, albeit hard work, was also a gift. I continued to play with her, which I knew she liked, and also behaved in a warm, maternal manner, reflecting good parental traits. Helen's wish to play with me with increasing regularity was normal in these circumstances; however, her expectations were unrealistic. I was exhausted and in need of a break so that I could stop to sort out the abundance of material that the study had generated to date.

Commentary

On this occasion, although found in the midst of enjoying herself with one of her peers, Helen displayed eagerness at the prospect of returning with me to the realm of play. This, in fact, was true on almost every occasion. This testifies both to the power of play in general and to its importance for this relationship.

Helen began relating to me much more actively, once we were alone and away from the more public sphere of her friend's family. As in the last session, our early conversation and relating took place over the topic of food. This topic and later the ritual of meal preparation were used by Helen to convey information about the self and its relationship to both her family and me, and to continue her controlling but caretaking role with me in the everyday realm. Our exchanges, first in the car and later in the kitchen, also underlined the view that, for Helen, power and caretaking were merged categories. My offer to make

Helen her favorite pie, in the face of some feelings of deprivation in relation to her mother, tended to play into Helen's views of me as the good, "protective," ideal mother, and stand in opposition to her conception of the bad or negative mother. Helen's caretaking alongside her dominant bossy behavior may in this instance be seen as a symbolic expression of some of her personal struggle. Her alignment of herself with her father on eating habits and the total absence of an overt mother figure in all her fictive creations so far suggest that this struggle may be of an unconscious nature.

It was during dinner that Helen first alluded to her earlier play with her friend. In mentioning their game with animals, she gave me my first orientation to the play realm that we would enter after dinner.

Once we were in the bedroom, the site of our "secret" dramas, Helen wasted little time in very directly suggesting that we should engage in playing. On previous occasions, she had tended first to ask me what we should do before finally suggesting the direction our play should take. This time, once I had agreed to her idea, she deferred to me by allowing me to have some say in the role she would play, although she circumscribed this by giving me only three alternatives from which to choose. When I suggested that she should be a dog, she agreed, and then once more sought her turn to sketch the main idea around which the play was jointly built. (Once again, Helen saw the game as being a performance to be recorded.)

Having introduced the nature of the game as being about a girl and a dog who were captured by some men, Helen then began to consult me about how the game should begin. Once again, I avoided influencing her story by providing suggestions of my own. My tendency to answer her with further questions was an attempt to elicit her ideas. This behavior on my part may be seen as akin to that of a therapist, although, unlike most therapists, I am largely acting as a participant in and co-creator of the child's dramas, rather than as an observer and interpreter.

Although, my motives dictate my nondirective pattern of behavior, especially during the planning of Helen's fictions, it is striking that, subsequent to Session 1, it was only during the planning phase of the play that Helen continued both to offer and allow me choice in negotiating the fictions. She displayed flexibility in sharing this planning activity with me but did not render the play performance realm to me. The latter was her domain and operated on rules that were very different from that of the everyday. It was a sphere of performance, excitement, passion, and evaluation, but it was subordinate to the inbuilt safeguards of play. It might be argued that she was fearful of evaluation in the everyday realm of metaplay activity; hence her wariness of the use of the tape recorder in the more public planning sphere. Activity in such a sphere is still too much under the control and logic of the everyday; it lacks the madness, paradox, and spontaneity of performance. In addition, for Helen it was the performance that really counted; it was this sphere that was to be recorded, evaluated, and reveled in. This was the sphere for power, dream, and autonomy.

Her main concern in setting up the play revolved around how to begin. For example, on five occasions she repeated her questions about what I wanted her to be and where the beginning would be. This was finally resolved when I suggested that we could improvise.

My concern was to find out what the plot was. After several attempts at getting some sense of what might be going on, I finally asked her how many characters the game had and who they were. For me, this was the first indication from Helen of what role I might play myself and play against. Finally, she began to be more directive about how I should behave, for example, by warning me about the robot dogs and how I should react. Her statement that, as the story starts, "I am a plain old girl, walking, having a good time," defines a character that is reminiscent of the one she played at the beginning of our previous session. This time, as then, she soon became transformed into someone greater.

As soon as Helen's major concern was resolved and she decided that we would improvise the details as we went along, she was ready to move into performance. It did not seem at all necessary for the child to know the details of the action to follow. A mere hint seemed all she needed. She also knew that, once within the play performance realm, she could come out of it in order to plan the next sequence, when we either got stuck or needed to redirect the action. Characteristically, her performance was punctuated from time to time with brief periods of time-out for discussion of matters of staging and management. As in the planning segment of our earlier Session 4 activity, Helen merely suggested very schematically how the plot would be shaped. Further, in this section, not only were her utterances more abbreviated but, as noted, there were also more invitations seeking my ideas about how the story might proceed. Such negotiations made for a very different pattern of syntax to that found in the play performance realm, where she was in control. She saw herself as responsible for making the performance effective; therefore, the performance was in her view no time for negotiation and a play of opinions. This was a liberty that she might take only before the performance.

Within the structure of the play itself, various changes were noticeable. On prior occasions, the theme of protection was more explicitly expressed in the everyday realm such as in Helen's relationship to her pet caterpillar (Session 2) as well as in Sessions 3 and 4. In this fifth session, protection was an explicit concern and expressed in relation to my character, who got to be protected. My point is that her behavior in prior plots, as well as in other realms, not only affected later plot behavior but also her actions in all realms.

In terms of agents or roles in the drama, an amazing reversal took place in terms of the everyday participants: Each took the other's role. I became a plain old girl, and Helen became me, Diana, who later on in the drama became synonymous with characteristics represented by the little dog, Sandy (i.e., power, protection, and wisdom). In taking Diana for her own identity, she merged the qualities of Diana, TV Wonder Woman, with Diana, her adult play partner, and the miniature but super powered Sandy, the dog. She thus provided herself with a symbol of power, adulthood, beauty, and moral goodness. In addition to the play-realm role reversals between Helen and me, there was an everyday character reversal. Helen became the powerful adult, and I became the plain, weak girl. All manner of transformation is clearly possible in play.

Helen's use of language in this context was extraordinary. She experimented with an alternative communication system and did so in accordance with her motives and the situation at hand. Language is not only a communication system but an agency for expressing and wielding power. It served Helen well, both in the plot she created and in allowing her to be autonomous and superior in performance. By using her barking system, she wittingly or otherwise had me (the adult) under complete control in her efforts at making meaning in the play realm. I became solely reliant on her communication signals, and often this experience felt like a guessing game where I was forced to read Helen's responses for clues about whether I was close to or far away from the meaning she wished to convey.

As the extract illustrates, one of the difficulties Helen met was that her barking system fell apart when it was required to yield more than simple yes or no answers. For example, when I asked her a question such as, "What's the matter?" she barked expressively but I found myself asking the question twice and, having failed to understand her response, rephrasing the question to, "Are you sensing danger?" The child was able to answer this second question effectively by nodding her head. Similarly, when I asked her whether she was angry, she was able to shake her head in negation. As an interactant in this process, I discovered that, in order to match her limited communicative potential, I needed to frame my questions according to her yes-or-no code because it was in response to such questions that she was able to give me clear information. This was necessary if we were to communicate and keep the enactment moving.

Helen also realized that she had to use conventional and clear referential gestures to accompany her vocal behavior, if she wished me to interpret her code. For example, in response to my question, "You think there's some evil around?" she nodded her head affirmatively and turned to look in a particular direction. "Is it coming from that direction?" I asked, and in response she barked very loudly, indicating that I was getting closer to the right answer. On another occasion, she barked once sharply and raised her paw to her forehead, which I correctly understood as meaning that she had an idea.

Although these devices helped us to communicate, they were as yet insufficient to sustain the development of a story as complicated as the one she had in mind, especially since we were improvising as we went along and the two of us had no clear idea of the plot outline. Therefore, Helen was forced to resort to using a combination of barking and whispering the details of her meaning, in order to keep the story moving. Eventually, the barking dog turned into a talking dog, for the same reason. What Helen was struggling with here was an issue of communication. Although she used barking to sustain her role as a dog, unless she stepped out of that role to correct and direct me as to the course of the story, using everyday speech, she discovered that she could not make her alternative communication system work for her.

In relation to its narrative structure, this play text appeared to be the most fully developed of the performances so far. It had a distinct beginning, a middle or developmental phase, and an end or resolution. In addition, there was also a coda for the restatement of major themes. In this story performance, Helen very adroitly picked up cues that she had introduced earlier. She elaborated these to lend the story coherence and provide the audience with narrative clues related to the unfolding of the plot. In addition, this story had a number of performance features that were common to her other enactments. These included direct speech, expressive sounds, sound effects, and motions and gestures, all of which are integral to making a story go effectively.

Some features of Helen's rhetoric were noteworthy. For instance, to communicate her story and point of view in performance, she built up suspense and excitement by maintaining her anonymity and secret identity, and by using the ploys of magic and the uncertainty. Helen had clearly learned a basic grammar of story and performance and had found in me a play partner whose interest was in enabling her to make her efforts successful. In fact, the high level of cooperation required for such a venture to succeed, given the uncertainty of the plot and story direction, may have been too difficult for her peers to sustain. Further, in this text, Helen manipulated up to six roles per page of dialogue, marking the changes in role by shifts in vocal register and other auditory cues. This device has been demonstrated with varying effectiveness in all her story scripts.

Helen's strategies and personal style as reflected in her negotiations in this performance were cooperative. While comparable to her efforts in Session 4, they were in contrast to her less cooperative and almost wholly solo efforts in the taped performance of Session 3. In a cooperative effort such as this performance, Helen was more often able to redirect and correct my efforts if they were not in keeping with her developing inner articulations of plot, without disrupting the story enactment. For example, when I say, "I feel different," Helen says, "I know it," and when I describe this difference as "feeling strong," she says as part of the dialogue, "No, you don't. You don't have muscles, but I made you *not* scared."

In another instance she used her behavior in the play realm to reveal her everyday feelings of love for me, her play partner, as well as to comment on her perceptions of those feelings. She reaffirmed and completed this personal statement by her strategic and symbolic gesture of identifying with the idealized or loved one, Diana. In addition, in this text as in others, Helen's style led her to engage in a physical enactment of the climax, even after it had been reached ideationally. In other words, she would first sketch the climax in fantasy and then, still within the play realm, recreate its excitement and arousal in direct experience, usually through mock physical fights.

The closeness of our sharing was also evident in Helen's behavior at the end of the performance. After we played together, instead of moving back into the everyday realm, we lingered in the intimate realm, to which this enactment had brought us. It was a time for closeness and celebration, for a spirit of risk and happy abandon. Left behind were the polarities and reversals of the everyday and play realm, in favor of a more integrated or synthesized set of meanings being brought into play. Dreams and fears reign side by side in moments of intimate sharing. This is known as festival play, rather than dramatic play. The latter, which forms the bulk of what we call play, is replete with the symbols of life in disguised and dialectical forms, as we have seen. It is passionate, urgent, and often difficult for the participants. Festival play, on the other hand, seems rather to be reserved for those who have reached consensus, either through dramatic play or by other roads to mutual identification. In festival play there is more release and regression.

Conclusion

This fifth session marked the end of the first phase of our relationship. By this time, Helen and I had established a close, intimate relationship and our own world of shared meaning and understanding. Helen's initial motive and desire for me to get to know her and accordingly to persuade me into her private world had been successfully achieved. In turn, my project of gaining access to this child's play and being a participant in it had also been securely launched.

5 The Middle Phase

The stage had been set for some change in the nature of the relationship between Helen and me. I was not aware of this at a conscious level, however, other than in my feeling overwhelmed by the masses of information I had collected and the increased pressures of my everyday life. Not only had Helen unknowingly been asking a great deal of me, but I had placed some heavy demands on myself, too. Nonetheless, the nature of the evolving relationship and the opportunity it afforded me to understand the play life of this child within the relationship were enormously rewarding. Thus, despite the toll on me, I failed to acknowledge and deal with the stress directly. Instead, I allowed a series of circumstances to insure that there would be a break in the relationship during which I could recover my energies for continuing to see Helen. I did not see Helen for the purposes of playing with her for three months, although in the interim I kept in contact with her by letter, telephone, and the giving of a Christmas gift.

As is too often the case with teachers and researchers who work with children, few of us pay attention to the feelings and needs of the children when it comes to setting up our schedules for working with them. The issues of separation or ending are seldom dealt with other than by marking these by some celebratory ritual. This was certainly true of my behavior. At the time, it seemed to me sufficient excuse that excessive work demands, an unforseen but necessary trip out of the country, and the end-of-year holidays would interrupt my plans for meeting Helen. She, however, felt quite differently, as did her parents, who had to deal with the hurt feelings of a child who acutely felt the loss of her adult play partner. My adult communications in the form of letters, cards, and telephone calls reassuring her that I was thinking of her did not seem to count for much in the child's mind.

In a telephone conversation I had with Don King during this time, he told me that Helen was confused and hurt, and he went on to chastise me for not protecting her feelings better. He was right. Although I thought that I was acting in a fair and responsible manner, I had failed to understand how involved the child had become with me and how vulnerable she was to my approval and disapproval. I realized it too late but was then eager to make amends and continue seeing her. Although I persuaded the Kings to allow me to resume my work with Helen, I decided that it would be better for us all if I regulated my visits to once a month and, further, ceased my duties as a baby-sitter. These decisions were governed by my feeling that I would not be able to meet satisfactorily the time commitment of baby-sitting. I also felt that this arrangement would be less taxing on me and, most important, would give the child a more structured sense of my visits and time with her. The Kings agreed to this plan. Although they seemed angry and disappointed in me, they were gracious enough to allow me to continue working with Helen.

After the new arrangement had been agreed upon, I called Pamela King early in February to make a suitable time for visiting Helen. We made a date, but she decided not to tell Helen in advance of my planned visit. I was somewhat confused by this decision but deferred to her judgment on this matter.

SESSION 6, FEBRUARY 15
Transition

As I set out for the Kings, I felt nervous and unsure of how I would be received by the family. In a sense it was a matter of facing another beginning not unlike school teachers do after a long vacation.

It was a bleak winter day; everything seemed grey and cold. I arrived at the house about 10:00 A.M. and walked hurriedly to the door. A fierce wind blew about me. I knocked twice and waited for an answer. Pamela met me at the door; after we had exchanged some remarks about the long cold winter, she informed me that Helen was playing upstairs with one of her school friends. Helen's mother called to the child, saying that she had a visitor who wished to see her. When Helen rather irritatedly asked her who it was, she said, "It's a surprise." By this time we had both ascended the stairs and were standing on the landing outside the room in which Helen was playing. It appeared to be a toy and junk room. As soon as Helen saw me, she stood up and smiled warmly. She said nothing but, to my relief, came toward my outstretched arms. Her friend had been told about me and wished to meet me. I greeted Helen with a hug and put my arm around her friend. By this time, Pamela had left the scene.

Helen introduced me to her friend, Anne, and both girls competed for my attention. When I asked them what they had been doing before I arrived, they said that they had both been reading. In fact, they were surrounded by books. Helen's main concern, as was mine, seemed to be to reestablish contact. She attempted to do this by giving me several back rubs and sitting in my lap and by other such shows of affection. Helen found it difficult to manage the situation because she lacked a sense of exclusive audience with me. In a bid to claim my attention, Anne often would enter into games of one-upmanship with Helen where she, too, would give me back rubs, tell me about herself, and so forth. In response to this Helen would surreptitiously suggest that it would be better if I came the next day, when she was alone. Both girls then told me about their school play, *Snow White*, and enacted various scenes from it. Helen tried to engage my exclusive attention by moving closer to me and following my gaze when I looked at Anne. Then she would step in front of Anne and block her from my view. Anne, who was not to be beaten, did the same to Helen from time to time. When I made attempts to tape what was going on, Helen became very agitated and whispered that she did not wish me to tape anything. She said, "That's only between us. It's for our secret tapes. I don't want to do it now." I respected her wish.

After awhile she asked me what we should do. I suggested that we could play a game. At first reluctant, she asked me how long I intended to stay and eventually said that she thought there would be time to play something. After some negotiation between Anne and herself, it was decided that we would play families. At this point, Helen insisted that we move to her bedroom, thus marking this shift in activity by a change in location. She decided that the game would revolve around a mother and a baby. To this Anne added, "and a sister of twelve." The plot concerned a very special baby, the strongest, most powerful, wonderful baby in the world, who was able to read words and perform miracles. Helen was to be this character, who was named Diana Aphrodite Artemis. She was an orphan who was sent down to Earth by her father and was adopted by Lois and Superman. Helen cast me in the role of Superman and seemed to ignore casting anyone as Lois. However, as the play enactments proceeded, she clearly looked to me to assume both the roles of Lois and Superman although this was never clearly articulated. Anne was to be her oldest sister and was simply called Anne. During their early days on Earth, it was my job to look after the girls, especially Diana. This involved my feeding them, putting them to sleep, and engaging them in childhood games such as "Ring-Around-the-Rosie" and skipping around with them to the accompaniment of songs from *Snow White*, which Helen sang in a very babyish voice.

During the game there was little cooperation between the two girls. Each of them did her best to advance her own cause and engage my attention. The game developed to the point where Diana and Anne began to demonstrate their superior powers. As the story went, the sisters were not daunted by various dangers they met on Earth because they had powers that allowed them to sense danger and enabled them to intervene, even in faraway places. Once there, they engaged in performing several feats, such as knife bending and spear throwing. Their powers enabled them to warn me, Superman, of numerous instances of evil, thereby helping me to save places from danger.

Episodes in this game were signaled by the girls eating and going to sleep. This was a recurrent gesture at points of transition. When I finally stated that I had to leave shortly but would return again soon, Helen suggested that she and Anne should continue playing the game after I left. In the meantime, however, she said I had to tuck them into bed once more and kiss them good night. She requested this as part of the play. Having done so, I left. It was 11:45 A.M.

Commentary

As I got into my car and began to drive home, I was struck by the warmth and welcome I felt from Helen. Furthermore, I felt relieved of the anxiety I had felt earlier on arriving at the Kings', as I had expected them to be aloof and critical. I had also thought that Helen might have returned to her cold, bossy self of our first meeting. However, neither of these things occurred, and I believe that it was my guilt at having so unwittingly hurt Helen that led to my anxiety.

In fact, Helen seemed pleased to see me, although somewhat frustrated by the competition she faced from Anne. This factor, however, was out of my control, although I did my best to respond to Helen's play for my exclusive attention. The thrust of the activity while we were in the toy room seemed to be for her to reestablish contact and convey her feelings of affection for me. It seemed clear, too, that Helen wished to continue seeing me, as indicated by her suggestion that I come the next day when she was by herself. She saw this activity as ours alone and in no way wished to share it with Anne. I was very relieved that the encounter had been so positive.

As I thought about my insensitivity to some of the issues involved in working so intensively with others, especially children, I was struck by the absurdity of studying behavior like play apart from the interpersonal relationship of which it is a part. And yet, few of us are ever made aware by our social science training of the complex dynamics of human relationships and, further, of the large extent to which we ourselves are part of the meaning of what transpires. Moreover, generally we are not prepared for the stress of working intensively with our informants or made aware of the ways in which human beings live, love, hate, and deceive themselves; nor of how we compromise, substitute, and evade personal problems of which much of the time we are not even aware. For my part, I had entered a situation in which I needed a great deal of assistance so that I could understand both the social and psychological dynamics of the situation. My own therapist, and my husband, also a psychoanalyst, formed a ready network for enabling me to deal with the many personal issues with which I was confronted in working so closely and intensively with Helen. Arranging for once-monthly and more structured meetings was one way in which I could be protected from a situation that I had come to find exacting, sometimes tedious, and very demanding of my time. I felt that, as their baby-sitter, the Kings would have liked me to come as much as possible, just as Helen would have. In such a situation, I had a difficult time saying no to them. Thus, it seemed useful and necessary for us all that we change the arrangement.

When thinking about the child's play, I was particularly struck by two features of an earlier story enactment, ones that had been indirectly introduced in the very first improvised story of Session 1. In the present session, they had been far more directly expressed. The first had to do with Helen's view of reading as something miraculous. She sees her decoding ability as power in many ways: as signifying intelligence, worthiness, superiority, and competence, and as making her different and appealing. It seems that Helen's self-worth is premised on her superordinate ability to read and, by extension, to be intellectual. At the same time, and not surprisingly, the second notable feature of similarity between the two sessions concerned her desire and longing to regress and be cared for—to become a baby, albeit a special one who could read. Helen further wished to keep this role for herself and was happy to deprive her friend of this regressed role by supporting Anne's wish to be an older sibling.

In contrast, something that was strikingly different from the first session was her casting of me as both Lois and Superman. She makes me both female and super, suggesting that she may have introjected me as the "good mother." This may further support the suggestion that Helen had a great desire to be mothered and cared for. Helen may have had me caretaking her in this play since, outside of our sessions, our everyday relationship or working alliance precluded such matters.

Helen's wish for exclusivity was in keeping with her behavior on previous occasions, where, for example, she wished to safeguard our relationship from my nieces (see Session 2) and from her parents (Sessions 1 and 2). Although her play with Anne was a measure of Helen's adequacy with her peers and a sign of normalcy, in this instance, it was clear that her relationship with me was, among other things, one of intimacy. Because our play was a crucial part of our sharing, it was this activity and its taping that Helen wished to protect most. Her attitude here indicated that the tape recorder and play-recording activity were part of a secret and intimate relationship. Helen's wish for reestablishing some intimate contact with me was especially noticeable in the play interaction between us just prior to my leaving. On hearing that I was about to depart, Helen incorporated my leaving into the play, thus successfully synthesizing intimate farewell behavior from the everyday world into the play world. This clearly suggests a spirit of flexibility in relation to transferring behavior from one realm to another.

This session also marks a transition to more mature sexual content, with both fathers and wives portrayed. I played both roles and was given my first wholly positive enactment. Helen even took a less powerful role in the play (as an orphaned baby), although, once again, she retained her other powerful roles. This brief play episode therefore contained a hint of a new set of roles, themes, and concerns that Helen was to introduce into the next set of stories she performed.

Conclusion

This session was one of transition. Not only did it mark a change in our pattern of meeting, it also marked a change from an intense and very varied relationship to a more structured one. Further, its story themes were the beginning of somewhat different preoccupations for Helen. It marked the onset of a more settled phase in our relationship, in contrast to the more scrutinizing, experimental, and intense initiating phase.

SESSION 7, MARCH 14
A New Beginning

This visit took place four weeks after the last one. Although during the last visit Helen had asked me to come the day after, I did not do so. Instead, I called her on the telephone to explain that I had prior commitments that prevented my coming to her for three weeks. Although somewhat resentful, she accepted my decision. In the end, it turned out to be four weeks later, since Helen was ill during the third week.

When I arrived at the Kings, Helen met me at the door, accompanied by her mother. She seemed excited. She greeted me by jumping up and down and clapping her hands. She had a dog made of balloons, which she thrust at me, and this toy formed the focus of our interactions for a few minutes. She bounced it in the air, sang, danced, and threw it at me. In the meanwhile, having said "hello," Pamela King left us and went upstairs. After she left, the first direct statement that Helen made to me was, "I was waiting for you. It's past 4:00." I had said I would arrive at 4:30 P.M. Looking at my watch I mentioned this to her, and she grimaced. She led me into the living room. Sitting alone with her on the settee, I began to recall our first encounter. This occasion would be another one for negotiation, but its form would be different.

I asked her whether her parents had told her that I would not be able to baby-sit regularly for her anymore. She said that they had and asked me why that was the case. I replied that I did not have the time to do so as often as she would wish me to be with her, so, rather than disappoint her, I felt it would be better if I came to see her once every three or four weeks. Helen did not like these terms at all and asked why I could not come once a week. I attempted to explain that I had too much work that had to be done during that semester and was not as free to visit her as I had been in the fall. Helen tried several times to get me to agree to coming more frequently. She insisted that I make an effort: "At least once a week," she said. "Try to come. At least try." I felt badly for her but also knew that I would not be able to cope with visiting more often. Helen was then anxious to discover how long I planned to stay that day. When I replied that it would be about two hours, she promptly said, "That's too short. Stay to dinner. I really like you to stay for a long time." She then added, "You know, it would be much better if you came for a whole day."

In the face of this, it was extremely difficult to insist on my original agreement. I did, however, and she reluctantly seemed to give in, saying, "Okay, let's not talk about this anymore; let's go upstairs." This was a direct invitation to her bedroom, where play was her main interest, and it marked a transition to the next phase of the activity.

Once we reached the bedroom, Helen closed the door. Almost as soon as we were inside she began jumping about, wiggling her hips at me, lifting her dress as she twirled around, singing and drawing my attention to various flying objects that she had recently acquired. After this, she showed me a copy of *A Child's Garden of Verses* by Robert Louis

Stevenson, which had belonged to her mother at age five and which she had kept for Helen. I admired the book, and Helen asked me whether I had a copy, too. I said that I had had one as a child. She went on to tell me that she liked the book of Aboriginal myths that I had given her for Christmas. "I've read it all. It's good. Very scary, though," she said, as she reached for it. She then turned to some of the pictures in the book and said, "I'm scared of the spirit pictures." We talked for awhile about ghosts and spirits after that.

After this, Helen laid the book aside and began to tell me about a new game that she was "into." She was very excited about it. She said that it was about a new planet, Battlestar Gallactica, and added that it was named after her new favorite television show. She giggled as she whispered that the show contained her new crush, Starbuck. She asked whether I knew the show and the various characters from it, which I did not. She then asked me whether I knew any Viking myths. I said that I did, after which she told me that she had been reading them and thought they were great. She asked me whether I knew who Athena and Thor were. She told me that Thor was the strongest god. She then mentioned Aphrodite, and when I said that she was the goddess of love, Helen added, "of Beauty, too." Then, almost instantly, she asked whether we could tape a story and wanted to switch the machine on for this purpose herself. She played with it for awhile and told me that her parents had given her one for Christmas but that she did not like using it by herself much. She then suggested that we should "do the story for the tape. It will be about the new game I told you, okay? About Viking gods and Battlestar Gallactica." I agreed with her suggestion, and from that point on we moved into the story-planning phase of the encounter.

The topic of concern in this last interaction was Helen's latest sources of fiction. It seemed essential to her purposes that she introduce me to the new worlds that were influencing her, because these were the worlds on which she planned to draw during our joint efforts at story making for the recorder. Also inserted in this segment of conversation was the fact that "Wonder Woman" was no longer her favorite program, since it had been dropped by the television network. Helen's talk about her new sources of fiction was used to orient me to her story world so that we could begin the actual story plotting.

With the opening of the story activity, we entered the play domain. This time, Helen was eager to have the planning phase taped. Her reluctance in the past to let me record her talk in these early stages suggested a distinction she made between preparatory activity and the "real thing," the enactment, which was what she wished most to have taped. The change on this occasion may indicate either that Helen had become used to the machine and wished it to capture all our talk, or else that she was beginning to find this planning segment to be an important prelude to the performance.

The planning phase took half an hour and was conversational in style. The main roles and barest plot details were introduced. Once again, Helen had the upper hand because she had a clearer outline of the characters and situation on which she planned to draw. In contrast, I found myself scrambling to keep abreast of the content and make sense of it so that I could participate as she wished me to. The following segment from the transcript illustrates this dynamic.

C: Now, do you want it to be . . . *How shall we get there* to this planet?

A: Well, we are both gods, right?

C: Goddesses.

A: Goddesses. But what about Thor? He's not a goddess.

C: Of course he isn't; he's a god.

A: Right. So we're having Athena as one goddess. Who's the other one, Odin?

C: No, he's a god.

A: Odin's a god as well?

C: Yeah, I told you from the Viking myth, two gods, and you know, two goddesses from the Greek myth, and a god.

A: Okay.

C: But I've told you they're gods.

A: Right. So that we've got Odin and Thor.

C: Yes.

A: And we've got Athena and, who's the other goddess?

C: Athena and Aphrodite.

A: And Aphrodite, okay—goddess of love.

C: Yeah, and beauty.

A: And beauty.

C: Now, you should . . . Who d'you want to be a mother and father?

A: You mean, who shall we make a mother and father?

C: Yeah.

A: Have they got to be, er, ordinary people or gods as well?

C: Gods. They *have to be* gods and goddesses—*they have to*—or we're immortal. Or we're not immortal, we're mortal.

A: Right, right, but in the game we're immortal.

C: No, we would be if we're, would be if we both have gods and goddesses as mothers. Now I'd like to get on with the game, but let's see, get started, but how will we get to this planet, because you don't want Thor to be angry at us?

A: No, we could, um . . . What kinds of things would make him happy? What are the things that please him?

C: Look, I thought that it would be—no, that wouldn't be good. I'll have to excuse. Why don't Athena put us there to help us?

A: Okay.

C: We're immortal.

A: Uh-huh.

C: And we'll be on here while we're babies, okay?

A: Okay.

C: Now you understand everything?

A: Right. So we're babies and we're on the planet. We've already been put there.

C: Uh-huh.

A: So we don't have to work out the whole problem of how we get there. That seems fine by me.

C: Okay . . . Now shall we start? We're on this planet which . . . *(continues)* only us can be quite okay.

A: Okay.

C: This will be how we grow up and then of course how we get to be there. Okay?

A: Okay.

C: I'll be the one who finds the gang.

A: Okay. And now, who's the gang?

C: The gang is Apollo.

A: Uh-huh.

C: Starbuck. (*Laughs, amused*)

A: Starbuck; right.

C: And, I forget his name, but the commander.

A: Okay.

C: Of the book.

A: Okay. And are they, are they? And when we find them . . .

C: They'll be prisoners.

A: Hm.

C: Hm (*amused*). I'm changing us around, them and us around. So that we won't be prisoners, but they will.

A: Right. And then how do, when we, you find them, and I, you bring me to them as well?

C: No, see, I do it secretly, and I say, "Here, let's kind of . . ." and I *pretend* them, I *pretend* because the others are mean. They were prisoners, so they capture them, and they put them on this planet and they can't breathe so well, and it's a very cold planet, but we can stand it.

A: Okay.

C: Because are we not gods? Goddesses?

A: We are gods and we can stand the cold.

C: God*esses.*

A: Goddesses. Right.[1]

Having laid out her plans thus far, Helen once again said, "Okay, now let's start playing," to which I agreed. Just at that point, however, she added another complication:

C: (*In a somewhat embarrassed manner*) Wait, there's one thing—look, they'll be in, only in, in only a panties and an undershirt (*all said giggling and unclearly*).

A: What?

C: (*Continues to giggle*) They'll only be in panties and an undershirt.

A: They'll only be in panties and an undershirt.

C: Um.

A: Right, but do we have our clothes on?

C: Oh, doesn't matter. Oh, wait, wait. I wanna get something. (*Goes to drawer*) Oh, rats, it isn't there!

A: Doesn't matter; we'll pretend.

C: Oh! That doesn't matter. (*Looks in the clothes hamper, finds her leotards and gym suit*) Doesn't matter if it's dirty, just for play. (*Drags clothes out, puts them on, and seems ready to begin playing*)

A: Right.

C: Yay! . . . Now, we are, now. I'll be always sewing that—really, I'll be getting ready—but at night, when we're supposed to be asleep,

---

[1]The problem Helen set for herself in this game was how to get to the planet without making Thor angry. She set this situation up in the beginning and remained interested in exploring it throughout the game. She quickly answered her own question by suggesting that Athena should put us there, in order to help us, and that we would be immortal and begin our lives on the planet as babies. Although she began by casting us both in the role of babies, which in itself was significant because it was the first time she cast us in apparently equal roles in a story, she then went on to cast herself in a star role, saying, "I'll be the one who finds the gang." This comment, in addition to giving her a key role, also added new information to the situation, which I needed to have elaborated. Upon identifying the gang as being Apollo, Starbuck, and "the commander of the book," and as being prisoners, Helen bemusedly commented on her version of the story: "I'm changing us around . . . so that we won't be prisoners but they will." With this twist, she had apparently rewritten for her own purposes the real television plot outline from which she seemed to be working.

I'll sneak it. You will also be pretending to sew that, okay? (*Refers to clothes she has unearthed*)

A: Okay.

The performance of the story may be divided into eight scenes. The story reflected new concerns, themes, characters, code, and location. It was the tale of two goddesses who found themselves on a freezing-cold planet, beginning at their babyhood and spanning seven years. It told of their origins and particularly of their discovery of and relationship to men, whom they first rescued from imprisonment and then nurtured.

Helen opened the performance of the story with the line, "Now let's go start. This is the beginning." This announcement was immediately followed by baby talk and gurgling and whimpering noises, which she signaled me to join in. "Remember, we're babies," she said as she continued gurgling. As in the stories in Sessions 4 and 5, once more she began the story by clearly establishing the scene and character via auditory cues. Her out-of-performance comment to me about our being babies was a reminder to me that we needed to establish this fact by our behavior.

However, as in the story where she chose barking as a system of communication, this system also presented some problems because of its limited scope for communicating shared meaning. Therefore, in response I said, "We have to have some words, or how are we going to make ourselves understood?" She replied, "No. First we go. Then we be one years old." She followed this with more baby sounds of various rhythms, then added, "Now this is when we're one years old. And we can talk very well but we have to crawl around." This helped to set the scene and served as an announcement within the performance to an imagined audience as well as an instruction to me. A scence was then enacted where much energy was spent on being babylike, which was represented by dancing, frolicking, singing, and making nonsense sounds and gurgling noises. After this had gone on for about ten minutes, Helen signaled the end of this scene by saying, "Let's stop this game."

The second scene was introduced by another narrative remark by the child, explaining both to the audience and me that the goddesses has gotten a little older: "Now you're five years old and I'm seven years old. Now we can walk." Turning to me, she said, "Stand up to me," after which we moved straight back into the performance.

During this scene, the young goddesses discussed their origins: who and where they were and how they came to learn language. This was in keeping with one of the main story concerns: how they got to the planet. The scene ended with the refrain, "Let's go to sleep, anyway." Helen used this for several purposes, including marking transitions from one phase to the next in the story and drifting in and out of scenes. Before moving into the third scene, however, there was an extension of the ending to the second, unwittingly prompted by my response to her refrain, which resulted in a further thirty or so lines of talk. The following is taken from the transcript:

C: Um. Let's go to sleep, anyway.
A: I think we should. We've had a taxing day.
C: Taxing?
A: Tiring. I hear that word, too—taxing. I think it was supposed to mean tiring.
C: You think? No that isn't that. Tiring is tiring, not taxing.
A: Right, but I think they use the word to mean tiring as well.
C: Oh! Taxi. Taxi is taxi. I just heard that.
A: You just heard it?
C: What is taxi anyway?
A: Taxing, taxing.
C: No. Taxi—i, i, i.
A: Oh! Taxi. Did you just hear that word?
C: Yes.
A: I think I know what is. It's a car.
C: (*Whispers to me:* "We're not supposed to know the right word.") No. It's not a car. It's little ants, I think. All little ants, don't you?
A: All these little ants? (*Pointing at imaginary creatures*)
C: Yes, these little things that go ee, ee, ee, ee (*making "ant" noises*), and so on.[2]

She finally signaled the close of this segment by once again saying, "Let's go to sleep, anyway."

_____

[2]Here the child clearly was taken by an idea that she then expanded to her own ends. It involved playing with the notion that words are arbitrary symbols and may be toyed with. She was not interested in the referential use of language but used it instead as a private symbol system. On the one hand, her communication served a poetic function in that its main focus was on the message for its own sake and on drawing attention to sound patterns, diction, and so forth. On the other hand, however, she used this piece of word play to check on whether her channel for communication worked and to prolong a playful exchange.

Scene three commenced with Helen's next narrative cue to the participants: "Now this is when we are six years old. We know a lot more, we know about every word." This was followed by a dance and song refrain. In this long and rambling scene, Helen reported a dream she had had that foretold the future. This is a well-known and sophisticated narrative device. As she put it, "Let me tell you how come I was so sound asleep. Um. I think it may be the future. I dreamt that I found these three people in underwear. (Laughs) Hee, hee, hee, hee . . . Men! . . . People around them are pointing guns to them . . . and we got them . . . were nice to them."

Subsequent scenes elaborated the ideas in this prophecy, albeit somewhat loosely.

The fourth scene was one of the more collaborative sections in the performance. There was a clear change in the structure and interaction of the play at this stage, as it had become smoother and displayed more spirit. Helen, as the seven-year-old goddess, took off to rescue the three men who were held prisoner, as foretold in her dream. The beginning of the scene was marked by her comment to her sister (me) that she was "off," which was uttered to the accompaniment of flying noises, thus making the shift in location clear to the listening audience.

I also played the role of the evil guard of the prisoners. When Helen, in role, arrived at her destination, there ensued an encounter between the goddess and the guard. The latter acted as provocateur in a by now familiar interaction similar to the routine verbal duels between the principal good and evil characters in earlier stories. As the guard, I taunted the goddess on issues that were certain to elicit a response: smartness versus dumbness, disparagement of the men in whom she was interested, and ridicule of her mysterious identity. Helen enjoyed these battles, especially when I became an active participant. They were occasions for quick verbal repartee and insults, in which she displayed a sophisticated level of thought and language use.

On this occasion, the goddess used her device of shape-shifting to take a disguise and thus confound the evil gatekeeper. While she concealed her identity from him, the twist was that, unlike in other stories, she was not a super being but a goddess who was both uncertain of her origins and possessed of an impenetrable identity. This was in keeping with a spirit of collusion and its link with power and control. For example, when the guard asked her to tell him who she was, Helen said, "I am a girl, as you said. I do not know what my name is. I do not know where I come from. And I do not know why I am here. I have lived here seven years." The scene ended with the goddess's mission being fulfilled: The imprisoned men were handed over to her and the gatekeeper climbed into his spaceship and left.

The fifth scene took place at the girl goddesses' place. The seven-year-old returned having gotten what she wanted. She made it quite clear that the three men who had accompanied her were those she saw in her dream. Then, rather quickly, she suggested that the men should be taken care of, after which the girls should vanish. "There. Now we got clothes for them, good health, and we better get invisible."

The sixth scene concerned a conversation between two of the men, Starbuck and Apollo, who discussed being on a freezing-cold planet that miraculously had turned warm.[3] They also talked about their amazing escape, then finding themselves provided with food that magically appeared. As they wondered about the source of all their good fortune, they heard far-off sounds suggesting that all this was being provided by spirits. The men became scared, fainted at the thought, and turned to sleep while the invisible goddesses took turns at guarding them. Later, the men awoke and discovered the sleeping goddesses, who had become visible. On seeing them, they fought about who would adopt them. The girls awoke in the midst of this argument, asked the men to stop their chatter, and suggested that they would decide this matter for themselves. The men agreed and once more went off to sleep.

Going to sleep became a motif throughout the text not only at points of transition but also when Helen wished to terminate a section because she did not wish or was unable to sustain the action any longer. This latter reason seemed to apply in this instance, a suggestion supported by the fact that there was a good deal of whispered discussion and redirection afterward, which left me still feeling confused. Consequently, I asked Helen to guide me as to the next stage of the action.

The seventh scene was once again diffuse and fragmented. I was not clear as to her direction, and she seemed vague as well. At this point, I came out of the game to tell her that I had to leave soon. She asked why, and when I explained that I needed to return home to cook dinner, she said, "I'll finish it soon."

This seventh scene centered around Helen making clothes, ones she said were destroyed in the battle as well as new ones for us both. She spent several minutes engaging in talk about her sewing prowess and the wonderful articles she turned out. Finally, she veered the

---

[3]The third man introduced as the commander of the book never was interpolated into the dramatic play.

conversation around to the men. They slept during the sewing activity but then awoke and returned to discussing their fate. Once again, it became clear that there was little coordination between Helen and me. As evidence of this, while in the game, I asked, "What on earth is going on? Could you clue me in?" Helen responded, "What d'you mean, could you clue me in?" She laughed and then said, "You do the funniest jokes," followed by more exaggerated laughter. I said, "Well, I just want to find out what all this is about. I don't feel very easy about it."

As my frustration mounted, it became clear that we needed another consultation. This occurred and at that point Helen began to initiate the last scene and end of the game. In this eighth and last scene, the girls magically returned the men to their own home and then set off for theirs, smelling their way back. When I asked Helen to lead the way, she reminded me that I should not be a sissy because I was then ten years old, having grown overnight. Even at this point, my responses within the enactment revealed uncertainty: "What are we supposed to do?" or, "Yes, but I feel very unsure of the way."

The story ended with the goddesses going back to the great Viking gods, Thor and Odin. These were prototypic, mythic figures, who were very different from the needy but sexual Starbuck and Apollo. Before finally closing the story, however, Helen introduced another snippet from the Viking myths when she alluded to the trickster, Loki, and killed him for being a brat. It seemed as if she could not resist this last act of physical aggression. She said, "Well, you see, you . . . I won't kill you," thus reassuring me of my safety. Then, "You grab a person like this, you get him by the head, and rip him apart. You just go like this," she said, demonstrating with a gesture. "There!"

Helen's final refrain was "Now we're home. Let's go to sleep," which told the audience that the story world had been closed. Our final chorused comment, "Goodnight Odin, goodnight Thor" marked the end of the performance.

As we moved back into our everyday-realm activity, it seemed clear that Helen did not wish me to leave. She attempted to delay my departure by returning to our conversation about the new arrangements for seeing her, by asking me to stay to dinner, and seeking in other ways to involve me with her. For example, during the latter part of the game, when she was involved with sewing clothes, she changed out of her leotards into another pair. As she did this, she giggled as she wiggled her hips while standing completely naked. She also spent some time showing me several mosquito bites. One, she said, was on her genitals, and she attempted to show it to me. When I asked her how she was so badly stung, she said she did not know. Finally, she wished to listen to the tape, but I had to suggest that she do this the next time because of the constraints on my time that night. She agreed and followed me downstairs in her play clothes.

When we reached the living room, we met her father, from whom Helen quickly hid. She tried to press herself into the wall and did not wish him to see her or comment on her appearance. This was an intrusion from the public world that she wished to avoid. He did comment, however, saying, "What's this?" and laughed. I said that it was part of our game. He then asked Helen to see me out of the door and wish me goodbye. She remained silent through all this but followed me out of the living room into the foyer. When out of her father's view, she threw her arms around me and said, "Goodbye."

I felt badly for Helen. Not only did she not wish her father to see her in her play clothes, but having just been in a rich fantasy of a childlike sexualized encounter with a father figure in her play, it appeared that she wished to hide from him. I said goodbye to her, reassuring her that I would be back to play and that if necessary she could telephone me. "Come soon," she said. "How about in two weeks?" she added, smiling. "I'll try," I said and left.

Commentary

This session marked the beginning of the middle phase of the relationship, with the previous session (the sixth) marking the transition between the beginning and middle phases.

Several features in the text marked this story as distinct from those that preceded it. First, my role as caretaker in the everyday realm was over. This had implications for the way Helen related to me in the play realm, particularly in the story enactments, through which she brought caretaking intimacies into this realm. It also affected her behavior in the everyday realm, where she tried hard to persuade me to spend more time with her. She did so in a number of ways: by chatting to me for longer periods before the play texts were planned and played out; by sharing more of her sources of fiction with me and seeking my opinions of them; by engaging in festival play prior to the story; and by outright requests that I stay longer and come more often.

Second, the players in this story were cast as equals or peers, so that the drama matched our feelings of everyday friendship. We were twins in the story.

Third, the story content was new. The more mature, perhaps "oedipal" concerns hinted at in Session 6 were apparent once more; in the story, the young goddesses protected and were nurturant to weaker men. Men, although prisoners, were positive and alive in comparison to earlier males, who were either unredeemable or negative and transformable. The men in this story were linked with sexuality, a concern that was evident in the use of sexual symbolism (underwear, guns, men, and embarrassment), which seemed to be instinctively picked up and used.

Fourth, an instrumental attitude toward the world was more apparent. For example, Helen was much more willing and eager to tape the planning activity. The attitude was instrumental in the sense of being regulatory and outer-oriented. In the prior sessions, the play was all consuming and planning was secondary and certainly uncertain. In this instance, she saw it as useful to her purposes and part of her managing and operating the action. This was not the case before. The taping always made it more official or certain and intended for an audience.

Fifth, in the play realm, there seemed to be a regression in relation to my cooperative efforts at enacting the story. The plot and performance displayed more disjuncture and dominance by the child than has been evident for awhile. These qualities are much more akin to her earlier efforts as in Session 3, for example. This may be explained in developmental terms, as she seemed to be in a new phase of growth. Puberty was probably on the horizon, so it was a time when she might have been dealing with new concerns such as sex, peerhood (so that I became an equal but nevertheless a rival within the drama), her female identity, and scientific and physical prowess. Thus the worlds she envisaged were more complex, and this was reflected in her struggles with new story themes and plots. As a result, although there were brief segments of zeal and passion, on the whole, her performance was poorer; it was fraught with contradiction, fragmentation, loose development, and a lack of cohesion.

Helen's tendency to reject my contributions in the performance may also have been exacerbated by some resentment left over from my long absence and changed arrangements for visiting. Further, the disjuncture was due at least in part to the fact that, although I was a coparticipant, I had no idea of the elements of the new plot. I was totally unfamiliar with Helen's use, her grammar, of the sources of fiction for this occasion. Both the public sources ("Battlestar Gallactica" and the Viking myths) and the private fantasies (sex, peerhood) upon which she drew were new. Not only was I uncertain of the details, but Helen may have been, too.

All of these factors influenced our relationship and could be seen to operate in the text. The developmental features recurred in later texts within this middle phase, but with less obfuscation. However, the high level of disjuncture that characterized this seventh session disappeared in subsequent sessions until the relationship entered its final phase.

What was striking about our initial contact on this occasion was Helen's early display of celebratory behavior. Her excitement at seeing me was obvious. She used the toy made of balloons to create a joint focus for our early interaction as well as to provide herself with a safer, less direct means of interacting. This toy, like the pet caterpillar in Session 2, became a transitional object for making contact and moving closer. It was, to follow Burke (1941; 1968), her choice of gesture, embodying her delight at the prospect of rekindling our private relationship. It spoke to the play world and was an effort to induce a corresponding attitude of excitement in me. Further, this celebrational tone was elaborated upon and revelled in, once we moved to Helen's bedroom. Before this occurred, however, there was a temporarily interruption in our playfulness and festivity, as we turned our attention to more serious matters in the everyday realm.

In this realm, Helen and I discussed our new relationship: the new terms on which I would visit her in the future and the demise of my caretaking function. This was a public negotiation and had involved Helen's parents, too. Accordingly, Helen and I sat in the living room, a public arena, for discussing the issue. The topic was introduced by me. It seems clear that such public-realm negotiations were more my concern as researcher and adult, than they were the child's. It was I, in consultation with Helen's parents, who wished to clarify and seal the terms of a new agreement. Although Helen was not pleased by the new contract, it seemed that she was far more interested in play and matters pertaining to our private relationship. Her comment, "Let's not talk about this anymore," not only lent that part of the encounter and its topic of concern closure but also signaled her main interest, our play activity and sharing within the private arena of her bedroom. This comment and her suggestion that we go upstairs marked a transition to the next phase of our session: the resuming of festival play in her bedroom.

Within the safety of the room, her initial strategy was to catch my attention by a show of celebration. Through a variety of strips of playful behavior, Helen attempted both to capture my interest as well as to express delight at our meeting after what had seemed like a long winter's absence. Helen had displayed such behavior on previous occasions, but it was usually after we had jointly shared in creating a story enactment. What was striking on this occasion was her use of this festival play beforehand to celebrate both a renewal of our relationship and the chance to engage in further story making. This demonstrated a flexibility of selves and actions that may have been based on the child's confidence in my acceptance of her and the stability of our private relationship. Such a view is supported elsewhere by Helen's increasingly open, risk-taking behavior with me, especially in the intimate and play realms.

After this, Helen moved to sharing more about her feelings for me. By alluding to her mother's gift to her of *A Child's Garden of Verses*, Helen was able to comment on my Christmas gift to her and then talk about how she felt about it. Having revealed her feelings of fondness for me and her delight at the renewal of our relationship, she was ready and able to move on to the next phase of the encounter: an introduction or prelude to the play realm that we were soon to enter.

The prelude to entering the play realm took the form of a conversation between us about the sources of fiction she would employ in our play. What was first striking about this conversation were the symbols Helen introduced, which were different from those she had used before and pertained to the new situation to be encompassed. They suggested battleships, war, cold, alien planets, the unknown, and vulnerability (Battlestar Gallactica); as well as males and sexuality (Starbuck and Apollo); awesome, prototypic males (Odin and Thor); and women of wisdom, beauty, and love (Athena and Aphrodite). The situation to be encompassed by these symbols consisted of her new interest in males and sexuality, her own femaleness and consequent identity, her interest in peerhood, and a cooperative and instrumental approach to the world. This prelude was an orientation to the play realm.

The first phase of activity in the play realm consisted of our plotting the story. Our conversation included details about how to begin, as well as a synopsis of the story. The strategic problem Helen set herself, of how to get to the planet, although solved in planning, was not explicated in the story enactment. Rather, it was used as a rationale or idea for how to begin the story. The assumption that we were placed on the planet by Athena was alluded to, however, when the goddesses explained their origins. This served the double purpose of illuminating the goddesses' identity and development as well as of providing a justification for their being in the vicinity of men whose attractiveness was clearly sexual.

The second phase of our play-realm activity involved our playing out the story or plot. The early scenes and actions dealt with the representation of different stages of growth and development. The progression from babyhood to maturity, which came at age seven (Helen's age), was represented by gurgling, crawling, talking, walking, knowing a great deal but having no powers at age six, and then finally at age seven being considered fit to undertake a mission involving men. The middle sections elaborated the encounters the goddesses had with the men, Starbuck and Apollo. Their actions here involved fighting evil to protect the men, and rescuing and caretaking them. This was the section in which veiled sexual interest was expressed. The men were protected by the girls, who were clearly in control. The final sections involved returning the men to their homes and restoring the situation to one of safety and nonsexuality. The girls aligned themselves with the gods at the end, rather than with men. Sexuality was therefore bracketed and held at bay by the larger, mythical, and asexual concerns of the goddesses' origins, marked by reference to Athena at the beginning and Thor at the end of the performance.

The acting out of the story was much more diffuse in this session, which may be explained by the complexity of what Helen was undertaking. I was not a full participant until scene four and very much in the dark as to the grammar of the game. In adult improvisation, once the plan or outline is suggested, participants work collaboratively with each other, adapting their behavior to the several viewpoints operating. Helen was as yet not fully able to do this, so the script was largely of her creation, as were the rules, which were not clearly explicated. Therefore, as usual, I needed to be very flexible, seek direction, and wait on her moves. In scenes where she knew the routines and rules and was more informed, as in the rescue scene where I played the guard, we were able to act the story out more collaboratively.

Helen's gestures at the end of the performance were in keeping with her initial purpose: to persuade me to spend more time playing with her. In a sense, the rhetoric she used was akin to that of a lover, as she made a bid to move our behavior into a more intimate realm. She introduced several physical intimacies into the drama, for example, changing her clothes, wiggling her body, and sitting on my lap while I played the role of one of the men. Further, her wish to listen to our taped performance was an attempt to share more time with me. My need to leave cut short several of these efforts.

Helen's final act of physical aggression at the end of the story, aimed at the character Loki, was consistent with her behavior on prior sessions. This gesture, as well as her bid to create a more intimate sharing between us, were part of her personal world and spoke to her struggles, needs, and desires.

Conclusion

In sum, we may claim, after Burke (1969a), that the actions in the drama realistically mirrored the situation to be encompassed; that is, a new stage and a new adventure were marked by cycling back for a new beginning. The onset of a new developmental stage for Helen was manifested by scenes that explored questions of origin and babyhood.

A developmental strand held the otherwise episodic story together. This thread was the schematic depiction of the growth of the main characters from babyhood to age seven. Each stage was characterized by particular features and competencies, governed by Helen's fantasy world. It is interesting to note that the child began her autobiographical account as far back as Session 1, as well as the story concerning the birth of new superheroes back in Session 3. Both of those sessions also marked beginnings; a new relationship in Session 1 and a new play frame (tape recording) in Session 3. These efforts were structured along a growth dimension and around the issue of birth. In these prior efforts as well as in the current session, gradations in maturity and character were conceived of developmentally. These gradations were mythic and functioned as a scheme for conceptualizing the future. The use of this device would suggest continuity of style, although the earlier attempts were more primitive in comparison with the detail and sophistication of the scheme used in this session.

In addition to being an organizational device, a means of conceptualizing the future, and a strategy for managing new beginnings, such a ritualistic cycling back may also be seen as rooted in Helen's metaphoric key. In this story she elaborated her view that power can grow out of nothingness.

SESSION 8, MARCH 28
Baby Talk

It was about 4:30 one afternoon about two weeks later that I met Helen again. This was in keeping with the promise I had made to her on the last occasion as I was leaving, about making an effort to see her sooner than I had suggested in the new agreement. As she opened the door to me, she said, "I'm just checking up on something." On going into the living room, I discovered that Helen was in the midst of sorting out some piece of Biblical history, with her mother's aid. She returned to her seat next to her mother and continued to pore over a large book that the latter had on her lap. In the meanwhile, I sat opposite them, waiting for their conversation to end. It was clear that I had no part in this interaction except as an onlooker. Pamela assumed the role of teacher and expert in explaining the various elements of Old Testament history and their relationship to current events in the Middle East. When it seemed that the matter had been resolved, Pamela said to Helen, "Now you can go and play with Diana." Helen's rather indignant reply to this was, "Play? You mean tape recording!" To this her mother said, "Oh! Excuse me. Whatever you wish." Her mother then left the living room, and Helen suggested that we should go upstairs. As I stood up to follow her, she turned around and took my bag containing the tape recorder and offered to carry it up herself.

On entering her room, she commented on its messiness and attempted to clean it up somewhat. She said, "You see, I was playing with the girl I don't like. That's how come there's this mess." When I asked her who this girl was, she told me that she lived next door.

When Helen was satisfied that the room was sufficiently neat, she reminded me that she would need to listen to the last story tape, in case she wished to continue the story. I switched this tape on, and Helen became intensely involved in listening to it. She seemed to relive the entire experience and expressed a real sense of delight at hearing the replay. She also said that the story was "Terrific! Really fun." While she was listening, she went to her chest of drawers once more and took out her play costume. She changed into it, in preparation for the play realm she was shortly to enter. This time, in addition to her tights and gym clothes, she added a cape to her costume.

After listening to the story, she insisted that I should take the old tape out and replace it with a new one for that day's efforts. I asked her to allow me to use the old tape, since there was room left on it. Reluctantly agreeing, she said, "Okay, but what shall we play now?" When I said that I was not quite sure, she said, "We'll do the Battlestar Gallactica again, but slightly different. This time *they'll* find *us*." I said okay to this and then found that, again, Helen wished to turn the tape off during the planning phase. I finally persuaded her to allow me to keep it on, and our conversation follows:

C: Okay—now, see, what we *do* do, is—oh, you see, I don't mean doo doo. I don't mean the *butt* doo doo. I mean that what we *will* do is we will pretend that the Battlestar Gallactica finds *us* and we will be the daughters of Odin and Freya.[4]

A: Uh-huh.

C: Okay?

A: Right.

C: You shall always be older than me, but I will always be smarter, stronger . . . okay?

A: And so on, right.

C: And we're, and we're . . . up, up and away. (*Begins to get very excited and jigs around*) Ya-da-da-do! (*Begins to laugh, coughs*) Well, we're into it.

A: Right.

C: Do the right thing, okay? Now you understand everything?

A: Ah-ha.

C: Oh, by the way, Freya's the Goddess of Love.

A: So Freya's the Goddess of Love. And Odin?

C: Odin's the All Father.

A: Odin's the father of all?

C: Yes, of all the gods.

A: What happened to Thor?

C: Thor? Oh, he's the Son of God. (*Simulates fighting with swishing noise; gets very excited and gets into exaggerated skit*) He dead . . . He de' dea'.

A: Okay, so he's not in here, right? This time? Or he may be? Don't know yet.

C: He is.

A: Okay.

C: All the, er . . . Okay now, is it run out? (*Referring to tape*)

A: No. We can start and then we can stop and I'll change it over.

---

[4]On her way to articulating the plot, Helen became involved in moments of word play, getting caught up with the sounds, rhythms, and associations of her own language, which in turn stimulated spontaneous transformations and modifications of the original stimulus. She began with a concern to take me into account and clarify her meaning. In the attempt, she manipulated the form and meaning of her statement, playing with the double positive, *do do*, and its scatological implications.

C: Then let's hear the plans.
A: Okay. (*We listen to the plans.*)

This was followed by much switching the tape recorder on and off and whispers about when the tape would end. Helen finally returned to saying that she wanted to start playing the game on a new tape. At this point, I agreed to change the tape and give in to her whim, since she seemed so set on the idea.

As the extract suggests, Helen began the planning section by briefly sketching the plot outline. This involved a basic reversal of the plot of the last story. Instead of the two of us as the goddesses finding the Battlestar Gallactica, this time members from the Battlestar Gallactica would discover us: Where her title for the last story had been "Us the Finders," this one she entitled "Them the Finders."

There were four characters in this story enactment: the two of us as the daughters of Freya, the Goddess of Love, and of Odin, the All Father; and the two men from Battlestar Gallactica, Starbuck and Apollo. As daughters of Freya and Odin, we were powerful goddesses, although we began as babies and were very young through the duration of the story.

The performance phase opened with a scene where two babies were cooing, gurgling, and communicating with each other in baby sounds. As in Sessions 1, 5, and 7, Helen established the status of her characters and the opening situation by making sounds characteristic of their babyhood and species. Unlike in the other stories, however, in this case the opening was not officially announced by a narrative voice. Instead, the audience was presented with the contextual sound cues right at the beginning. Several lines of sound dialogue followed, suggesting communication between the two babies:

C: Ge ga—ga ga—ga ga—goo (*softly*).
A: Gee (*very softly*) ga (*sotto voce*).
C: Ga ga—ge ga—go goo! Goo ga ga gaa? Ku—koo . . . Koo koo! (*Quickly, excitedly, and in shrieky tone*) Ku Kook—ku koo . . . Kook—kuk koo—kuk koo (*very rhythmically*).
A: Kuke—ku—koo?
C: Kook, (*rapidly and sharply*) Ku Koo!
A: Ke koo.
C: Ke—ko—ku—koo?

A: (*Very soft, almost sibilant sound*) Ke, ke, ke . . . ke ke.
C: Cook! (*Sharply*)[5]

After this spate of language play, we stepped out of the performance to renegotiate the next section of the action. A lengthy, whispered conversation pertaining to this ensued, followed by a long pause
and more baby talk.

C: Ku koo kook kaa. Kook ku kaa (*slight tremble*).
A: Kook—kook—kee (*high-pitched and soft*).
C: Ga—ga—gaa (*very strong voice*).
A: Ku kooo (*low with downward inflection*).
C: (*Baby gurgles; pause; more baby gurgling; whispering; more gurgling*)
A: (*More gurgling*)
C: (*Baby crying; more whispering; a period of whimpering; long crying episode*)

In addition to the whispering indicated, this section also contained
two further occasions for whispering, due to the need for discussion
and explanation of events between the participants, in order that a
collaborative performance might occur. In this session, as with the
barking in Session 5, Helen's choice of code and channel for communication necessitated added translation because of their arbitrary and
limited expressive nature. Once again, she knew the system and I was
left guessing.

The scene then expanded to include two other characters: Apollo,
played by Helen, and Starbuck, played by me. These men stumbled upon
the scene of the crying and whimpering babies and were surprised:

---

[5]The striking features of these communications were their sound modulations,
varying rhythms, and speed. They were fuguelike in that the passage resembled a musical dialogue. The partners payed attention to the phonological
shape of one another's utterances and slightly modified the sequences each of
them produced in turn. Although referentially meaningless, these sequences
displayed a textual coherence in that they were related by a similar phonological
shape to each other. However, unlike later examples, these routines were high
pitched and often staccato, and did not follow usual rhythmic contours of
conversation.

In this instance, too, as alluded to in Session 7, the child's play responses
were prompted by her ideas on the origins and acquisition of language and its
beginnings in undifferentiated sound patterns. In playing with the formal
conventions of language, Helen restricted the code in a bid to establish an
alternative form—baby language. The formal features of language with which
she played were pitch, rhythm, timing, and volume.

C: Starbuck, do you see those babies?

A: Oh! Those babies? Gosh! . . . They're babies. Babies crying and whimpering.

C: (*Screech, followed by more crying; whispering; more crying; babies distressed. Playing baby role*) You've got to take this (*muffled*). (*Back to playing man*) I think they're frightened of us.

A: They look frightened.

C: Starbuck, well . . . what will that mean? We take them or not?

A: Take them?

C: They must be starving.

A: They sure look as if they are starving.

C: (*Correcting my response by feeding me a new line; said in a lower voice, in my role*) But, *Apollo*, they *must* be starving, I know; but what happens if we *do* take them?

A: (*Not getting her point*) Well, I don't know. Maybe we should just take them and figure out later on.

C: Well, they will be on our te . . . team.

A: But they're only babies!

C: But they will grow up! Don't you know they'll grow up? Well, (*pause*) they *will* grow up about a year or so. Don't you know?

A: Okay, well, maybe we'll take them. Shall we go and just grab them?

C: *Not grab them!* Take them with, or . . . Be careful, they must not have a mother here, or she would feed them.

A: No, they mustn't have a mother here, or she would feed them. (*pause*) No, they mustn't have a mother.

C: Then take them *quietly*.

A: Okay, Starbuck. Do you want me to take them?

C: I'll take one, and you'll take the other.

A: Okay. Ready?

C: Get set.

A: Go!

C: (*Whispering, more crying*)

A: Oh, they're yelping and crying, Starbuck.

C: One, but not the other.

A: Well, why don't you pick *her* up?

C: Because I don't wanta.

A: Well, be . . . D'you mean we should take one, and leave one behind?

C: Maybe.

A: Okay, I'll . . . (*Sounds of baby crying*) She's crying . . . Come on (*to baby*).

C: Well, okay. (*Gestures of picking up baby; gurgles*)

A: She seems to be comforted now that you've picked her up, Starbuck.

C: Must have wanted a friend.

A: Must have wanted a friend. Hmmm. (*pause*)
Is she saying anything to you?

C: Nope! Just seems to be talking to the other.

A: Hmmm. I don't understand a word of what they're saying, Do you?

C: (*Baby squeaks, whimpers*)

A: They're just making little squeaks.

C: (*More baby sounds*)

A: Making these noises.

C: Well . . . they *do* seem like they're talking.

A: Do you think they're twins?

C: They might be!

A: Humph. (*Whispers*) Well, Starbuck . . . Look. I feel . . . babies are . . .
I think we have to do something with them. I'm just going to leave
them down, now, again.

C: *Don't!* We have to take care of them!

A: We don't have any place to leave them, Starbuck.

C: *Take them to the Battlestar Gallactica!* We need more women, anyway.

A: Okay. We . . . These two sure are gonna be women. I wonder what
their names are. I suppose they don't even . . .

C: (*As man, in authoritative tone*) Well! (*As baby, yelps at men in response*) War!
Zap! Zap! Zap!

A: What? Do you think she understood me?

C: She might've.

A: Pretty weird babies.

C: (*As child*) Ba . . . Thor . . .

A: Thor? Did she say Thor?

C: (*As translator, interprets baby language*) Nope. I think she said nope,
nope.

A: Nope, nope. Well, you know, they're pretty advanced babies. I
mean, they only look about one year old.

C: (*Baby noises*) Da de da. (*In response to me*)

A: Oh, she's not even one year old. Is that what she said?

C: She's ten months.

The performance continued for twenty pages of transcript, during
which the men's early relationship with the babies was charted and
developed alongside the babies' own developmental process. Their development consisted of learning to be more in control and powerful via

the steady acquisition of language. The men worked to understand the babies; they moved from not knowing what to do with them, to some mismanagement and moments of friction, finally to understanding and supplying their needs successfully. This resulted in a friendly and warm relationship between the men and children, and the performance ended with the babies sitting in the men's laps and dancing with them in celebration.[6]

Although the need to end was first suggested by me, Helen finally decided upon the point at which she would conclude the action for the day. She said, "We'll do up to, up to at least four, three, okay." As soon as she announced that the babies had turned three years old, in accordance with our agreement, she began to initiate the closing segment of the play, as follows:

C: (*As man*) And they've been so friendly.

C: (*Baby response*) What d'you mean we've been friendly? (*Pause; another baby response*) Oh well! So beautiful . . . Green, everything nice.

A: What is she saying, Starbuck? Queen?

C: Green. I . . . that's what I found out.

C: (*Baby response*) Isn't it pretty? So beautiful there?

A: (*Baby response*) It's wonderful. Quite different from here.

C: (*Baby voice*) I know, and there we can travel 'round and all we see is green—except for the pollution.

A: (*As child*) But there's not too much pollution.

C: (*As child*) True! We cleaned it up. No! . . . No, no, no. Father—yep—my Father did it.

A: (*As baby*) Right. (*As man, in undertone*) What are they talking about, Starbuck?

C: Us! (*As man, very forcefully*)

A: (*As baby*) We don't want to tell you.

C: (*As baby*) We *told* you.

A: (*As man*) But we don't understand you . . .

C: (*As baby*) Us! The place (*singing*). Well, it's a daydream from here. It's so beautiful. It's terrific. E-e-e. Come on, let's do the dance.

A: Okay. (*We stand up to dance.*)

C: It's so ter-ri-fic (*clap, clap*).

---

[6]The song-and-dance routine with which the performance closed was influenced by Helen's experience of participating in a school production of "Snow White." It was typical of her other frequent play with various verbal modes, such as word play, sound play, repetition games, and singing.

A: Beautiful (*carrying melody*).
C: (*Dancing*) E. E. E. E. E. It te ta te. Te ta, te tee (*rhythmic and tuneful*). La da daa da, le da de de dee (*Whispers*) The way we . . . the . . . way . . . we . . . great (leave?) you, if you will, a smile. De da da de de der . . . da . . . da la de da . . . la de da . . . We tired. Goodnight.
A: (*As child*) Goodnight.

The key images in this closing section were those of beauty, dream, and green, suggesting Arcadia. Although disjointed, the talk in this section foreshadowed the finale, the song-and-dance routine. The ending was reinforced and sealed by the child's comment, "We tired. Goodnight." This is a familiar and formulaic close for her.

On this occasion the session ended fairly quickly after the end of the story because Helen had to accompany her parents on a shopping trip. She made it clear, however, that she would have preferred to continue our game. I left at 6:20 P.M., promising Helen that I would return in three weeks so that we could continue this text, which had not been completed but, rather, interrupted by demands from the everyday world.

Commentary

Although Helen was expecting me on this occasion, my arrival intruded upon an interaction in which she was already involved. Since neither she nor her mother sought to include me in any way, I waited until they were finished. This was signaled by Pamela saying to Helen, "Now you can go play with Diana," and served as an exit line for the mother. Helen's response to her mother was interesting in that she attempted to deny that we played. Her comment both aggrandized and sought to disguise our activity. By emphasizing our use of the tape recorder, Helen asserted the value and validity of her relationship to me. It may be argued that, if the child's ultimate purpose was to have a relationship with me and thereby to transform herself into a powerful, beautiful, and wise being, then her behavior in this instance was an example of her wish to protect our doings. Tape recording thus was viewed as prestigious as well as a defense against the adult public world (her mother). It symbolized adult doings and was associated with the intellect. Therefore, in the public world, it was more important than playing. This instrument and its activity had thus become assimilated into Helen's myth or metaphoric key, signifying language control, power, and wisdom. Ultimately, as will be shown, Helen came to do nothing but plan and talk instead of playing.

Once this interchange with her mother was over, Helen was ready to shift her attention to me. Her gesture of carrying my bag seemed to express her interest in what we would be doing, once inside her room. The life she lived out there was in contrast to the one lived on more public stages.

Helen engaged in a series of activities in her room: clearing the mess, listening to the last story tape, and dressing up in play clothes. This series of rituals marked a transition from the everyday realm to the play realm. The former activity faced outward, while the latter ones (listening and dressing up) faced inward. In fact, these latter actions served as a direct warm-up to the play, by plunging her into the excitement and resonance of the fantasies of the previous occasion. They were her aids for bringing about the transformations necessary for her to move into the play realm.

Having recaptured the spirit of fantasy, Helen signaled her readiness to embark on another story-making game by her insistence on using a new tape. This designated the beginning of activity in the play realm and marked the third juncture in the occasion. Her repeated insistence on using a fresh tape may have symbolized her intention to create a story signifying a new step in her fantasy world. In fact, in the light of her adamance about the fresh tape, some of Helen's earlier talk may have been her way of filling in time in order to use up the old tape. This is suggested by her inquiries at the end about whether the tape had run out, her stalling to listen to the plans, and, finally, her directly stating a wish for a new spool.

Helen began the planning phase with enthusiasm but was once again self-conscious about having this activity taped. As has been suggested before, she may have felt that recording this activity was too risky, given its closeness to the everyday realm, while the playing out of the story occurred in the arena of fantasy, where she felt utterly autonomous. Such an interpretation is supported by her brief episode of language play. In the face of my insistence that the tape be left on, her spontaneous reaction was to digress into a playful spate of regressive, scatological language.

Although the planning episode was fairly brief, it revealed a great deal of information about Helen's view of planning. The grammar she supplied simply stated the situation to be embodied in performance and delineated the characters involved. She did assume a certain degree of shared knowledge, however, based on our play during the last session. This was shown by her suggestion, "We'll do the Battlestar Gallactica again, but slightly different. This time *they'll* find *us*." In addition, Helen included her key symbols: powerful goddesses of love, suggested by their connections with Thor and Freya, and sexual human males who were adventurous, symbolized by Starbuck and Apollo of the battle-star.

In stereotypic terms, this was a much more overt expression of Helen's interest in sexuality than had occurred previously. However, it is more interesting to note that this little girl, like others I've observed, is quite able to express her own interest in sexuality and the male sex from a distinctly female perspective. I have noted elsewhere (Kelly-Byrne, 1988) that little girls are full of sexual initiative and able to attribute sexuality to themselves and women if not suppressed or thwarted.

The immediate situation to be encompassed by these symbols was the development of a scene in which men discovered girls and had a domestic relationship with them. The men turned out to be good and nurturant, qualities that contrasted with Helen's earlier representations of men. This may have grown out of her earlier and similar differentiation of me in the everyday realm. The more general situation involved continued development and sharing of an intimate relationship with me.

Further, in delineating her symbols, Helen displayed her attitude toward them. Once again, there was the intimation that the goddesses were powerful and in control. More specifically, the child reiterated some of her essential metaphoric concerns—power, strength, and smartness—which added validation to the hypothesis, first sounded in Session 1, about Helen's metaphoric key.

Her comments, "Do the right thing, okay?" followed by, "Now you understand everything" were significant. On the one hand, they were both orientations to the performance to follow, with the first also revealing the value she placed on this activity. It was to be perfect, or executed in a proper manner. It could also have meant do the morally correct thing. The second comment, on the other hand, suggested a somewhat magical idea of what planning might accomplish. Despite the minimal details she provided, Helen expected that this could function to inform me about how to behave in performance.

My role throughout the planning sequence, while still nondirective, was informed by Helen's story plan on this occasion as well as her story and play world in general. Therefore, my responses were mainly interrogative and repetitive of her answers. They were designed to clarify details of the plot as well as maintain the dialogue by my taking a turn without adding too much to Helen's plans.

What was most striking about the performance itself was Helen's choice of code and channel for communication. Language continued to be her agency, but, as in Session 5, she set up a system that necessitated translation before long. Its very arbitrariness, however, lent her the control and power she sought in this situation. Language clearly became a symbol of power, as well as her main means of creating her systems of meaning. Language was also crucial to our relationship, as it was a symbol system through which we shared a great deal. She and I identified with this system from the very onset, through our ability to fable and create nonsense and secret languages. Thus, for Helen, the power associated with language played into both her biography and her relationship with me.

In considering Helen's use of language as a symbol system in this story, we find that here, as in Session 7, the babies' developmental process consisted of learning to be more in control and more powerful through the steady acquisition of language. This was a further elaboration of Helen's view of language as a symbol and agency of wisdom and control, and therefore of power. The men had to work at language, too, in order to understand the babies and establish a relationship with them. In fact, the main strategy for developing and expanding the story revolved around the dynamic between the two parties, men and babies. On one level, the dialogue developed from the men's desire to make sense of the babies' communications. On another, it was sustained by the expressive restrictions and the resulting challenge of communicating in the face of such difficulties.

The strategy was based on a guessing-game model, where the men engaged in decoding an unknown communication system. The babies' responses consisted of gurgles, cries, shrieks, outbursts, and beginning language sounds, all of which were part of the currency of exchange for conveying meaning. It was to these codes that the men reacted. The communication system used was akin to a secret language and like the barking Helen used in Session 5. It was modified and accompanied by distinct and more conventional facial and bodily gestures, which were aids to negotiating meaning in an otherwise restricted and "foreign" code. In addition, its form was based on conversational conventions such as turn taking and sequencing, for example, which created a sense of conversational cooperation and demonstrated Helen's metalinguistic awareness.

The arbitrary and unfamiliar code required constant translation into standard English so that the game might proceed. This was introduced in two ways: in the form of out-of-performance whispers and as part of the performance. In the latter case, Helen, as the smarter and more privileged character, discovered that she was curiously able to tune into the babies' language system and began translating her baby talk for the benefit of her partner, Apollo. This was Helen's solution to the problem of how to communicate her message and thus build scope for further dialogue and the exchange of information, the latter of which took the form of a commentary on the babies' antics and oral responses. Not only did this enlarge the scope for making meaning, it also advanced the action and gave Helen a sense of power.

The notion around which the game revolved thus was that of communication as a problem-solving activity. The process generally consisted of my making hypotheses about what was going on, followed by Helen making contradictions and counterstatements. Then there would be the positing of alternative hypotheses or answers, by Helen, who had access to more information about what was going on, especially in relation to the babies' internal states. Being at such an advantage allowed her to control the game, create suspense and tension, and produce a "no-win" situation for my character, who was forced to defer to Helen's better judgment. Given her intention to communicate via this alternative system, it was Helen's prerogative to *select* the signals, channels, and messages to be negotiated.

In the end, the men succeeded in understanding and keeping the babies happy. In fact, a friendly and warm relationship was established between the men and the girls. The performance ended with the characters sharing in a gesture of intimacy, when the girls sat in the men's laps and danced with them in celebration.

What was most notable about this performance was the way Helen used language to set up a bipolar meaning structure. On the one hand, her baby talk was very regressed. As such, it could be associated with vulnerability, intimacy, and a private system of shared meanings. Moreover, it was also employed for festival making, for singing, dancing, and other playful, shared routines. On the other hand, this alternative language system provided its agent with control. As translator, Helen controlled all the other characters as well as the plot; hence, she controlled adults and males. Her playful and regressed language also served as protection against the dangers of inquiry and logic. Thus, all relationships were negotiated via a language that served simultaneously to draw one closer and to keep one at a distance. It was an ideal system through which Helen could express her interest in and exploration of sexuality, adulthood, and intimacy, as well as her ambivalence toward and denial of all this, as she sought to control it. With its competing dialectic of desire and control, language was both her symbol and her rhetoric, as it was her plot, for encompassing the situation.

Finally, Helen used several strategies for staging her story action. She organized the sequence of this story in terms of the babies' chronological development. They were discovered at a very young age by the men and then grew during the course of the story. This device underlay the progression of time and events and lent the story a sense of unfolding. These stages were announced by Helen from time to time and signaled major junctures in the story. This occurred, for example, when Helen said to me, in an offstage comment, "We'll go to sleep until we're two years old, okay? or when she told the audience, "This is when we get to be three."

Helen also alerted the listener through her story cues to changes in location of action. This, too, created a sense of the unfolding of events in time and space. For example, when in role, I say: "Shall I get some milk?" Helen said, "You *can't* until we're back in the Battlestar Gallactica." Then she made a swishing noise simulating the flight back to the battlestar, after which she said, "Now we are (there)." On another occasion, she simply announced the different location: "This is when we're in bed."

Changes in role were suggested by shifts in register. For example, when in the role of a man Helen used an exasperated and authoritative tone of voice and also changed her pacing, discourse style, and manner when she said, "Well, (pause) they *will* grow up about a year or so. Don't you know?"

Such staging strategies suggest a clear awareness on Helen's part of a text/audience relationship and illustrate her ploys for making the structure effective.

Conclusion

This story-making effort was rather long and drawn out and rather low on action. Nothing of major import really occurred throughout its course. There were no real complications, although small points of tension were created via mismanagement of communication between the two parties. In comparison with the Session 7 storying effort, however, this was a much more collaborative venture. For instance, if Helen redirected my responses, she accomplished it within the story and often either by simply taking over my part quietly, or by suggesting that I must not have meant what I said or had imagined something, or by some other more tactful means.

Helen's preference to continue playing rather than go shopping is noteworthy. For Helen, as for many children, there is little that is more exciting than being in a relationship (although usually with a peer) where play is paramount. These times are not only exciting for those who regularly play together, but they are opportunities for children to use the many sources of fiction around them to weave myths about life with a sense of ease, as Helen did. As with all myths, hers were also structures that attempted to reconstruct events of significance in her world, events that she could pattern anew according to her desires, fantasies, fears, and ambitions.

I also thought that this eighth session recalled some of the harmony from the later sessions of the first phase. It was certainly free of the ambivalences and irritations that had emerged during the previous session. As I recalled the difficulties that were part of this study, I felt certain that they were consonant with a dynamic view of a relationship, which views events and their meaning as socially constructed.

The harmoniousness in this session was due to my being familiar with Helen's basic script and to being once more an involved participant. I had no agenda burdening and constraining me, only my wish to be with Helen and go where she led me. Consequently, negotiations were easier and occurred less often; there was more spontaneity and friendship between us; and the session may be seen as typical of the feelings of settlement and enjoyment that were to characterize much of the middle phase of our relationship.

SESSION 9, APRIL 24, PART 1
Coming of Age

This session deals with our efforts at concluding the last story and then embarking on another; therefore, it is divided into two descriptive parts. In this section I describe what happened to initiate the session.

A few days prior to the twenty-fourth of April, Don King telephoned to ask whether I could assist him by baby-sitting Helen for about four hours because Pamela was away on a business trip and he had to work late. He added that Helen and he would also like me to join them for some light supper that night. Having agreed to the arrangement, I arrived at the Kings' house at 3:30 P.M., in time to meet Helen on her return from school.

Helen stepped off the school bus, rushed into the house, excitedly greeted me, and began talking rapidly. She put her bag away and followed me into the kitchen as I got her a drink. She was annoyed at how long the bus ride took, she said. Then she began to enact a short drama. "Now stop it," she said. "You're just a brat! What's that?" Then, turning to me, "My brother is such a dope. He doesn't know anything." All this was said with a knowingly exaggerated expression on her face, to cue me as to the nature of her behavior. I simply watched it all but said nothing. She then engaged in a mock fight with the brother and pushed him off a chair, which she then sat in herself with a smug air. At the end of this, she laughed. I smiled.

Standing up from her seated position, Helen then suggested that we should go upstairs, thus marking the second phase of activity for the afternoon. Once inside her room, Helen came and sat very close to me on the bed, placing her arm around my shoulder. "Let's sit on the floor and listen to the last tape recording," she said. "Then, we'll finish the story. It'll be very short, I think." I followed her onto the floor and began replaying sections from the last tape. She listened in a somewhat bemused manner and, after a few minutes, switched the recorder off. At this, she moved her position on the floor, so I asked her whether we were planning to complete the story from our last session. She said yes and began to describe the situation that we would jointly enact. Listening to the tape was thus a warm-up and served to orient Helen to the play realm. It bridged the gap between her last story-making efforts and those in which she was shortly to engage. Her gesture of switching off the recorder signaled her readiness to begin composing for the day.

In the third phase of activity, planning required very little time and went as follows:

C: It's going to be very short.
A: A'right. So, we can talk perfectly. And where are we continuing it on from?
C: When we were four years old.
A: Okay.
C: And . . . and we'll be sleeping?
A: Oh! We're still sleeping.
C: Yes. We're sleeping. Now we can dress a little by ourselves. (*Very softly*) Turn it on (*referring to the machine*).
A: It is on.
C: Fine.

The brevity of the planning phase may be explained by the fact that, in this instance, it was needed only to help resume and complete an already developed story, rather than to initiate a new one.

This dialogue was followed by a long pause, during which Helen seemed to be preparing herself to come onstage. She moved straight into the role of one of the four-year-old girls, saying, "Look! They are asleep," referring to the two men. This statement opened the performance realm and marked the fourth phase of activity. The siblings were quite irritated to discover that their male caretakers were fast asleep.

The men awoke, however, as the girls were commenting on the fact that it was their birthday and were busy opening their presents. The girls talked about the fact that they had progressed to four and a half years of age. Both the men and girls then engaged in several early morning rituals, including stretching, jogging, and breakfasting. Finally, this phase of activity was terminated by the girls' suggestion that they all go to sleep.

This was followed by a narrative conversation between Helen and me, which functioned to explain what happened next as well as to advance time and action in the plot. Thus, after sleeping, Helen said,

C: We'll skip five and we'll do six as we learn everything as quick as one day. Everything.
A: Aha!
C: Everything. Everything. Everything needed.
A: Okay.
C: Now we're almost seven . . . Now let's go to—to—to—
A: Where?
C: Work.
A: Okay.
C: Remember that we're supposed to do stuff. Oh! Here they come (*referring to the men*).

Helen proceeded to act out this piece of the action quickly and schematically and then, almost as soon as she had begun, added, "Let's go to sleep," thus signaling the end of this phase of activity. She then whispered the directions for the next stage of the story, which was very different from what had gone on so far, both in pace and action.

Helen set up a story line that revolved around a fire that broke out in the middle of the night in the recess room of the spaceship. The men woke the girls, and one (Helen) decided to accompany the men to the scene of the fire, where she rescued Boxie, a man who was trapped in the flames. The fire eventually affected Helen, who found that her life was in danger. The next scene took place in a hospital where the girl (Helen) eventually died. The other girl and the two men stood talking at her deathbed, describing the feats that Helen had performed as she rescued the men and the ship. They talked about her smartness, strength, and courage and celebrated her risk-taking achievements.

Helen enjoyed the action and excitement of this scene immensely. She also liked her clear role as heroine and rescuer of the men. After it was over, she resurrected herself and delineated another short scene in which the men refused to allow the girls to accompany them on one of their trips into outer space. She suggested that she would become very frustrated at the men but vent her anger on her sister by kicking her on her vagina. She said, "Now, when I do something bad to you, you get angry at me, and then I'll say sorry." The following is how this went:

A: You kicked me!

C: Well, I'm sorry. Oh rats!

A: Well, calm down, because you don't get to go with them anyway.

C: (*Redirects my lines, in a whisper.*) Oh rats!

A: Oh, stop kicking me!

C: (*Asks me to tell her where she kicked me*)

A: Oh, my stomach.

C: (*Shakes her head, indicating wrong response*)

A: Er, on my "zip"!

C: Oh! You mean right here? (*Pointing to my crotch*)

A: (*Angrily*) Yes!

C: Hm! You mean your V?

A: Yes.

C: And then a G?

A: Yes.

C: And then an N?

A: Yes.

C: And then an N?

A: Yes.

C: And then an I?

A: Yes.

C: Sorry. (*Helen giggles.*)

This scene was followed by another complication, also related to the girls' wish to accompany the men. They discovered through an alarm system that the men were lost in space. This catastrophe acted to confirm their judgment that they should have insisted on going with the men. They then decided to launch themselves into space, find the men, and return to the ship with them. Their mission accomplished, the girls went to bed. Apollo and Starbuck then talked about the girls' feat in saving their lives, even though they had denied it when the girls were around. Just as they were doing so, the girls awoke and rushed in singing the refrain from the musical, "Snow White," in celebration of their saving the men's lives. They danced and made several baby sounds to accompany their frolicking. They also further explained and demonstrated how they had done this deed and, with the story having reached this resolution, flew off into outer space forever, chorusing, "Goodbye." The performance was brought to an end with Helen coming out of role to assume a narrator's voice and saying, "And that's the end."

As soon as this was over, Helen said, "That was great. Okay—I already have an idea for our new story. It's going to be really, really great."

Commentary, Part 1

This occasion was different from the last three in that once more I had resumed the baby-sitting role. Consequently, our meeting was not mediated by either one of Helen's parents. In addition, the child also knew that, under such circumstances, I would spend an extended period of time with her, which was much more in accordance with her wishes. The particular ramifications of these situational factors were reflected in Helen's behavior in all realms.

The first incident of interest was the child's spontaneous and brief preliminary make-believe performance in the kitchen. For the first time, Helen showed sufficient confidence to act out a bit of play in a setting that was public and outside her bedroom. This move, in addition to the content of the play itself, implied a freedom to be more than "an ordinary girl" in the everyday realm. Perhaps because of the absence of her mother, Helen was able to take the role of a more powerful character in this realm, and play this strength against an imaginary brother, whom I suggest was also herself. She was thus able to put herself down openly. This interpretation is based in part on the conjecture that, on the child's return from school, her parents often questioned her, as would be typical. So, this snippet may be seen as her parody of such behavior. It also is based on consistencies throughout the study, the details of which are withheld to protect the family's privacy.

Her early playful gesture was thus an orientation to me about her new sense of freedom about her status. It also reaffirmed our shared beliefs about the impossible worlds that might be inhabited in play.

This occasion presented a chance for recreating some of the intimacy of the early sessions. Helen's behavior in the bedroom revealed her feeling of affection for me as well as a spirit of intimacy. Of course, these characteristics were always features of our developing relationship. On this occasion, however, it is not unreasonable to suggest that her mother's absence affected her very direct expression of both affection for me and excitement about our play-making activities.

In listening to the tape of our prior story performance, she oriented both herself and me to the play realm. By switching the recorder off, she signaled her readiness to begin composing the finishing section to the last time's efforts. The brief time spent planning was another indication of her excitement and eagerness to begin.

In the performance of the final section, the first situation of interest was the girls' relationship to the men. It was essentially a domestic relationship, complete with early morning rituals. The tenor of the scene was one of ease and mild amusement. Symbolically, such actions suggest access to men as quasi-lovers and fathers, within the familiar context of domesticity. This double aspect of maleness (father/lover) remains consistent throughout the performance. For example, the main point of this latter part of the story was to demonstrate how the girls, especially Helen, saved the men; in other words, how they made themselves valuable to adult males. The series of heroic actions in which they engaged had two sets of implications. On the one hand, they suggested Helen's competence, her need for achievement and for task accomplishment. On the other, such actions engendered admiration for the character who was victorious. Helen herself celebrated being valued for her accomplishments. Her smartness, strength, and courage were validated through risk-taking achievements. Both the situation and action provoke such an attitude in the audience.

Toward the end of the story, the men treated the girls as children in rejecting their wishes to accompany them on their adventures, as well as in dispatching them to bed. However, the men finally acknowledged the girls' feats, and this was also celebrated, through singing, dancing, and baby sounds. This not only suggests a structural link with the earlier parts of the story, but connotes a sense of intimacy through regressive action. It would seem that, to be more than "ordinary" is to be useful, adult, smart, and, in this instance, the "parentified child." This is an ironic reversal of the title of the story, "Them the Finders." It could, in the end, read, "Us the Caretakers or Rescuers." Once again, such details suggest Helen's view of how one might get closer to men. Being indispensable (and perhaps lover/parent/adult) to men, in the face of earlier rejections, may be not only her poetic meaning in this story but also a personal equation.

The second situation of interest concerns Helen's view of adulthood and her accompanying attitude toward childhood. In this performance, being "six, almost seven" represented the girls' fully-grown or adult status. This was symbolized by the completion of all learning, which meant being fully equipped to act in the world or "do stuff." To be a child was seen as being deficient. Accordingly, life was perceived as organized in terms of stages through which one progressed in order to reach efficiency and perfection. To Helen, adulthood meant having reached a state of possessing everything needed in life: beauty, wisdom, and power.

In this story, however, adulthood was represented as being risky. Once the girls were seven years old and knew "everything," they encountered danger: fire broke out while they were asleep. Men were involved in this situation, and the girls decided to enter the scene of danger. Although overtly the situation suggested that the men were endangered and in need of rescue, what was risked by the girls in their decision to involve themselves with men (and sex) was incapacitation or even death. (One of the girls, Helen, who was the most daring, was fatally hurt in the fire, although she saved a man.)

If the sexual connotations I have attributed the symbols and actions seem farfetched, Helen's next act within the performance more openly corroborated sexuality as a concern of hers. The girls wished to accompany the men on their trip, but their request was refused. Helen took out her frustration and anger on her sister by attacking her sexually. In this instance, her sister may be viewed as a displacement for her mother, the real cause of her lack of easy access to men.

The grammar, symbolism, and rhetoric of both situations elaborated her motives: to explore, comment on, and in some way resolve her relationship with men and, through success and achievement, to arouse an attitude of admiration for herself.

Three features of the text as a dramatic story were of particular interest. First, there is a striking difference between the child's behavior in the opening scene of the drama as opposed to the second and third scenes that followed. The spirit of the first was nonserious, lazy, and playful. This mood matched the domestic nature of the scene with its well-worn rituals. In contrast, in the second scene, Helen broke into performance accompanied by a strong sense of excitement. Here, one felt a build-up of tension as she approached the climax of the story and her own inner impulses. Second, it was interesting to note how the child signaled different stages of the action, different characters, and her relationship to objects. Much of this was accomplished and marked by shifts in linguistic register or variety. Helen had learned that there are many spoken registers or language varieties that are used in different situations having regard to the subject, addressee, and context at hand. Thus, here, as in other stories, Helen used appropriate changes in language style, tone, mood, and the like to effectively indicate changes in character, action, and scene. Third, the manner in which Helen introduced and elaborated the main theme of the story and the coherence she maintained throughout it were most impressive. She carefully and consistently led her listener through an explication, development, and resolution of plot details. In addition, she worked to highlight the main point of the story.

Finally, just as the story began with the discovery of the girls on the planet by the men, they disappeared at the end of the story into outer space. Their exit was as mysterious as their entrance and gave a sense of overall design and shape to the story. Having fulfilled their mission of growing up and saving their caretakers, the girls departed to another realm not of this Earth.

Conclusion

This tale highlights the risks of being grown-up and of pursuing men. However, it also points to the ambivalence the child experienced about the perceived role of adult men; although it was they whom she hoped would save her, it turns out that in the fray of life, she, the child, saves the adult men. The tale is also quite stylishly bounded by an idyllic and peaceful beginning.

SESSION 9, APRIL 24, PART 2
"The Beautiful Life of the Gods"

In the second part of this session, Helen and I improvised a story text called "The Beautiful Life of the Gods." The planning section consisted of the first half hour and belonged to the play realm. It dealt with the basic plot/situation to be developed in performance and went as follows:

A: Okay now, what were you saying?

C: Well, we, see, you'll be our, my mother, and I'll be the one who saves Viking gods. Okay? Athena and Thor will be my mother and father.

A: Uh-huh.

C: You will be Athena.

A: Uh-huh.

C: And we will do it from the very, very beginning. (*Continues*) This will be like the story of (*pause*) a beautiful life of the gods, which we think of them. Well, I do.

A: Mm-hm.

C: Okay? Do you want to be Diana? I don't mean like yourself, but I mean the Goddess of Hunt?

A: But she's a Greek god, isn't she?

C: Yes. They're both Greek gods and . . . which do you want to be— my father? Thor, Odin, (*pause*) or Beautiful One, the One of Light? Which?

A: Which is that? What's his name?

C: Buddha, Buddha . . .

A: Mm-hm . . . (*In a softer voice*) You choose. Anyone you choose. I don't mind.

C: Well, Thor . . . But which do you want to be? Diana, the Goddess of Hunt, or Athena, the Goddess of Wis, Wisdom?

A: Do you have any preferences?

C: What do you mean by "preferences"?

A: Do you prefer one to another? Which would you rather?

C: No, I don't have . . . prefer any.

A: You don't prefer any? Maybe I just be . . . ah . . . if I be Diana, maybe it'll all get confused.

C: No, it won't, because I'll call you Artemis.

A: Oh, okay. So maybe I'll be Artemis.

C: (*Clapping her hands gleefully*) Yaaa . . . I wanted you to be. (*Laughs babyishly*)

A: Uh-huh.

C: Okay. So you'll be the Goddess of Hunt. You really make a good match with Thor . . . but (*in a softer voice*) you aren't married to him.

A: I'm not? Why not?

C: You made a quest with your father . . . "Do *not* force me. Do not let me marry anyone."

A: Uh-huh.

C: Understand?

A: Right.

C: So that's what you made with your father, Zeus.

A: Okay. Now . . . so I . . .

C: Apollo is your brother.

A: Uh-huh.

C: Okay?

A: So I'm not married to Thor?

C: Yeah, but you . . . hmmmmm! (*Pause*) Maybe you could . . . (*Pause*) No—you *have* me.

A: "Have you"?

C: And Thor's my father. (*Pause*)

A: But we weren't married?

C: No. (*Pause*) It's adultery.

A: Okay.

C: But that doesn't matter with the Greek gods.

A: It doesn't matter with the gods?

C: Ah-aah. No. Not at all . . . because Zeus must have let you.

A: Okay. And so, if my father let's me, it's okay?

C: Of course . . . He's the chief, he's the king of Greek gods. (*Pause, looks at me and laughs*)

A: Okay.

C: (*Quickly*) Now come on.

A: Okay.

C: Now. This is exactly when I'm born from you . . . (*Pause*) Do you want me to be *born* from your head (*laughs*) or from the usual way?

A: Which do you want to be?

C: I don't mind . . . any . . . either . . . It's your decision.

A: Maybe from my head.

C: Ahh . . . Athena was born from her father's head. (*Laughs*) No, wait. I'd rather be born the usual way.

A: Okay.

C: Now, this is from exactly when I was born, okay? (*In an announcing voice*) Le-e-et's *beeegin*.[7]

With this remark, Helen formally marked the opening of the performance realm, at which point an imaginary curtain rose to reveal a baby being born, implied by about thirty seconds of crying noises made by Helen. The fact of the birth was then reinforced by me, as her mother, by comments on what has been happening and attempts to quiet the crying infant by attending to her needs.

At this point, Helen stepped out of the performance to whisper the next stage of story development, which required me to leave the baby with Cupid while I went out on one of my hunts. This little scene both established my role as Goddess of the Hunt as well as introduced Cupid as a carefree, young, spoiled-child god. What also became clear was that, during the planning section, although the opening scene had been suggested, information was not exchanged about what would occur next. Therefore, it was imperative for Helen to clue me in. Besides, since Helen herself was in the role of baby, she was restricted in her

---

[7]This planning section marked the beginning of the participants' story-making activity. Helen emphasized that it would be enacted from the very beginning, which meant from her birth. Although the performance, as we shall see, depicted her development, growth, and final crowning as Princess of the Gods, which took place when she was seven years old, these details were not spelled out in the planning section. Rather, they became incorporated into the performance and were concepts for the organizing of experience through the largely "free-talk" performance.

communications to me, which might otherwise have prompted further action on my part.

After this second vignette, Helen stepped out of role to announce a further stage in her development and consequently that of the story, too. Marking scene three, she said: "One month more . . . two months later . . . Well, Hermes at birth could do almost everything. When I'm one years old I can do everything, almost everything." This piece of narrative commentary was part of the performance and seemed to look both backward and forward in orienting the actors and audience to shifts in time and development. It further served to build plausibility for improbable events and actions. Such events become permissible as long as they are accounted for or motivated in some way.

To indicate the new phase of development in scene three, Helen began to make the noises of a slightly older baby. Then, once more, she came out of role to explain that "this is when [she] can do certain goo-goo sounds and so on," further informing her audience of what was going on. Having established her older status, Helen whispered the next stage of development to me. At this point, another character, Athena, came on the scene, and series of interactions between Athena, Artemis, and the baby took place. The conversation revolved around admiring the baby. The scene served the function of introducing a further slice from the life of the gods through the interactions among the characters. The brief portraits of Cupid and Athena were drawn in relation to the main characters, Artemis and the baby, Diana.

Again, Helen stepped out of role to announce the next stage: "Now this is when I'm one month old, when I crawl and do most baby stuff . . . Well, Let's say, eleven months old." During this fourth scene of the story, Helen, as Diana, involved herself in two main activities. First, made up a dance, wiggled her hips excitedly, and chanted to the sounds of "ga" and "goo." Second, she engaged her mother in teaching her how to use bows and arrows. She had her first lesson in this sport, successfully killing deer, and delighted in her early talent at hunting as she celebrated being the daughter of Artemis. She and her mother killed deer and cleaned, cooked, and feasted on their flesh.

The fifth stage of development also was clearly marked by Helen: "This time, I'm past one years old. I'm five years old, okay? This is just when you wake me up, and this is my first really deer, deer hunt . . . And I'm gonna get a bow and arrow and, and every weapon, even pistols, even guns." This served to inform the audience and players of the context and rationale for the coming spate of action.[8] It opened with Helen being awakened by her mother. She arose with excitement, remembering it to be the day of the hunt. They duly prepared for this event and then went forth. After successfully killing 100 deer, which was their goal, they returned home overjoyed. During the hunt, allusions were made to other Greek mythic figures such as Hermes and Hercules, in order to evoke appropriate notions of swift help and inordinate strength. Diana and Artemis, upon their return, prepared a grand feast from their kill.

The next phase of this scene resulted from a complication introduced by Helen. She responded to an imaginary voice issuing a prohibition. It turned out to be Zeus, forbidding them to partake of the feast, which made the goddesses tremendously angry and disappointed. However, Zeus's mind was fixed. Helen then explained to me, in an offstage whisper, what was going on. The next scene, the sixth revealed the reason for Zeus's decision, as well as how Artemis and Diana coped with the situation.

Another new character, Hera, came onstage at this point, and we discovered that it was she who had influenced Zeus's decision. A verbal battle ensued between Hera and the irate Diana. During this battle, it was revealed that Hera was Diana's stepgrandmother and Zeus's queen, whom he loved and to whom he had to listen. Hera, in a provocative move, set Artemis's throne on fire, tied her up, and generally behaved in a high-handed manner. All this was only alluded to in conversation, however; it was not shown.

Diana responded to all this with fury, first shooting an arrow at Hera, which "skimmed" her clothes and finally setting her alight and burning her "to a crisp." This was followed by much celebration. Interestingly enough, Zeus was delighted by his granddaughter's bravery and offered to make her one of "high rank." In fact, he decided to crown her for her victory in overcoming the evil Hera.

Before she could be crowned, however, there was a further initiation that the young goddess had to undergo. As Zeus said, "Now, first I must teach her . . . She will go down to men, I will speak to Wonder

---

[8]This was a narrative explanation, which Helen used instead of incorporating its content into the performance so that the audience could deduce the state of affairs through the action. In making this statement, she did not address a third party (audience) but instead directed her comments to me. As such, it was akin to an unself-conscious offstage whisper. This mixture of direct enactment supplemented by narrative explanations was characteristic of Helen's story style in the performances I took part in.

Woman and she will be taught the ways of superheroes." Diana was thrilled about the idea, although Artemis wondered whether she could manage on Earth alone. Diana persuaded her that she was capable of hunting and defending herself, and Zeus decided to test her by sending her to Earth immediately.

Scenes seven and eight centered around Diana's adventures on Earth, where she met Diana Wonder Woman, Batman, and several other superheroes. She was taken to the Hall of Justice at her request, learned the ways of superheroes, demonstrated her prowess in several areas of godhood and heroism, and was finally taken by these heroes on their missions. She left Earth having become a fully fledged superbeing. This entitled her to become Princess of the Gods, which, as she remarked, was the point of her journey to Earth.

In this process of initiation, Diana went through a series of actions where she magically acquired superhero powers such as catching air, reading superheroes' minds, flying airplanes, hunting, and so on. During these scenes, the audience was given a further sense of the kind of life these superbeings lived and what they valued. Information was divulged through the action and dialogue about the life of gods, Diana's history, and her role on Earth.

I have given the details of what occurred up to this point in a tightly summarized form in these sections, in order to highlight the essential points of the story and the motivation for all the rhetoric. What I see as the main thrust of the story occurred next.

Once Diana had met the superheroes and learned their ways, Helen led us through some scenes from her life after her initiation. She announced this clearly: "Now afterwards, when every superhero knows that she's become the strongest girl in the world." In scene nine, Helen presented Diana in superhero terms as she miraculously combatted criminals and destroyed them, thus illustrating and fulfilling one of her main tasks in life: fighting and overcoming evil. Her final feat on Earth was to save her father, Thor, and his Viking allies. Having successfully accomplished this, she returned to Mount Olympus riding her horse.

With another set of whispers, Helen explained the next set of developments. In scene ten, Diana returned home and was met by Artemis. When her mother inquired about Diana's adventures on Earth, Diana casually mentioned that she had "saved all the Viking gods." This surprised her mother, who asked whether she had rescued Thor as well. When Diana said that she did, Artemis revealed that Thor was Diana's father, who had been "spirited away." The young goddess was jubilant at her accomplishment and was then given a special suit of clothes appropriate for fighting evil and ruling the land. At this juncture, only Apollo and Zeus knew of these plans for Diana, that is, that she was to become the princess who would rule over all the gods. By this time she had grown to be seven years old.

Diana alluded to Hera and her evil disposition, vowing not to be like her when in power. She explained that, unlike the other gods, Hera was mortal because of her evil deeds. "Good deeds make you great," Diana explained, and they make you immortal, according to the "rules of superheroism." Just prior to Diana's crowning, Cupid was introduced onstage as an obstreperous figure. He challenged his cousin Diana's rise to power and acted in a characteristically spoiled fashion. Once more, Diana used her shooting prowess to demonstrate her power over him, taking a bit of Cupid's hair off with a flying arrow. Diana then explained that Cupid was so angry because "he either wishes to be on the throne or wants Diana to be his wife." Finally, she pacified Cupid by offering to accompany him to play.

Further whispers between Helen and me served to plot the eleventh and final scene of the story, featuring Cupid and Diana as they went off to play. They "played fun" by shooting arrows that injected feelings such as anger and hate into unsuspecting humans. The story closed with these cousins going back to Olympus after their time of fun. Helen officially ended the performance in a narrator's announcing voice: "And *that's* the end of the story."

Helen was thrilled with this story performance. She said that she loved the story and wished to listen to it. Before doing so, however, she said that she wanted to tell me something. It seemed that her friend Jill and she played many games together, and Helen wondered whether I would like to meet her. I said I would. She said that she would arrange a meeting between us, but that Jill did not know anything about tape recording. Helen wanted us to show Jill how it worked, once more suggesting the importance attached to this activity. I reassured Helen that we could introduce Jill to the tape recorder when we all met.

I then replayed part of the story, to which Helen listened with a spirit of anticipation and delight. While listening to the tape she insisted on lying in my lap. This seemed to be a time of quiet comfort and enjoyment of our shared efforts. This activity was interrupted by her father's arrival. He called out to her from downstairs and mentioned that he had brought us some dinner. If you recall, in setting up Helen's and my meeting for that afternoon, he had asked me whether I would stay to dinner as well. He said that it was Helen's special request that I do so. I had agreed but made it clear that I would have to leave shortly after the meal. Therefore, in keeping with my agreement, I joined Helen and her father for dinner.

Dinner consisted of pizza and orange juice. During this time, we talked of food and eating preferences and a host of incidental matters. I left promptly after dinner, at 8:30 P.M. Both Helen and her father saw me to the door. He seemed very grateful that I had done him the favor of babysitting that evening, and Helen displayed clear signs of enjoying the length and nature of my visit on this occasion. Her behavior demonstrated patterns of ease, delight, and closeness which were characteristic of many of the earlier sessions. These were occasions when I had had caretaking responsibilities for her while her parents were not at home, and I had spent longer periods of time with her.

Commentary, Part 2

This was a story of celebration. The underlying situation to be elaborated concerned the birth and development of an idealized or perfect being, played by Helen. Accordingly, a situation was chosen where the characters were, by definition, the embodiment of power, heroism, beauty, wisdom, strength, and so on, in that they were all gods. For example, Athena is the Goddess of Wisdom and Beauty; Thor is the all-powerful father in Viking mythology; Artemis is the Goddess of Hunting and Chastity; Apollo is the Sun God and God of Intellect; and Zeus is the supreme patriarchal God of Greek mythology. This was an impressive lineup.

More specifically, the story presented a series of situations designed to arouse admiration for and the celebration of a superbeing, as her story unfolded from birth to age seven, when she reached perfection and was accordingly crowned Princess of the Gods. This was fleshed out by a cast of central characters, some information about their relationships to one another, and some direct and indirect information about the setting. The main point (the presentation of the quality of life of a loved and idealized being) became the major organizing principle of the other story and a central topic of concern in the planning section.

On considering the details Helen proposed, what is apparent is that there was neither a clear problem to be solved nor a carefully sequenced series of actions included in the plot outline. Rather, as in most of her story texts, this performance depicted and elaborated a *situation* thought by Helen to be worthy of exemplification. The situation and its symbols, rather, suggested certain actions—those that would delineate and highlight Diana's development and behavior and bring her applause and glory. Helen used this overall design as a means of depicting her view of the good and beautiful life; it is her paradigm for a possible world of experience, created through the power of fiction.

During this particular planning activity, Helen's style of plotting and negotiation was much more fluent. She seemed to be much more in charge of her thoughts and eager to keep things moving. It may be that, in this instance, she had had a chance to warm up to the composing activity, through the story performance we had just completed. In addition, given the nature of the tale, her mother's absence may have allowed her to feel more freedom than usual, also accounting for her more economical and less diffuse style on this occasion.

After delineating the bare essentials of the plot, Helen began to involve me more actively in planning a few more of the details. She did this by asking whether I wished to be Athena or Diana, and by asking me to decide on which god I wished her father to be: Odin, Thor, or Buddha. I decided on Diana/Artemis, and Helen decided on Thor, thus reserving one of the choices for herself.

It also became clear that Helen had not as yet learned to plot with a sense of the whole in mind. Further, she seemed unable to communicate an entire outline or an equal amount of information to her partner in play. Although some of this was due to her enjoyment of experimenting with the unknown, with its resultant spirit of excitement, the rest of this style may be explained by her stage of conceptual and narrative development. Her style was to posit characters who themselves implied and carried much meaning in terms of their role attributes, and who thereby suggest story possibilities and constraints and generate some of the action. In addition, Helen suggested a theme or issue for elaboration, as well as some initial sense of mythic space and time. Once these things were done, she was ready to develop the story in conjoint performance with me.

The information exchanged in the planning section was transformed and elaborated in performance. In order to launch this story situation, Helen used strategies that she had used before with success. For example, she used the device of chronological development to delineate a progression of events and thereby organize the story. Each developmental stage was used to represent a more exciting period in the child's life. Further, she used auditory cues, such as crying, gurgling, and the sounds of flying arrows, to establish several scenes. Out-of-role comments were used to orient the audience and signal shifts in time and space. As mentioned earlier, she also built plausibility via the explanations she offered for improbable events and actions, showing her intention to hold the audience's attention.

Drawing on all these strategies to establish her privileged and remarkable early years, Helen then introduced a complication in the plot. Although this was not part of the plan, it was the conflict she required to develop the story structure and bring her purposes to full completion. As the story went, the young goddess and her mother had been up all night demonstrating their incredible hunting prowess. They had hunted and killed 100 deer and cleaned and cooked them in preparation for a large feast for all the gods. At the last minute, Zeus ordered that the child and her mother be disallowed from partaking of the feast. This prohibition had the effect of arresting the flow of action. It angered the characters, especially the young Diana, while it simultaneously engendered in the audience an attitude of sympathy for them, due to this unexpected and unfair turn of events.

Then, in accordance with her grammar and rhetoric, Helen brought Zeus and Hera to center stage, to become the primary symbols associated with the scene: Zeus, the prototypic father figure, and Hera, the wicked queen, his stepwife. In the story these two figures were given the somewhat distant status of grandparents to the young goddess, Diana. Further, Hera was presented as being in competition with Artemis, Diana's mother, an idealized figure. Hera sought to destroy her, set her throne on fire, and wreck her daughter's favored position.

I cannot help wondering at the personal symbolism underlying these more universal symbols. The situation would suggest that, in Freudian terms, Hera was a thin disguise for Helen's bad mother, while Artemis represented her idealized mother. Further, the child's view of the relationship between Zeus and Hera is interesting and supports an oedipal translation. Note how she implied her ambivalence: On the one hand, she suggested that Hera was Zeus's queen, whom he loved and therefore had to obey; however, on the other hand, Zeus is shown to be delighted when Hera is burned up and destroyed by his granddaughter. This act led to victory and celebration. Symbolically, this was a gesture of liberation that removed the impediment to Diana's growth toward and final attainment of a state of perfection and value.

Before perfection was finally attained, however, the child worked through other feats, all of which were rites of initiation designed to elaborate facets of learning, wisdom, bravery, and power. They all involved scenes that presented the heroine in a favorable light and entitled her to be crowned Princess of the Gods, the beautiful, wise, and powerful ruler. Thus it became apparent that the scenes, actions, symbols, and strategies in this story were all in keeping with Helen's purpose and the underlying situation to be exemplified.

Conclusion

This tale may be seen to elaborate Helen's autobiographical account, as rendered in Session 1. This was a story of ennoblement and enthronement. Through it, Helen reached perfection, a process that included saving her father and killing the witch-stepmother, thereby preserving good and destroying evil. At last, she became worthy of her father, being no more a "plain ordinary girl." It was a story of the desire for and celebration of power and perfection, which may also be translated into an oedipal personal myth. As this story and the others have illustrated, however, this desire was not absolute. It was relative and involved the subtleties of superiority and inferiority, with reflections going back and forth between these states.

6 The Final Phase

SESSION 10, MAY 9
The Game of "Darlene"

Our meeting on May 9th added a new dimension to our encounters because, on this occasion, Helen had invited a friend to join us in our activity of story making and tape recording. This was an important occasion for Helen. She seemed very invested in its success and arranged it entirely on her own initiative. Helen had mentioned Jill briefly during our last meeting (April 24th), commenting that she was a "really neat kid" whom she had told about our tape recording. She had also suggested that I would like meeting her.

On May 4th, Helen telephoned me, something she had never done of her own accord before. She told me that she had arranged a meeting among Jill, herself, and me. She said, "She can come on Saturday. So can you come in the afternoon?" Unfortunately, I had planned to be in New York that weekend and was unable to alter my plans. Helen was very disappointed at this news and lapsed into what seemed like an interminable silence. I felt badly for her and offered to come for a threesome as soon as possible during the following week, reassuring her that I was excited about her idea. She offered to call her friend immediately and reschedule the date.

On May 6, I called Helen to ask whether she had succeeded in setting an alternative date and gathered that she had spent a great deal of energy arranging an alternative time for us to meet. The new date was to be Wednesday, May 9th. She said that it would be "safe" at 3:45 or 4:45 P.M. Several times Helen mentioned that she could hardly wait for Wednesday and that she would like us to meet sooner but was wary about having too much homework to do earlier in the week. Before concluding our conversation, she said, "You will bring the tape recorder, won't you?" I assured her that I would.

At about 3:30 P.M. on May 9, when I arrived at Helen's house, I was met by Don, who invited me to join them in having some coffee. Pamela was in the living room and encouraged me to do so, too. Neither Helen nor her friend was in sight. I decided to sit with Helen's parents briefly, and after a short while Pamela went inside to alert her daughter to my presence. Helen came downstairs accompanied by her friend, whom she introduced to me: "This is Jill."

I quickly noted that Helen's friend was slim and tall. She seemed older than Helen. Later I gathered that being nine years old she was closer in age to Helen than she appeared to be. Jill and Helen were friends, however, and this age difference did not seem to stand in their way. Later in the afternoon, Jill revealed that she suffered from epilepsy and in a phone call between the Kings and myself after this session, I gathered that Jill had been a very sickly child, had missed a great deal of schooling, and consequently was a year behind her age level peers at school.

I greeted Jill, who smiled shyly, and then before I had a chance to say more, Helen turned to her mother and complained that she was very hot and wished to change into something cooler. Jill, too, was interested in changing out of what she had on because she had lost a button off one of the straps of her overalls. It was finally decided that both girls should change and that Jill would wear one of Helen's dresses while her overalls were being fixed by Pamela. The girls then left to change but did not invite me with them. At about the same time, the phone rang and Helen's father left to answer it.

At that juncture, I excused myself from Pamela's company and went upstairs to use the bathroom. It was also a bid to move away from the parents' company and attempt to locate the girls. As I came out of the bathroom, Helen called out to me, telling me that they were in the bedroom. When I went in, I found that they had already carried my bag containing my writing pad and tape recorder into the bedroom. Helen was very eager for me to show Jill the tape recorder, and we spent some time talking about it. Helen took pride in pointing out various features of the machine to her friend, who looked admiringly at it. I turned the recorder on fairly promptly after this inspection, so that most of the talk from that point on was recorded. I spent about two and a half to three hours with Helen and Jill.

During this occasion, our activity took place in Helen's bedroom, then moved into the bathroom, and finally moved back to the bedroom, where the event ended as I left. It was a different occasion in that, although I clearly interacted with the girls and was an important member of the group, I was not a participant in the acting out and the snippets of performance in which the girls engaged. I was clearly an audience to them. As such, I asked several questions that pertained to their activity, somewhat similar to those I asked Helen during the planning phases of our story activity together. Much of the girls' behavior was directed toward me. I was to be informed, persuaded, and entertained by their efforts. In addition, just as Jill was being allowed access to a special part of Helen's world—the tape-recording activity, play and story making, and me—I was being allowed access to Helen's close friend, Jill, and her world, to which Helen was already privy. Much of this world contained a preadolescent interest in sexual behavior.

As the afternoon progressed, at various junctures I felt that I was being allowed special access to the worlds of these children, which were very much a part of their own childhood culture; worlds from which adults were usually excluded. The following is a transcript of what took place in the room (note that H denotes Helen; J, Jill; and A, adult researcher):

H: Put it on . . . Did you put it on? (*In reference to the tape recorder, in a whisper*)

A: I'm gonna put it on, ya. So, no . . . Do you want to take a bath in the middle of the game, a real bath? (*Taking a bath had been suggested earlier.*)

H: A real bath.

A: Well, we'll try and see if it's possible.

H: But we're so sweaty . . . and hot . . . and uncomfortable.

J: I feel a bit cooler now. (*She'd just changed.*)

A: You feel cooler now? Maybe . . . I'll tell you what . . . Why don't you plan to take a bath somewhere through it but maybe towards the end? Something like that. Or, if you're feeling like it, we could just switch it off and bring the tape recorder in there (*bathroom*). We'll see how it goes, according to our plan.

H: Okay.

A: Do you want to shut the door or leave it open?

H: Doesn't matter. (*Mother calls from downstairs at this point, to inquire if everything is all right with the dress-changing episode. Helen says, "Yep."*)

A: Now, are you going to tell me about your game, or what?

H: Well, you see (*in a much more animated voice than that of the prior conversation*), we, er, it, we'll start inside and we'll keep on inside, okay?

J: Hm . . . Okay. But I'd like to go outside sometime in the game, too.

A: Okay.

J: Well, I'll tell you about it because I'm the one that made it up. Well, there was this girl, and Da, her Darlene. That's the main character. That's why the game is called "Darlene." And, she has all these friends. You know, it's a kind of serious game, sort've, you know. And, it's about. And her oldest sister always gets teased by Darlene's friends. But her older sister does have friends.

H: (*Interrupts Jill to correct her; speaks to me over Jill's last sentence*) And Darlene.

J: Yeah, and Darlene. But her older sister does have friends.

H: But, the older sister is *so* stupid, she falls asleep in the lecture. She was switched to second grade but she should quit, but she should be put in kindergarten.

A: Hm.

H: She *really* is stupid.

A: This is the big sister, the older sister?

H: Yeah.

J: Yeah . . . No, actually, actually Helen, Phyllis stayed back and she should be in, er, third grade. Er, she stayed back in second grade.

A: Who's Phyllis?

J: Sister, the girl.

A: Oh. Phyllis is the girl. Is this a real story?

H & J: (*In unison*) No . . .

A: It's a made-up story?

J: Yes, made up, but it could be real. You know how . . .

H: (*Again talking on top of Jill's last sentence*) It *sounds*. Do you know?

J: Darlene Carr, the actress?

A: Roughly, roughly. But you're telling me a whole new world.

J: Yeah, and, er, that's what the girl's name. Darlene Carr. Phyllis Carr and Darlene Carr.

H: And Julie, which I'm playing, mainly.

J: Julie Tinberg.

H: Is really, really . . . She really. She scares Phyllis like this. "I'm gonna beat you up." (*Puts on a gruff, scary voice; girls laugh*)

A: So Phyllis is a friend?

J: Friend?

H: (*Quizzically*) A friend? No, see, we love teasing her. And what we sometimes do is, what we do is, we say, "Phyllis, me and Darlene don't know how we do without you." And she says, and (*turns to Jill*) you say what Phyllis would say . . .

J: What?

H: You say what Phyllis would say.

J: Um, (*puts on an exaggerated voice*) Oh really?

H: Yes, we *love* teasing you.

J: (*In Phyllis's voice*) What? (*Both girls laugh.*) That's the first, that's just like Charlie Brown.

A: Right. So . . .

J: Oh yeah, it's exactly like Charlie Brown, except, except, er, Charlie Brown's little sister, you know, Sally? She always get full of . . . Darlene is just the opposite of Sally.

A: Okay. Sounds marvelous.

J: Darlene

H: Wait, let's say what happens when

J: And as for the Disneyland . . . Have you ever heard of M.S. Readathon?

A: Yeah, vaguely. Tell me about it.

J: Yeah, there is . . . You know, M.S. stands for multiple sclerosis.

A: Right.

J: And the children often, children are told, in the school, in school meeting, they're told, to . . .

H: Sign up.

J: Go around, get, take a kit, a M.S. Readathon kit that they're given.

A: Mm-hm.

J: And go around to people they know, and ask them to sponsor them for the readathon.

A: Right.

J: And, er . . .

H: For how many books they've read.

J: Yeah, and they get money for how many books they read.

A: Have you been in one?

J: Yeah. And I read fifteen books, and fifteen's the magic number. And, I win a prize for it, I think. And they say the magic number fifteen, and I win a prize for it . . . But, I mailed them the kit, a long time ago, I mailed 'em. If I win a prize or not, I don't know.

A: But you could, potentially.

J: Yeah. I hope I do. They said the person who reads the most books gets a trip to Disneyland, and their family. And, um, let's do the M.S. Readathon today, and, er, Darlene and Julie are the closest and, Phyllis only read (*switches to telethon announcer's voice*) two books and only got one sponsor and only had five dollars and ten cents. And, Darlene read thirty books, got twenty-five sponsors, and forty-four dollars and twenty cents.

H: And let's say that Jule, Jule, let's say that Julie got, a hundred dollars . . . because she . . . Julie can read very much, okay?

J: (*Softly*) Um.

H: As much as I like to . . . I didn't sign up, because, you know something, I would win a prize. And I wouldn't know how many books I've read.

J: No . . . Julie didn't get a hundred dollars. That's more than Darlene.

H: Okay. How much did Julie get?

J: Julie got, forty-three dollars . . . and thirty cents.

H: Well, let's do the time when they all go to Disneyworld, okay. The whole class . . . We'll show you what happens, okay?

J: (*says something, but it is inaudible because Helen speaks her last sentence over Jill's line*)

H: Now, let's start relating.

J: And, Phyllis doesn't get to go to Disneyland. The whole class ran, read about, read thirty books. Wait. Julie read twenty-nine, too. Um. How's that?

H: No. I want to be the same as you.

J: All right. Well, Julie read thirty books, but she got a little one, one penny less than Darlene.

H: Okay. Just one, so I wasn't . . . Yeah. She had forty-four dollars and twenty-four cents.

A: And Darlene got forty-four dollars and twenty-five cents.

H: Okay.

A: Okay.

H: Now, we'll start playing it, but a little different way.

J: Not in a different way.

H: No. We'll change it a little.

J: Change it? No, we won't change it, because, um, because it's the M.S. Readathon and Phyllis's team.

H: I know, I know.

J: We'll come in.

H: But we'll make it a little bit longer.

J: Yeah.

H: Or should we, or should we do it also the Pied Piper?

J: No, let's not do the Pied Piper.

H: Oh! The Pied Piper, I love it.

J: We'll do the Pied Piper later.

A: Is that another game?

J: Yes. Another game.

H: No, it isn't. It's the same game, but in a, in another series.

J: Um. Yeah, yeah! A different series.

A: Okay, but it's still a Darlene game.

J: Yes, still a Darlene game.

H: And now,

J: Now, um, now, the M.S. Readathon is starting. You sit down (*to Helen*). I'll be the person who describes the M.S. Readathon. Do you have any stuffed dogs?

H: Stuffed dogs?

J: Yeah.

A: Just one thing—don't go very far, because it is only a small tape, okay? Or you'll have to talk loud.

J: Okay.

H: (*Goes out of the room to look for a stuffed toy*)

A: So "Darlene" wasn't a game that you made up?

J: It is.

A: In other words, it's not written anywhere, you made it up totally by yourself?

J: Yes.

A: That's great.

J: Hm. (*Smiles*) . . . You know what?

A: What?

J: Phyllis's life, Phyllis's life actually happened to me in our family, you know—the teasing part, you know.

A: Really?

J: When I was eight years old, my sister was five . . . (*Helen returns and hands dog to Jill.*) Thank you, Helen. But, er . . . When I was eight and my sister was five, my sister had friends that were always used to tease me, and I was like Phyllis when I was eight. That's how I got this game.

A: Oh.

J: Piece by . . . But I added a little, more and more. Phyllis has a little bit more bad luck than me.

A: But it's got some truth in it.

J: Yeah. A lot of truth, because, um . . . Once, there was once Darlene's friend, Jeanie John Tucker . . . Er, have you ever read the Katie John books?

A: No.

J: They're really good . . . Er, Darlene's friend, Katie John Tucker, was on the NBYCU, and this is what she told Darlene. Um . . . Its about sexual stuff. Do you mind? (*As I shake my head, she continues*) "Santa Claus (*inaudible*) pulls down your pants." This is what she said to Phyllis in the summertime (*laughs*).

A: Oh no!

J: It's true. Yeah.

A: What did you make of that?

J: Um, actually, that . . . That's what happened, you know. That's what happened with me.

A: You mean, they really did it?

J: Yes, a boy named Joey, told my sister (*whispers*), "We're gonna pull down Jill's pants. Santa Claus going ter give you a screw." Really!

A: And what did you think?

J: And, well, I thought, I . . . Well, I was very upset, you know. I didn't say anything, because I, I was only eight then, you know. And they, they did pull down my underwear.

A: Did they?

J: Yeah . . . And, my Dad didn't know about it. And there were million times when I got into a lot of trouble, and . . . for hitting Sally, and I had to be punished and things like that . . .

H: You couldn't help it.

J: I know, 'cos I . . . couldn't help it (*inaudible*).

A: We could almost have a whole composition about that some other time.

H: Now come on . . . Stop getting those tears in your eyes, Diana.

A: They're spilling over into a pool. (*Laughter from girls*)

J: You sit down, and I'll get this thing . . . (*Children talk together about the next move; inaudible. Jill begins, in narrative orientation.*) Okay, now . . . This dog I have in my hand, you don't know about it yet, but this dog is the Mystery Spoof, and it tries its best to keep away the Battler that brings multiple sclerosis. And there's no cure for multiple sclerosis. It's a disease of the brain. Many people have been killed by it. More people will be killed if we *don't act now*. So, when you see this movie, you'll understand who the Mystery Spoof and who the Battler is. And, afterwards, I'll explain the whole thing about what the children are doing. Now, here is the movie. (*To us*) Now, I'm going to act out the movie.

A: All right.

J: (*Begins performance by making humming noise and then puts on a gruff, resonant man's voice, very caricatured, and announces*) Multiple Sclerosis: A very bad disease of the brain. Right here, this is a brain, and this is a Battler. While this Battler causes Multiple Sclerosis—and this is what he does (*buzzing noise*)—he grabs hold of the brain and the brain can't tell him exactly what to do. This is exactly what cerebral palsy is. Although it is a bit different. Now. What did Battler . . . This Battler has got to stop. At the very start of the M.S. Readathon, that's what these children are doing. (*Changes voice*) Now . . . (*Turns and addresses next comment to us*) Now I'm the teacher.

A: You're who?

J: Er, I'm the, I'm the teacher. (*Puts on a quite different, teacherly voice*) Now, we just get our sponsors, get some sponsors, get those sponsors (*tries out a different voice pitch on each phrase*) and tell them about the M.S. Readathon and get some money for each book you read. (*Moves to another point in the room, affects a different stance, and gets ready to play the role of a sponsor in interaction with a child. Helen watches all this with a mild air of amusement. Jill makes sound of a door chime; answers as person at door*) Hello. (*In different voice*) Hello. We're collecting money for charity, er, for the M.S. Readathon. And M.S. stands for multiple sclerosis, and there isn't any cure yet. So, I'm reading books and I need money for each book I read. And, I think I'm going ter, I mean, I need money for each book I read. (*In sponsor's voice*) Yes, and how many books will you read? (*As child*) I think I'm going to read ten books. How much will you pay me? (*As sponsor*) Oh . . . I guess I'll pay you ten cents. (*As child*) Thank you very much. Goodbye. (*Moves on to another sponsor by shifting her position in the room and quickly reruns the preceding conversation, in shorthand. As child*) Eleven books. How much will you pay me? (*As second sponsor*) Fifteen cents. (*As child*) Twelve books. How much will you pay me? (*As third sponsor*) Five cents. (*Back to exaggerated commentator's voice*) And on and on like that. (*As narrator*) And that's the end of the movie. (*As teacher to children*) You liked that movie, didn't you?

H: Um, yeah.

J: (*As teacher*) Now, do you like the Mystery Spoof?

H: (*As children*) Yeah, yeah, yeah!

J: (*As teacher*) Did you like the Battler?

H: (*As children*) No!

J: (*As teacher*) Now, the way to help it. The way to get rid of the Battler is: You *both* receive a kit like this. The one I have in my hand, and it will show you what to do about it, er, the readathon. Well, I'll read it. First, you go to, er, to a person's house, a person that you know, and you ask them to be your sponsor. And you need money for each book you read. And, you tell them how much money, how much books, that you intend to, that you think you'll read. And the sponsor will give you, will write down how much money he or she will, wants to pay. And it goes on like that. And you keep on reading books. And remember: No comics or picture books allowed. Just books, like these books (*holds up a book from Helen's shelf*). Like that. And it goes on and on like that. And in between, you get little notes from Doug Collins telling you, "Keep reading." But in four weeks you receive a red card that says, "Time out." That means that readathon has ended. So you can stop your reading and then you go and see your sponsors and collect the money, and tell them how much—tell them how many books you read and then you can collect the money that your sponsors said they'll pay. If you get ten sponsors and you read ten books, and all the sponsors get ten cents, it'll, it'll collect ten dollars for M.S. Remember, the more sponsors you get, the more money you can send to M.S. And as soon as all your money is paid, have your father write a check and either put the check in a little envelope and send it to M.S. or take it to the bank and the bank will send it to M.S. And don't send any cash in the mail. It won't reach the M.S. and you can send it in check or money order. And, that is the thing of M.S. Are there any questions before you go? Julie? You.

H: (*As Julie*) I wanna know, can we do it to strangers?

J: (*As teacher*) No. No strangers.

H: (*as Julie*) How come?

J: (*As teacher*) Because they might not know what you are talking about. You might not meet anyone who's had multiple sclerosis and they might not know what you are talking about. And you might meet robbers and burglars, and things like that. Did you read about the little boy who went trick-or-treating and got shot in the head and died? (*Steps out of character*) Really, Helen, that really happened—at Halloween.

H: No, I didn't hear.

J: (*As teacher*) Well, no strangers. Remember, do it to people you know.

H: (*Raises her hand, as Phyllis*)

J: (*As teacher*) You.

H: (*As Phyllis*) Er, what's a sponsor? I don't understand what a sponsor is. And what's this about M.S. Readathon, er, writing a check and sending it to the bank and (*Breaks in as teacher*) I think you've got it, dear. (*As Phyllis*) What? (*As teacher*) I said, I think you've got it. (*As Phyllis, softly*) Got what? (*Helen discusses with Jill this series of exchanges; Helen barged in and said what she did, there's now a need for explanation of this to Jill.*)

J: (*As Phyllis*) Oh, no, I don't have it. I'm just not listening. (*Jill renegotiates and takes her role as teacher back.*) Oh! You're not listening. Well, you should listen more. (*Looks for other questioners*) Okay, you.

H: (*As Julie*) To tell the truth, shall I tell you what happened?

J: (*As teacher*) Yes.

H: (*As Julie*) I'm afraid she may have it—that stupid idiot. (*Breaks into peals of laughter*)

J: (*As teacher*) Er, I don't think she has it. 'Cos if she did have it, she'll be screaming and yelling. Because a disease of the brain is *not* not listening. It isn't just not listening. A disease of the brain is doing things you don't intend to do. Like this is an imitation of cerebral palsy—of M.S.—(*Puts on a spastic act*) and you don't want to do all the stuff that I'm doing. That's multiple sclerosis. That's something that's wrong with your brain . . . um . . . your brain can't tell your muscles what to do, so your muscles just do anything they want to do. And you just jerk your arms without meaning to, or kick your leg . . . You might even kick somebody (*kicks*) without even meaning to. And that's what cerebral palsy is—M.S.—or whatever. (*Negotiation between the girls; inaudible; Jill continues as teacher.*) Phyllis, you didn't understand it, did you?

H: (*As Phyllis*) No, I didn't.

J: (*As teacher*) Well, I'll tell you what it's all about. How. A sponsor . . . Do you know who a sponsor is? Well, I'll tell you. (*Jill goes through her whole speech again, emphasizing that a sponsor is somebody you go to for help. Emphasizes fact of collecting money for a charity and fact of not going to strangers. Emphasizes fact of no cure. Then she hurries her speech and concludes.*) If you understand it, you do, and if you don't, you don't. (*As Phyllis*) I understand it a little (*falteringly*). I tell you I know where to get sponsors, and to read book . . . Yeah, I understand it now. (*As teacher*) Well, go with Julie. (*More negotiations; inaudible whispers*) (*As teacher, harshly*) Well, go to Julie or Darlene or anybody and ask them to be a sponsor.

H: (*As Julie, mockingly*) Oh no! Oh not that stupid Julie! (*Made a mistake; meant Phyllis*)

J: (*As teacher*) All right now, that's enough, girls. Now, Phyllis, I want you to understand this.

J: (*As Phyllis*) Okay, I understand, I'll find a sponsor. (*Girls negotiate. Helen delegated to be a sponsor and Jill to be Phyllis. Jill simulates ringing doorbell.*)

H: Yes?

J: Hello, I need a sponsor. (*Goes through entire routine, doing it well*)

H: (*Unable to contain herself, switches the flow of script and cries out as Julie*) Oh, look at Phyllis. Phyllis! No! Get out of the way! Run, Phyllis!

J: (*As Phyllis, acts retardedly*) Wha? Wha? Wha?

H: I'll tell you. She said not to go to strangers. That's about the only time I'll save you. You stupid old fool. (*Drags Phyllis away; scuffles*)

J: (*As Phyllis*) Stop it. (*More negotiations between girls; Jill becomes both sponsor and Phyllis; simulates doorbell sound. As sponsor*) Who are you? (*As Phyllis, said very stupidly*) My name is Phyllis, er, and I'm working for a charity for the M.S. Readathon. I need a sponsor. I think I'm going to read ten books. How much will you pay me? (*As sponsor*) Wha? (*As Phyllis*) I already explained it. (*As Darlene, who happens along*) Listen, Phyllis, you're not supposed to go to strangers. (*As Phyllis*) Oh! I forgot.

H: (*Very nervously*) No, get out of here—quick! Now that calls for a beating. (*Hits Jill/Phyllis*)

J: (*As Phyllis*) Stop it, Julie . . . No! Stop!

H: Darlene, come on and help me with Phyllis.

J: (*As Darlene*) Now, Phyllis, I heard you had ten books read. Aha! (*Mocks her*)

H: Guess what! She went to a stranger. Aha! (*Also mocks her*) This calls for action. (*They hit her and fight with her.*)

J: (*As Phyllis*) Stop it. Oh, Darlene! Stop! I'm her (*referring to Darlene*) older sister.

H: Oh yeah? You may be older, but you aren't stronger.

J: (*As Phyllis*) Stop it! Julie, you'll kill me! (*Screams*) (*As narrator*) Okay, now let's pretend it's the end of the readathon.

H: The end has come, and I read about . . . the same as . . .

J: Darlene.

H: Darlene.

J: Okay, let's pretend we're watching television. I'll be Bugs Bunny and you be something, too . . . (*Goofs off, using some scrambled sounds*)

H: (*Begins to wiggle her hips, lifts her skirt, dances about, using nonsense sounds*) Do-da-de-do-da . . .[1]

---

[1]In this section, the two girls really had their play in sequence. Each followed her own dictates, with Helen bossing, teasing, hitting, and mocking Phyllis and Jill running the show. There was no real collaboration, despite all the whispers.

The main interest in this part of the show was that Helen was clearly secondary to Jill. It was Jill's show, and she played the star role in a manner unlike Helen's acting with me. Jill did not look to me at all for prompting (as Helen often did) and she seemed very certain of the script and its shape. Much of the difference may be attributed to Jill being older and more competent at scripting and making her plans operational. Helen cast herself as a star but was far less fluent and in control.

Helen collaborated occasionally, but more often than not she butted in with her own agenda. This usually had to do with being extremely insulting to the scapegoat, laughing at her, beating her, scolding and shouting at her, and pointing out how stupid she was. She wiggled her hips, danced, sang and goofed off very similarly to her festival celebrations with me. She was generally much more lively, loud, and "naughty." As subsequent dialogue shows, she also shared more intimate feelings with Jill.

In the scene that followed this, Helen became very absorbed in being a TV character as well as in talking to the Disney-world creatures such as Donald Duck and Mickey Mouse. As the story developed, Darlene and Julie discovered that they were chosen to go to Disneyland, but not Phyllis. They had won the M. S. Readathon prize and were very excited about it. They whooped it up, commenting on how excited they were and, at the same time, putting Phyllis down and taunting her because she was not chosen to go. Here is some of their conversation:

J: Hi, Mickey Mouse; hi, Donald Duck; hi . . .

H: I wish Phyllis was here to tease. Let's go get a ride. They said it was free for us.

J: Oh! I can't wait, can you? The Flying Bed.

H: Phyllis is never, never going to see us for a week and we're at Disneyland.

J: Yeah. Oh just feel it.

H: I know what you mean by feel it. So cozy. You know that time we all slept over.

J: Yeah.

H: Boy, was she a stupe. So stupid. I always love sleeping over.

J: Yeah, me too.

H: How?

J: It's so romantic in this place. Oh! The witches' chant will put me to sleep. Oh . . . I'm going to sleep. (*Simulates sleeping sounds; silence*)

H: I thought I heard a cock.

J: (*Startled*) A what?

H: A cock. Crowing. (*She crows; speaks out of role to Jill*) No, wait. I'll pretend I just woke up before going to sleep. (*As Julie*) At least we don't have to listen to Phyllis snoring all the time. Oh. Like this. (*Makes exaggerated snoring sounds*)

J: Yeah, Julie, good night. (*They sing a song.*)

H: Good night. We got each other for a week. (*They laugh.*)

J: Good night.

H: (*Helen begins to sing softly and then they both fall asleep*)

J: (*short silence; heralds the morning with a crow sound*) Morning. I'm Donald Duck and I wake you up. Wake up! Wake up!

H: (*Scolding*) Donald!

J: (*Out of role*) No. You don't say that. Act surprised.

H: Donald. Oh, just wait for me, please. I want to make sure.

J: (*Mimics being greeted by the various Disneyland animals*) Wouldn't it be nice to go into a pool? (*They run the bath and decide to jump in.*) Can we put on our bathing suits?

H: No, I'm going to go naked.

J: Isn't there a bathing suit or something?

H: No. I'm going naked. You go, too. Jill, if my father comes, you can just go like this (bends down).

At this point, there were prolonged discussions about the water, height of water, bathing suits, and so forth; and much turning the taps on and off. Helen's mother came in to check up on things and condoned the activity. Jill, after using the toilet with all of us there, resumed the game with Helen, in a sort of mock way. From this point on, there was a real mixture of enactment play, shy talk, singing, goofing off, and personal sharing. The girls also asked my permission in a whisper, about whether they could discuss a range of "sexual stuff," as they called it.

H: I didn't know you were getting your breasts.

J: Oh! (*Covers them*)

H: Well, you don't have to do that. (*Laughs*)

J: (*Shyly*) I know. (*In a whisper*) I'm also getting my period.

H: (*Incredulous*) You are?

J: (*Softly*) Yes.

They then talked about periods in soft terms. Helen asked about when it came and how long it lasted, and Jill admitted she was embarrassed. Helen was really enjoying the water and splashing about. She began to introduce Peter Pan, flying through the window, but Jill showed no interest. Helen said to Jill, "Let me get on your back," to which Jill replied, "I'd rather not."[2]

While they were still in the bath together, I announced my decision to leave. The girls promptly hopped out and dried themselves. They persuaded me to stay awhile longer so they could hear a replay of the tape. Jill was interested in hearing most of it, while Helen tired of it after awhile, perhaps because so much of it featured Jill's performance. Jill asked me whether we could involve other children in "making up a

---

[2]In this second half, Helen took over and was far more controlling, talkative, and funny. She initiated most of the talk, while Jill was clearly quieter. This was Helen's show, and she enjoyed every minute of it. They were aware of me as an adult supervisor of the bath activity. They occasionally became aware of the recorder and would put on voices for it, or periodically resume the Darlene-in-Disneyland game, but in a very caricatured and nonserious way.

whole big play," as she put it. "We could record it and even make a film," she said. Both girls were taken by the idea, and I suggested that we could perhaps plan to make a videotape soon. During this conversation, Helen unearthed a box of candy and offered some of it to Jill. They were very secretive about this and asked that I not divulge this information to their parents. At this point, I decided to leave and, wishing them goodbye, walked out of the room. Helen's last comment to me was, "We'll do the film soon, okay?" I suggested that we would talk about that next time we met. It was 6:30 P.M.

Commentary

Before commenting on the various aspects of this play enactment, I would like to make some general notes. Unlike in many prior play sessions, in this instance I have included most of the transcript of the "Darlene" story, as I feel that it is quite an extraordinary play session and also different from those we have had so far. For one thing, Jill was a friend of Helen's with whom she played regularly and one she wished to share with me. This was different from her attitude to her friend Anne, with whom she played in Session 6 and with whom she was not eager to share much of me or our play. In contrast, on this occasion, it was clear from the beginning that Helen was invested in sharing with me both Jill herself and her play with Jill. Moreover, she also desired to share with Jill our tape-recording and story-making activity, which Helen valued. Further, the episode is a good example of peer play or "chumship" (Sullivan, 1970, p. 158) between girls in the latency or preadolescent period of development, where there is intense involvement with one another emotionally, in terms of secret interests such as their emerging sexuality, their performance in relation to the outside world, popularity, scape-goating, and peer competitiveness.

Again, this play was entirely motivated by the girls' agenda and initiated and controlled by them. "Darlene" was interesting to me on at least two broad levels. First, it was a wonderful example of these children's interest in their own value and their fears and insecurities about it. Helen and Jill were scared of being dumb (stupid) and as a result unpopular.

The theme of the game was scape-goating, the essential purpose of which is to reassure oneself of one's own worth by projecting onto one's target that of which one is most afraid. In this instance, the girls cast Phyllis as stupid in the context of a game that was a spoof about a readathon to help cure multiple sclerosis, a disease that, in fact, damages the brain and, in their terms, makes you "dumb" and unable to control your behavior. Through this story, the girls reassured themselves that it was Phyllis who was dumb and not themselves.

Alongside this, the second level on which the game functioned concerned Jill. By recreating a scene from her own life in such a way that the situation reversed what actually happened to her, we might suggest that she was engaging in some type of self-therapy. It was Moreno (1972), the originator of the notion of psychodrama, who claimed that people heal some aspects of psychological illness by re-enacting troublesome scenes from their lives. Not only did Jill reveal directly that she had been humiliated by her younger sister and her sister's friends in real life, but she also suffered from epilepsy and had periodic fits. These, of course, scared her and also led to her peers excluding her and treating her as someone who was simple minded or brain damaged. It seemed no accident that "Darlene" was Jill's game. However, Helen too felt a colossal pressure to be seen as smart and had suffered the effects of peer taunting and lock-out, as she admitted early in our relationship, especially in reference to Michael, the boy in her class who did not like her.

There were several other noteworthy features of this text. As I looked for the underlying situation in this session, it seemed to me as if this story was an opportunity for Helen to mesh her current interest in sexual matters pertaining to puberty with what she perceived as my adult interest in her, namely, the tape recording of her stories. In introducing me to Jill, she was orienting me to one of her main informational sources about the preadolescent sexual world. Thus, to have Jill and the games she initiated approved by me and tape recorded, was to legitimize the whole endeavor and the accompanying interest in sexual matters. Such an interpretation is supported by Helen's recurrent interest in sex, marriage, procreation, dating behavior, and so on, which became even more evident in the three sessions that succeeded this one. In fact, in addition, and in accordance with normal patterns of adolescent activity, this session introduced a new way of relating, one that characterized Helen's behavior in the session to follow. We saw here the beginnings of a major new means of sharing meaning: discussion and conversation about intimate matters. Talk, rather than played-out stories, began to assume importance. As part of this exchange, there were frequent narrative explanations within conversations or discussions. In addition, planning assumed a principal status; in the end, it became the game rather than a precursor to it.

The strategies the girls used to encompass the situation involved (1) the game, "Darlene," which Jill introduced, and (2) the running conversation they used as a backdrop. Each of these will be explained in turn.

First, as concerned the game, "Darlene," the primary symbols were the three characters—Darlene Carr (the star), Phyllis Carr (Darlene's sister and the victim of extreme teasing due to her stupidity), and Julie Tinberg (a friend and supporter of Darlene). These, as well as the other characters who peopled the world of "Darlene," were influenced by radio, television, cartoons, and fiction. The adult roles they played and caricatured were those of teacher, homemaker/sponsor, and television master of ceremonies. The children represented were their own age. They also animated some of the Disneyland characters, such as Bugs Bunny and Donald Duck.

Their actions involved a series of peer exchanges at school, at home, and in other social contexts, such as a class excursion to Disneyland. The interactions highlighted brightness and achievement on the one hand and stupidity on the other. Stupidity was manifested in general as social retardation, especially among peers. Phyllis Carr embodied such stupidity and vulnerability. In contrast, Darlene and Julie were smart; they were prolific readers and had access to sexual knowledge, which was associated with smartness and intellect. Thus, in this situation, intellectual superiority and school achievement were used to do symbolic service for sexual power, peer solidarity, and popularity.

The attitudes expressed by the symbols suggest the pain and stigma of being lonely, on the outside, and different from one's peers; the power of peer pressure; and the anxiety at the prospect of being a victim of teasing. The virtues and prowess chosen to signify being on the inside were a high level of school achievement and mastery of reading, which both girls valued. These indices of popularity were particular to the girls' school and family contexts and not in any way typical of all groups of seven-to-ten-year-olds.

The interaction between the girls involved much more negotiation than had occurred between Helen and me. This is in keeping with the literature on peer play (Garvey, 1977; Schwartzman, 1976). Much more time typically is spent in negotiation than in play, in most peer situations. Helen clearly liked and admired Jill but in no respect wished to play second fiddle to her. Jill, however, was not interested in giving her game over to Helen, and, although something suitable was finally worked out, there was evidence of Helen wishing to be the "brightest, best, and star" character, although she did not succeed in controlling the game on this occasion.

During this session, too, the behavior may be seen to fall into the three realms: everyday, play, and intimate. As on many previous occasions, the boundaries between the realms were fluid; it was with ease that the children moved in and out of these realms, each dictated by their various concerns and realities. For example, conversation and activity in the play realm provided a context for intimate sharing: Within the context of splashing in a pool in Disneyland, sexual matters such as emerging breasts and menstruation were discussed. In fact, the two children's behavior displayed a high level of sophistication. They invested a great deal of their energy in planning and explaining "Darlene." Jill then initiated a performance, with Helen's support from time to time. When they tired of it, they shifted their location to the bathroom. Although a semblance of the game continued there, the girls were really running two games at once, each pertaining to a different realm. On the one hand, they played out a scene of Darlene and her peers at Disneyland that was extremely regressed, influenced by cartoon snippets and on the whole a tired effort. This was the game that was played out for the tape recorder, which they insisted be left on. On the other hand, interspersed with the "Darlene" dialogue was a conversation involving their most romantic and sexual interests. These underlying interests were first expressed in whispered tones, as my reactions to them were being tested. In fact, they sought my permission, saying, "You don't mind if we tell you about, er, well, it's a secret, about sexual stuff, do you?" When I assured them that I did not, they proceeded to include me in their exchanges about several tabooed topics such as boys pulling down their pants, intimate bodily functions like menstruation, and secondary sexual characteristics such as emerging breasts.

What is interesting about this activity is that they used the tape-recorded fiction-making effort as a mask for their real concerns. There were two sets of behavior, frontstage and backstage, and on this occasion the frontstage behavior (tape-recording play stories), which had hitherto been valued, was rendered hollow. This became a trend during the remaining sessions between Helen and me and was a notable factor in the final phase of the relationship.

Conclusion

This tenth session much more clearly foreshadowed a post-oedipal or prepubescent stage. It was a time of peer interaction and of relying on the use of talk and discussion for understanding the external world as well as for exploring a newly developing sense of identity.

SESSION 11, JUNE 6
Play Under Duress

I phoned Helen on May 29th to ask whether I could visit her on June 6th. She told me that she would need to ask her parents and left the conversation for a minute to do so. On returning, she said, "Maybe yes and no." She then said that she would smack me if I did not come. She also talked of the character Starbuck and imitated him in a low voice. Helen next mentioned that she foresaw a problem with my coming on the sixth. When I inquired about it, she said that she thought she would have a great deal of homework to do. However, she rather quickly added that she wanted me to come anyway. I was struck by this hint of ambivalence about my visit, which I had not sensed before.

On June 4th I phoned Helen's parents to confirm the appointment. I spoke to her mother, who said that she did not know why Helen had said "Maybe yes and no," unless she had meant that she had to ask permission first. At any rate, Pamela assured me that I could come on that date. After that, I spoke to Helen, who seemed very excited. She said, "I'm trying not to remind myself you're coming, so I won't be bored before." We then talked briefly about one of her friends, Jane, after which Helen said, "I'm supposed to be playing with a two- or three-year-old from next door. Her name is Corrie. Could I say good-bye?" The conversation was concluded at this point. What struck me about both these conversations was the extremely quiet and low voice Helen used in speaking to me, as though she feared being overheard. In addition, she was not easy to engage and follow on the phone, which is not uncommon for many children of her age when talking to adults.

On June 6th, I arrived at about 3:30 P.M. I was met by Pamela, who invited me to join her husband and her for some coffee, as Helen had not yet arrived home from school. She came in about 3:45 P.M.

While we waited, her parents and I talked about a range of topics, most notably that Helen was "into Shakespeare." Pamela added that Helen was sure to tell me of her newly found love, especially because "adults loved it when she mentioned Shakespeare." She laughed. She said that Helen had taken the book of Shakespearean stories to school and that her teacher was passing it around and letting people know of Helen's interest. When I asked them how Helen was introduced to Shakespeare, they both began to tell me how it happened. They said that a baby-sitter, who was another student, was reading Shakespeare while minding Helen and told her one of the stories when the child inquired about what she was reading. Helen in turn told her parents the story and asked her mother who Shakespeare was. She was told that he was the greatest writer and poet who had ever lived, and this, according to them, caught Helen's imagination. At that, Pamela said, Helen had to have a book on him, which they got for her from the library. Don said that he had told her the story of *King Lear*, and she wished to hear more of these stories. Pamela added that Helen had rebuked her father for not introducing her to Shakespeare earlier and for giving her that "stupid stuff on *Snow White*." She emphasized her daughter's rebuke, saying that Helen was mad that they had not given her "the truth" earlier, especially since *Snow White* had "nothing to say about the truth." Such vignettes underline the value placed on learning, truth, and the intellect in Helen's home.

It was at the end of this conversation between the three of us that Helen returned from school. She came in looking somewhat flustered and quickly stated that she had not had much lunch. Don greeted her in the language of the home, and the three of them continued talking in it. I gathered that he wished Pamela to get Helen something to eat. Helen followed her mother into the kitchen, repeating that she was hungry and wished for something to eat. Then she returned to the living room and sat down, while Don continued reminding his wife about food for Helen. Shortly, Pamela returned with a bowl of cottage cheese for Helen and lightheartedly teased her by suggesting that what she had for her were cupcakes and candy, at which Helen made a face.

We resumed our conversation, first about schools and education in general and then moved to discussing Helen's schooling while she was in our presence. During this, Helen began to tell us how she hated gym and "flunked" it in second grade. At this her mother warned her that, if she continued to flunk gym, she would end up having to run daily like her father and that she should begin to take an interest in it. Helen began debating the point with them, but her parents adopted a teasing tone, needling her into reasoning on their adult level, at which the child grew exceedingly frustrated. When Helen could take no more, she went into the kitchen; on her return to her parents' midst, she stamped her feet, indicating impatience. Don rebuked her. She retaliated by saying that God had given her patience but that she had none left, at which she once more stamped her feet and took off up the stairs. Her father then began to chastise her for ignoring her invited guest, meaning me, while Helen mumbled something about going to the bathroom. Then, turning to me, he said, "Oh! She's gone to the bathroom; she takes long there," and laughed mildly.

The Kings and I continued to talk in Helen's absence. It was then that I asked their permission to take Helen and her friend Jill to one of the colleges so that I could videotape their play. They seemed not to object to this request and so approved it. Just then the telephone rang and Don excused himself to answer it. While he was away, Pamela expressed surprise that I would wish to take Helen out of her "natural environment" in order to videotape her. She thought this seemed useless, adding that she had tried to keep her opinions out of the work I was doing with her daughter. I agreed with her general point but explained that my chief interest was to observe the girls' interactions together somewhat more and felt that spending time with them on an excursion that they had partly suggested might yield interesting information about Helen, of course, and about their relationship and their play-story performance in a new environment with strange equipment. Her response to this was, "Well, all you can do is see. If you get nothing, you get nothing." With that, she took me upstairs to look for Helen. We found her and discovered that she had been crying. Since she seemed to ignore me, I felt that she might wish to talk to her mother first and so returned downstairs.

I heard Pamela tell Helen that I was waiting for her and ask what she intended to do about that. Helen replied that she expected me to come up. Her mother suggested that she should indicate that, at which Helen said, "She should guess my thoughts." Her mother said that she thought that was unfair and that Helen should tell people what she wanted of them. I then heard Helen say that she would send me a message via airplane, at which her mother laughed. When she asked her why she had been crying, Helen said that she had forgotten the reason and began to laugh. It was after this that Helen threw down a paper airplane to me, with a message that read, "I'm waiting for you." I picked this up and went to her immediately; I found her in the bathroom. On seeing me, she said, "I'm not even sitting on the pot. See, I have all my clothes on." We then quietly proceeded to her bedroom.

Helen was very upset. She kept bemoaning the great deal of time that we had lost and asked me whether I could stay longer. I said that I would do so. At this juncture, she went out of the room and returned with a soft toy which she held close to her. She began to cry silently. I placed my arm around her and asked her whether she was feeling angry. She said, "I'm angry. Well, not so much. I don't know what I feel. But what'll we do now?" When I asked her if she would like to play "Battlestar Gallactica," she told me that that program was now over. She said, "I have to get a new program and a new crush because 'Battlestar Gallactica,' to my knowledge, won't be on any more." She then sobbed a little more and said, "I have no one else to have a crush on. You can't get on without a crush." When I asked her why this was the case, she said that she would rather not tell me.

I then asked her what she had been doing in my absence, and she said, "I haven't been doing anything much." Then, rather impatiently, she added, "Now come on, let's go on. What d'you want it to be about?" When I asked her what the possibilities were for a game, she replied, "Battlestar Gallactica." She then said, "Or Darlene, which I couldn't do without Jill. And the reason she couldn't come was because I didn't ask her. Okay. Now, what's it gonna be?" At this point, rather than answer her question with a suggestion, I asked her what she had been reading of late. She said, "Shakespeare." When I asked her whether that suggested any story lines that we could play with once again her response was, "What is it going to be?" At this point, I realized that Helen was looking to me for ideas. Reluctantly, I offered her some suggestions, which did not seem to interest her.

Finally, after several unsuccessful attempts to restore harmony and engage Helen's interest, I said, "Well, I don't have any more ideas. You'll have to tell me what you want to do, because it's very hard to guess." To this, Helen replied, "Why don't we just play house?" "What do you want to be?" I asked. Helen said, "Baby." In response to my further questions about the plot, she said that she did not care what I was, as long as she was old enough to read. In fact, she said that she would be one year old. When I asked her whether she was a superbaby or a human baby, she said, "Why don't we play Super Reader? Something where we could read?" Helen was very quiet and noncommittal about the game. The only details that I managed to draw out of her suggested that it was to be a game about a baby who was born with a knowledge of reading. She then went out of the room and returned with a book of Shakespearean tales, which she sat on the floor and proceeded to read quietly.

At this stage it was more than clear that I would have to choose a role in relation to Helen and structure it in my own terms. Therefore, I decided to be a friend who would come to visit her. She seemed interested enough to find out what kind of a friend I was to be and also added that the game was to take place in a house. I told her that I would be a neighbor who was out with my dog and would stop by to see her. Helen then said, "You don't come for me. You come to chat. And I'm not the mother." It was clear that Helen wished not to be an active participant in the game, although she was not able to refrain from indirectly instructing me about certain details of it. She especially wanted to structure the game in such a way that she would have to say nothing but could read her book, which is what she really wanted to do. She seemed unable to ask for this directly, however, and also wished to have me work hard to sustain a game by myself. In fact, I kept this game going for quite awhile, playing two roles: my own, and that of the child's mother. As I did this, Helen whispered that her name was Wendy and from time to time whispered further details about herself. For example, at one point, when she did not respond to my questions to her, she whispered that she was deaf. Just then her parents called out to her that they were going out and would be back in about an hour. This marked the point at which Helen began to emerge from her withdrawn state, although very slowly.

She began by allowing me to ask a number of questions, which she either ignored or responded to by shaking her head. She also left the room and returned with a Lego construction set, which she placed on the floor beside her. In response to this, I asked her whether she wished to play a game with me. She nodded. As she moved closer to me, I also asked her whether she would like to sit in my lap, and she promptly moved onto my lap for awhile. She then began to whisper some directions about what she wished to do. She mentioned that she was going to build something with Legos and that I was to pretend that I had taught her how to do so. It seemed clear that, at this point, I had also shifted to playing her mother in the game, rather than a friend, as I had done earlier.

Helen built a man on a bike and drove him around a trail on the floor. She whispered to me that she wished me to play this game with her, by sending the figure back and forth between us. From time to time she clapped at her own efforts in a very regressed, babyish way; however, she said nothing while I continued to comment on her behavior, talk to her, compliment her, ask her questions which she ignored, and so forth. It seemed as though she was indeed engaging me in a guessing game as to what was on her mind and what would humor her. While playing this game, Helen told me that she wished to go to the bathroom. I said that I would wait for her and change the tape while she was away. However, she insisted that I accompany her into the bathroom with the recorder and change the tape in there. This marked a further juncture in the session.

As soon as Helen got to the bathroom, she resumed her normal voice and became quite talkative. While seated on the toilet, she said, "Let's play 'Battlestar Gallactica'—that game got me ready to play." She was referring to the "super-reader" and construction games that we had played before. I agreed to her plan and asked her to tell me more about the TV program having ended. She said that the new show she would watch would be "Mork and Mindy" and proceeded to tell me about it. When I commented that it seemed very different from "Wonder Woman," Helen talked about several different television programs.

We talked about the merits of watching television, and Helen rather adamantly stated that she only watched a little. She said that her parents disapproved of her watching more than a couple of hours a week, because they felt that "television hurt your mind." She con-trasted her viewing habits with those of her friend next door, who she said watched several hours a day: "She doesn't do what I do. I make it up into a whole great big play. I *use* it with my imagination. She doesn't. She just sits still, watching it." Then, rather abruptly, she said, "But now let's start to play, okay?" The conversation so far and a part of what followed took place in the bathroom, with Helen seated on the toilet seat and me seated on the edge of the bathtub.

Helen was intent on playing "Battlestar Gallactica." She began in a characteristic fashion by asking my opinion about how I wished it to proceed: "What d'you want it to be?" She then added, "I'm daughter of Captain Apollo." The rest of the conversation went like this:

A: Okay.

C: You are a . . . You could be Athena, my mother.

A: Um.

C: The Goddess of Wisdom. Or, you could be whatever you want.

A: What are some other choices?

C: Well, Apollo's sister.

A: What was her name?

C: I don't know her name, but she sure is Apollo's sister.

A: Okay. So I will be your aunt, then?

C: Yeah.

A: Okay. Maybe I'll be your, maybe I'll be Apollo's sister, because I haven't been that before.

C: I mean, there's also another choice, then. A few others. You can be a waitress.

A: Of a ship?

C: Yeah.

A: Okay.

C: You could be the Goddess of Wisdom, Athena. I was going to say the favoritest of Zeus. Favorite daughter.

A: Um. That sounds pretty nice. I'll be her.

C: Okay, you're my mother. (*Laughs*)

A: All right. Okay, I'll be Athena, then. Then, there's Apollo, right? He's gone off on one of his missions.

C: You can disappear like this. (*Clicks her fingers and gets excited*)

A: But you're not Apollo, are you? You're his daughter?

C: Yes, I'm Apollo's daughter. I've a mission to go to find Earth.

A: Okay. What's your name?

C: My name? You name me.

A: What would you like to be called? Let's make, let's get the parts we like.

C: Okay, I'll give you a clue. I'd like a name of a god, a Greek god or Thor, a god from Thor.

A: Well, a Greek god or goddess is Venus.

C: You could call me Venus Aphrodite.

A: Okay.

C: You could call me Diana. (*Gives a small, embarrassed laugh*)

A: Right. Is that what you'd like?

C: Oh! I don't mind, as long as I have a Greek name.

A: Well, you could choose. I like either Venus Aphrodite or Diana Artemis.

C: It's your choice. You're gonna play my mother.

A: Okay, why not be Venus?

C: Okay, I'll be Venus . . . Although Artemis would suit me I think better.

A: All right, you're Artemis.

C: You're on my trip, because I'm your daughter.

A: Right. And now, how . . .

C: I, I was sent out when I was about six years old to find Earth. I found out the Earth. I went to a planet which was called . . . I went to Earth without trouble, to find Cylons, all my enemies, and now I am coming back to tell Apollo, to tell actually the commander, Adam.

A: Okay. Now, if you are six, you don't need me to look after you.

C: No, I'm seven.

A: You're seven? Well, then, I'm here as a friend.

C: No. You're a mother.

A: But I keep you company?

C: Well, yeah, but you also help me.

A: Yeah, sure. I take you because your father has given you this mission, and . . .

C: Well, actually, he has, but I mean, he didn't want to give it, because I was so born a favorite of . . . I was about the only child because the brother was turned into a Cylon, or I mean, he got killed. So, my brother . . . actually, he's my stepbrother, I'd say.

A: Yeah, but even though he's your stepbrother, is he still a Cylon?

C: No. He's dead.

A: So, it's only you. So your father *had* to give you the mission.

C: Well, no . . . He didn't have to, but . . . and he was very uncomfortable that he had to, but I mean, he wanted to, because he knew that I was, I could get out of a lot of things, like I could kill Cylons because, um, you, Aphrodite, all the gods have given me all their blessing, so I was better than all of them. And you have given me the blessing, of course . . . And you should know, because I'm your daughter and you gave me the blessing wisdom.

A: Okay.

C: And I could write, and I have this beautiful cloth to wrap myself in.

A: Okay, so not only are you wise but you are beautiful?

C: Yes . . . Okay. Now let's start playing. Okay?

With this, we concluded the planning segment of our play, after which she and I launched into its performance. This occurred in the bathroom, too. We continue in role for about forty lines, and then there occurred what may be seen as a failure or break in performance. Helen seemed to become somewhat anxious, and her ability to handle her real concerns through performance and story gave way to a more direct articulation of her preoccupations. Her real concerns were with sexuality, the mother's and father's relationship, and, more particularly, her origins. The dialogue went as follows:

C: (*Whispers within the performance to me, inaudibly*)

A: What? You're gonna tell me a story?

C: No, you're gonna tell *me* a story, or, er, in this game. What it means is, you're gonna tell me how I (was) born.

A: Um.

C: The story is, what happens is, Apollo didn't know it, but you have fallen in love with him.

A: Okay.

C: Which is your (*inaudible*), and so you have asked, you had asked Zeus to give eternal youth, and for the whole ship.

A: Okay.

C: And, internal, um, and, er, eternity, to live forever.

A: Okay.

C: So, he hasn't . . . but Zeus could not permit it . . . but still, he did let a gray hair come. He said, "Your daughter will be—if you have a daughter, you will become, um, you'll have mostly everything." So, you disguise as a beautiful woman, for you knew what to do (*laughs amusedly*), um, got his attention, and he has to marry you. So it happened that, um, you did get married because you loved him.

But what happened was—this is how you told, tell me the story of how I born—and so, one day, he said, only . . . See, er, you see, he was sleeping and so you became, what you can do is, make a light come, and it's a different way of making love.

A: Uh-huh.

C: Um, well, if you like me talking about those words.

A: Sure.

C: Do you?

A: Yeah, I like them.

C: Because, actually, I feel very uncomfortable not being able to talk about the right words.

A: But why do you feel uncomfortable?

C: I mean, I mean.

A: You can talk about whatever.

C: I know that, but people feel uncomfortable with, when you talk about those words. But the point is, one day—see, he would *not* make love with you—but one day it happened that, um, you came upon him, er, like a light and made love.

A: Uh-huh.

C: And you tell me the story all over again; what he said when he got up and he had a daughter, okay? (*Mildly amused*)

A: Okay.[3]

The gist of this somewhat muddled story concerns me, her mother Athena, who fell in love with Apollo and then plotted to seduce him. According to Helen's story, I asked my father, Zeus, to give me both eternal youth and life. Zeus granted me this, although he did allow one grey hair to emerge. He told me that, if I had a daughter, she would have almost everything she wanted. Therefore, I disguised myself as a beautiful woman in order to get Apollo's attention and indeed was

---

[3]As the dialogue shows, what occurred at this break in the performance was that Helen decided that, as part of the play, I as her mother would tell her a story about how she was born. She stressed that this was part of the game. As the transcript illustrates, she then proceeded to tell me this story, which consisted of fragments of adult explanations about sexuality and human relationships, interwoven with her own representations and fantasies. What was striking about her story was its halting quality. Her thinking did not seem to be clearly organized or articulated. The plot shifted about, and the audience was not very carefully cued as to what was occurring. Further, it was entirely her own construct, and it was not dialogically developed. In this section, she controlled much larger portions of speech but with repeatedly unfinished thoughts.

successful, so that he ended up marrying me. However, I discovered that he would not make love to me. So, one day when Apollo was asleep, I came upon him "like a light and made love," which resulted in a daughter being born. Helen explained that making a light appear was a different way of making love. This was the story she wished me to tell as part of the performance. As she says, "And you tell me the story all over again; what he said when he got up and he had a daughter." Helen was noticeably amused at her own invention and slightly embarrassed at the whole thing. It was some time later when the opportunity for this retelling arose.

After this interlude, Helen resumed her performance as Artemis and became somewhat more focused and easier for an audience to follow. She left to find the Battlestar Gallactica and there met her father, who did not know who she was. He believed that his daughter had been killed by the Cylons, his arch enemies. The main point of this episode was convincing Apollo that she was indeed his daughter and worthy of being so.

Helen then moved into a scene where she gave her father and his men instructions for finding Earth. At this juncture, she also moved her location out of the bathroom and into the bedroom. After this, she went on a journey to another planet, called Clemens. She played the role of giving people advice on how to reach various planets. In the course of the performance, we discovered that, besides finding Earth, her father wished her to stop Starbuck, one of his men, from gambling and dating girls. She said, addressing me as her mother, "Um! I thought my father said, 'Why don't you get Starbuck to stop gambling and dating with girls? He gets in a lot of trouble that way. Don't you remember the time when he got a steam burn for dating with some girl and then moving to another?' . . . We wouldn't date with men."

Artemis (Helen), while talking to her mother, asked her, "How come he (her father, Apollo) finished to love you (Athena) so much?" It is significant that not only did her mother seduce her father by her beauty but she also tricked him into making love. This resulted in the birth of a female daughter for Apollo, which is a comical aspect of the child's story. This was her strategy for incorporating her myth about her parents and her birth into the performance. She eagerly encouraged her mother to tell her the story of how she met and married her father. While I related the story to Helen, it became clear that there were several details that she wanted included in the telling. To that end, she actively prompted me if I overlooked anything. For example, she said, "Er, Mommie, you skipped out a part. He first asked you for a date, don't you remember?" Her prompting and additions were all included with the performance and explained in terms of my forgetting or excluding important details that I had mentioned to her before. My story, which closely followed the outline she had delineated earlier, ended with my saying, "And, of course, that was the beginning of you." At this point, she spontaneously drew my attention to an egg that she had made out of plasticine and said, "Look, an egg, just like those eggs when you get a period." She thus raised the subject of menstruation and described a friend's embarrassment over the issue. I responded reassuringly to her concerns as Athena, her mother, after which she returned to the character Starbuck.

Starbuck (played by me) came back to ask for money for gambling. Artemis rebuked him for his request, on the grounds that he was breaking the law by gambling. She pointed out that it was her mission to stop him from gambling and stressed the fact that laws are right and that we have to observe them. As she said, "Excuse me. Have you forgotten the rule for gambling? . . . *No* gambling on Earth . . . Now, don't you know, this country is a law. And it isn't free from law. You gotta remember, law is right."

The story ended arbitrarily when the tape ran out and Helen said, "Oh, good! Let's end it. It'll have a mysterious ending." She added, "It was a great story. Such a good one."

After this, Helen spontaneously broke into snippets of play. She began to talk of journeying to mysterious lands, to fairyland, to science-fiction lands, to gods' and goddesses' lands, and to dreamland. She pretended to telephone various characters in these lands but then reported that "all lines were busy." Then she decided to visit Balalula-land, where she talked to small animals, whose names included Black Beauty and Winter. She also talked to a kitten, and she was very affectionate toward all of them, called them cute, and simulated letting them jump out of her arms.

She then suggested that we go on an adventure where we would catch animals. I agreed and asked her what kinds of animals we should chase. She replied, "A llama. Big animals are too hard to catch. I'll get my men to get them." She then ordered her imaginary men in a secret language. As she continued speaking in it, she said, "It's great! You only have to say a few words for a long sentence." Helen demonstrated what she meant by uttering a short segment of sounds, which she translated as, "I love you." After another spurt, she said, "This means, 'Get some animals.' You can make so many different sentences and meanings, it's great. But I don't tell anyone about it, only you because you're special . . . and Anne [her friend whom I met during Session 6]. She knows a great deal, even the same as me."

Then, turning away from this language game, she said, "Let's do sword fighting. Do you know how to do it? I'll show you. Let's do it. I won't hurt you." We played at sword fighting for a couple of minutes, during which she was physically very active. Following this, Helen came toward me, put her arms around me and said, "I love you." I told her that I was very fond of her, too, and asked her whether she had felt sad earlier on. She said that she had been angry instead. She added that she was angry with me but did not wish to talk about it because she would only get into a bad mood again. "I was in a bad mood then. I don't get in them very often. Now, come on, what shall we play?"

At this point I told her that we should look for her parents, because I had to leave. So, we went downstairs and found her mother in the kitchen. Pamela invited me to stay to dinner, but I was not able to do so. Helen followed me as I made my way out, saying, "Come here in the corner, I want to do something." As I did so, she flung her arms around me and gave me several kisses. In turn, I said, "You're a sweet one" and put my arm around her as I walked out of the house and toward my car. Our earlier contretemps had ended in reconciliation. It was 7:00 P.M.

Commentary

Before discussing the child's play during this session, I want to take a few minutes to review my own state of affairs at the end of it. Although I felt great relief at the way the session had finally ended, I also felt exhausted as I left the Kings' house that night. On my return home, I was glad for the opportunity to talk with my husband about my frustration with the complications that the evening had presented.

What I discovered was how trapped I had felt while witnessing the early events of my time with Helen. I had wished to extricate Helen from the conversation with her parents and take her upstairs to play. I also had felt that, given the course of our relationship, Helen might not have liked me socializing with her parents. I had felt in somewhat of a bind, however, because I had perceived the Kings' invitation to me to join them for coffee quite reasonable and also felt it unwise to interfere with the interactions within the family. I took the only available course, which was to be an observer to the situation.

During the argument, I had felt Helen's frustration and anger mounting and wished that her parents would not make fun of her, despite their lighthearted and nonmalicious attitude toward it all. I thought of the numerous ways in which adults in general win at the cost of children, who in turn are hurt, unmasked, and often confused by the adults' apparently jocular behavior. In this instance, Helen was hurt and angry at both of her parents but had little recourse but to go upstairs and cry silently. As yet, she had not learned to tell her parents directly of how she felt about their teasing behavior. My presence may have made it more difficult for the child, and it is little wonder that our subsequent interactions were affected by her hurt and angry feelings. As I comment on the particulars of this session, I will take up this situation further.

Our second telephone conversation prior to the session had suggested Helen's continued eagerness at the prospect of seeing me. On this occasion, as on the last, however, Helen witnessed me spending time socializing and making a relationship with her parents. One wonders what effect this had on the child, given her consistent earlier attempts to exclude her parents from our relationship. It would not be unreasonable to suggest that she may have felt betrayed by my interactions with them and fearful that she no longer had exclusive access to me. Such feelings may have contributed to her unhappiness at the time we had lost that afternoon. Her bemoaning the loss of someone to have a crush on may also have been an expression of feeling a sense of desertion. Thus, the loss of her television program became a symbol for the plight in which she felt herself to be on this occasion, in terms of her relationship with me.

The text suggests that, in a state of distress and frustration, the child was unable to participate in any creative activity. All she wished to do was to be regressed, passive, and labile, which is most uncharacteristic of Helen in normal circumstances. Symbols of her regressed state were her suggestions that we play house, that she take the role of a baby, and that she would be a baby who could read silently, denoting the need for minimal involvement. It was evident that the immediate scene in the everyday realm dictated the fictive scene, which in turn suggested the actions to be engaged in. The purpose of these actions was to guarantee her being on the outside and me being the active participant in the game. This was further confirmed by her choice of the name Wendy for herself, reminiscent of the character in *Peter Pan*, which had been her favorite story at age three. The soft toy she cuddled and the Lego construction set were also symbols of an earlier stage of play. Finally, by making herself a deaf baby with super reading powers, she abrogated herself from all responsibility to participate.

What can be said about her strategy for setting me up the way she did? By making me wholly responsible for sustaining the game, Helen was using me to coax her into being an active participant. My efforts may be seen as providing her with a means of transition from her state of anger and withdrawal to one of interest and engagement. My added gesture of mothering her as I shifted from playing the role of friend to mother was my personal response to Helen's communications about her needs for intimacy and being babied. The interpretation that she was making a play for intimacy was supported by her next request: that I come in with her to the bathroom, accompanied by the tape recorder.

All the regressed play activity prior to entering the bathroom may be considered as a warm-up to Helen's subsequent involvement in initiating more active play as well as relating to me more fully. In fact, Helen herself said as much when she stated, in her normal voice rather than her former baby tones, that our earlier activity had prepared her for playing "Battlestar Gallactica." This also suggested a high level of self-consciousness on Helen's part, about her own behavior.

It would be an oversight not to call attention to the role of the bathroom in this session. This location had figured previously (and as early as in Session 1) in our interactions, where it had been both a test of and a gateway to intimacy. In this session, however, it also became the location and source of Helen's creativity. As such, the bathroom became a symbol of a passageway to intimacy, especially in her particularly regressed state on this occasion. This location, like her bedroom, seemed to be a refuge for the child, a place in which she could lock herself and get away from it all. Thus there was a mesh between the scene and the actions, where each influenced the other.

In the planning of the story, Helen was intent on casting three roles: her father, Captain Apollo of Battlestar Gallactica; her mother, Athena, Goddess of Wisdom and favored daughter of Zeus; and herself, Diana Artemis, the offspring of these characters. Since Session 9, my fictive role as her mother had become stabilized and so had hers as an accomplished and favored seven-year-old child of the gods. She was a symbol of Wisdom and Beauty, as well as being a huntress and strategist par excellence. Her representation of herself was a mirror image of the way she symbolized the adult, her idealized mother. These symbols agrandized the child and shaped her own attitudes toward herself as heroine. They also enhanced the core features of the three situations she enacted. In the first of these, she demonstrated her worthiness in relation to her father's expectations; in the second, she displayed her wisdom and competence and dispelled any doubts due to her being female; and in the third, she supervises the retelling of the story of her origins and birth. The emphasis in this third situation was on courtship, sexuality, and the birth of a female child.

Two basic conflicts underlay these situations and were elaborated in different scenes throughout the story. They concerned sexual identity on the one hand and, on the other, involvement in sexual activity where the father/child relationship may be a target of her love. The first conflict was symbolically resolved through her favored status, great wisdom, powers, and success in fulfilling Apollo's missions for her. Such accomplishment validates her femaleness and allows her to accept her mother clearly as being the point of her origin and the source of her wisdom, beauty and power. One might speculate for a moment on how this female child has been affected by the sexist, socio-cultural scripts around her. For although her mother in everyday life is an autonomous, professionally successful woman, nevertheless Helen feels a need to endear herself to males and do so in terms of her intellect and powerful feats. In stereotypic terms, it is an identification with symbols associated with maleness, that is to say, the sun, the intellect, physical feats, and prowess. Of course, in addition, the home tended to uphold these values as markers of success.

The second conflict was resolved by Helen's assuming a regulatory role for herself. She accepted the responsibility of preventing Starbuck, who functioned as a sexual symbol in the text, from gambling and dating girls. He was threatened with steam burns, perhaps signifying fire, and other danger if he broke the law on these two counts. In Freudian terms, this would suggest a resolution in terms of her superego functioning. One can speculate that, after giving reign to her sexual curiosities via her interest about her parents' meeting and mating and her own birth, she became a superego figure, concerned with law and order. After all, her mission was to do good and destroy evil. Therefore, although she was curious about sex, she also felt ambivalent about it. Several examples of her behavior in the story, including her use of confutation, support such an opinion.

As a co-participant, I found myself often bewildered by what was going on. There was a regressed quality to much of the play, and Helen's periodic whispering about what was occurring often failed to make sense. This was almost entirely her story. Very often, she blatantly fed me the next line or corrected what I said within the performance. Time and scene were often not clearly delineated, and the story did not have clear beginning and terminal markers. Performance was marked by shifts in voice pitch and register.

Much of this regressed quality may be explained by the original frustration and aggression Helen experienced earlier on in the afternoon. In addition, there were many new strivings at hand pertaining to her interest in sexuality and puberty. These topics were a very real part of her everyday circumstances, and exploring them was encouraged by both her friends' experiences and sex education classes at school. Although they were not launched until her activity moved into the bathroom, these issues were still veiled in ambiguity, hence the rambling, disordered nature of much of the talk. Thus, in addition to her story concerns and her rhetoric for managing them, such larger contextual features distinctly affected the grammar of Helen's text.

Finally, her brief play vignettes at the end of the session were all part of her previous repertoire. Her physical activity in particular was a consistent part of every play session and may have functioned as a culmination of her creative efforts. In this session, she also played with language, demonstrating her own awareness of its symbolic nature. Further, she represented herself as a motherly or protective agent for little animals. These snippets were very reminiscent of her playful acts in the early sessions, especially the first and second. The recycling of this early material may have been in part presaging the end of the particular style of play activities we had shared and the beginning of a new cycle of action. This point will be elaborated in the last two sessions of the relationship.

Conclusion

This extremely long and rambling story was thus concerned with several themes: sexuality and the origin of babies, especially herself; pleasing her father and fulfilling his expectations as she succeeds in her mission to find Earth, rout the enemies, and stop Starbuck's gambling; and demonstrating how special she is and her overall prowess and importance. She also made Athena (me) into the "good" mother in this story, that is, one who is beautiful, wise, and eternally young; and one who begins to initiate her into womanhood and sexuality.

SESSION 12, JUNE 12
Emerging Discontents

This session was unusual in that we met in a different location from the one in which we usually met. If you recall, during Session 10, Helen and her friend, Jill, showed interest in making a videotape of their play, and I was quick to support their request. In addition, I wanted to have another occasion on which to observe Helen with Jill and also to see how she would fare in a location away from the home.

The arrangement for the session had been set up prior to our meeting, as I had to seek the cooperation of the Kings, the children, and another friend of mine, who was to provide us with the equipment and recording studio. This was all done, and six days after our last meeting Helen arrived at about mid-morning at my house, accompanied by her mother. Pamela and I talked briefly about our respective plans for the day; then she left. On walking into my apartment, Helen asked for something "to snack on" and settled herself into a chair at the dining room table. We sat chatting for awhile as she ate. She mentioned a forthcoming trip overseas to visit her grandparents, which excited her. She felt, however, that it was to occur too soon and then wished not to speak further about it.

She walked around the apartment rather quickly and curiously; however, on coming to my study, she stopped and commented on the number of books in it. She went to the shelves in search of children's books. I showed her some of my collection, and she wanted to borrow a few on her return from overseas. I agreed to this. Helen then reminded me that we would be late for meeting Jill if we did not hurry. With that I locked up the apartment and we left.

During the car ride to Jill's house, Helen continued to talk some more about her trip abroad. She talked about her love for her grandparents and some other details about her family. Then, rather swiftly, she became interested in my family and began asking questions about my parents, siblings, and childhood. She was most interested in my sister and the nature of our relationship. She wondered whether we played together as children and whether she knew about my secret languages and lands. "I really want to know more about what you did with your sister," she said, just as we drew up alongside Jill's house.

Helen had rarely been interested in the details of my life, other than her curiosity about whether I played with other children or not. The interest on this occasion was obviously generated by her being in my territory and may also suggest that she was beginning to see me more realistically as having a life of my own, rather than as the idealized one who was solely her play partner. In any event, I was relieved when we arrived at Jill's house and our conversation stopped short. I found that it was difficult to talk to Helen about myself, except in a superficial way. This is a part of the relationship with an informant for which researchers do not bargain, although neither had I anticipated the course of much else in this relationship! In addition, it is difficult to talk to very young children in much other than a somewhat detached way, because of the gap in understanding that exists. There is little doubt, however, that Helen observed my reticence and was affected by my behavior. Her level of interest in me was entirely dictated by her own needs and agenda.

We collected Jill quickly,[4] and both girls decided to sit in the back seat, chatting, teasing each other, singing, and playing song and hand-clapping games. They were quite boisterous. We stopped for lunch, during which the girls talked about the kind of film they would make. Both used the criterion of being "a good reader" when deciding to include or exclude their peers in the film they planned. Jill also talked briefly about a game called "Cats." When I asked about it, she said, "Oh! It's just like Darlene and Superheroes. It's about good and evil people and stuff like that." I had also discovered from a colleague that many elementary-aged children played this game called cats in the schoolyard (C. Sarett, personal communication, March 10, 1979).

As I reflected on Helen's behavior with Jill as they rode in the car, I was struck by the familiarity of the routines in which they engaged. The jokes they told, songs they sang, and clapping games they played were similar to those I had seen many children of their age group engage in, especially when they traveled in cars or buses. Although Helen was a special child in some respects, she was also very typical of others in her peer group. Moreover, some of her later boisterous, bossy, and controlling behavior with Jill also suggested that these patterns, which I observed in her interactions with me, were part of her personality style in general and not specific to our relationship.

After lunch, we drove a few blocks further to our destination. We walked into the building in which the taping was to take place and had to wait for awhile before my friend, Brenda, arrived to help with the activity. While waiting, the girls were very active and excited. Helen kept on climbing all over Jill, wanted Jill to kiss her foot, tickled her, kissed her neck, pretended that she was a baby, sang "Hush a bye, Baby" to her, and teased her. Although Jill did little to discourage her, she kept telling Helen that her behavior was embarrassing to her. Helen took little notice of this and seemed generally amused.

We then met Brenda, who took us to the room where the filming was to take place. The girls asked where the cameras were and then proceeded to rearrange several of the chairs in the room. The girls insisted that I stay in the room with them and be part of their play. Consequently, it was left to Brenda to do the filming. They began

---

[4]I had phoned Jill's parents to tell them I'd pick their daughter up to take her to play with Helen at one of the colleges. They were quite matter of fact about it, said that the Kings had mentioned this to them, and that it was fine by them. Since they both worked, neither was at home when I picked Jill up. She was in the care of an older brother.

playing "Darlene" and cast me in the role of the teacher. I did not wish to participate in the game, however, and offered to be a member of the audience instead. They reluctantly agreed. What followed was a playing out of several segments from "Darlene," followed by snippets from other games such as "Superheroes" and "The Beautiful Life of the Gods." The content of their performances was made up of familiar material, and the actual enactments were sketchy in comparison to the long, carefully planned and staged dramas that Helen initiated in her home.

In their first game, the theme was teasing. In the second, the action centered around themes of good and evil and the overcoming of evil in order to gain favor with an angry father, Thor. There was also much talk about penises, sperm, kissing, sex, taking off clothes, and nudity, which took place as they crawled under chairs and tables in the room and tumbled over one another. At the end of their performances, they were eager to watch a replay of the tape and seemed very involved in reviewing their antics. They laughed heartily, repeated some of the lines along with the recording, and commented on their performances in an evaluative manner. As in Session 10, once again, Helen became restless more quickly than Jill and proceeded to pinch Jill at junctures where she thought Jill had made mistakes on the tape. She then began to kiss her, give her back rubs, and attempted lifting up Jill's T-shirt to touch her breasts. Jill became annoyed at Helen and sternly reprimanded her for bothering her. After the playback, we thanked Brenda and left.

On the way home, the girls continued to sing, joke, and chat incessantly. When we finally arrived at Helen's house, she suddenly became very quiet, and, when her mother opened the front door, Helen looked very doleful. She was quiet and noncommunicative, despite some of her mother's efforts to engage her. But then she said, rather suddenly, "You know, I like Diana. It's not fair that I have to go away. I don't want to go so soon." To this her mother responded, "Oh! I could never have guessed. Come on, let's not have any more of this stuff." She smiled at her daughter, and Helen asked whether I could come over to see her the day after she returned. "You'll have to ask Diana about that," Pamela said, looking at me. Saying that we would plan on meeting soon after she returned from overseas, I gave her a hug, reassured her that I would miss her, said goodbye, and left with Jill. Helen shyly waved at us and then disappeared.

I drove Jill home. As we rode along, she mentioned that she thought Helen was about to cry when we left. She said, "I think she's sad because she'll miss us when she's away. You know, Helen is a neat kid. I like her." After a moment, she added, "Helen's lucky to have you. You're nice." I was touched by the largesse of these children's feelings, their vulnerabilities and honesty. Just as they are often seen to be resilient, they are also easily and deeply wounded by all manner of events which as adults we often deny, trivialize, and fail to understand.

Jill told me a ghost story and told me about the games that Helen, other friends, and she played at school. "Darlene" and "The Beautiful Life of the Gods" were among them. She added that they were also into teasing boys. On reaching her house, I escorted her to her front door and expressed an interest in seeing her when Helen got back. "Yeah! That'll be great, but I'll have to talk to Helen about it," she said. "Okay. Take care," I said, and left. It was 3:30 P.M.

Commentary

My final conversation with Jill corroborated the fact that the games Helen played with me were at some level part of the peer culture of which she was a part. I also realized, however, that the structure and dynamics of the play between Helen and me were different and were particular to our relationship.

What was most striking about this session was not only the undeveloped dramas but Helen's boisterous behavior. There were intimations of this in her play with me, but on this occasion she was more physically aggressive and almost solely into rough-housing behavior. On the whole, the play enactments were schematic, repetitive, and disjointed. The girls were very self-conscious in front of the cameras, tended to giggle, and in general seemed less involved in the play. It seemed as if, in these stressful circumstances, the girls could do little else than use very familiar themes and scripts. The session was the least interesting in terms of innovativeness, complication, and plot development. Such observations may be of interest to adults who expect to see children play at their most competent and creative in unfamiliar circumstances or public places. In such instances, as this experience demonstrates, they fall back on well-rehearsed scripts.

I also felt that Jill's presence made the play more public, although no less furtive. It was public not only because we were in an unfamiliar and public place, but also because we were a triad and in a situation where the girls were more interested in clowning around and teasing than in making lengthy make-believe dramas.

This session contained many differences of note. In particular, several characteristics of the everyday realm bear commenting upon. The most striking feature was Helen's apparent comfort in moving to more outer-directed and wider spheres of behavior than had previously been the case. This became evident in several ways. For one thing, the locations in which the activity took place were different, public, and new; and for another, her actions in them toward those she knew (Jill and me) and others (such as my friend, Brenda) were friendly and far from reserved. Third, she showed new interests and behaviors in these realms, in relation to both Jill and me. With regard to this third difference, in relation to me Helen evinced an interest in my world. Her desire to know the details of my personal life not only suggested a wider focus of interest but also an interest in personal narratives, as opposed to pure fantasy narratives. This interest was first glimpsed in Session 11, in which Helen showed an interest in the fantasized details of my personal life within the play realm. Thus, her interest in me at that time was as a fictive character, and, although this tale was told to aggrandize her, nevertheless it was the first time that I was allowed an extended turn to relate the details of my life in our conjoint story-making efforts. With regard to her friend, Jill, Helen displayed an enthusiasm for the form of riddles and jokes that were more Jill's domain. Despite Helen not having mastered these forms, which would be usual at her age, her interest in them belongs to a more public domain than does her own fantasy making.

These changes may be explained in developmental terms as well as in terms of the relationship. Not only was she much more interested in peerhood and the intricacies of the outside world, but she had come to share a much more stabilized relationship with me. This fact, together with her being with her friend, may also have accounted for her friendly behavior toward Brenda and her general excitability, which were both in contrast to her usually withdrawn behavior in public situations. I had been her peer in the play realm and, since Session 9, had also consistently played the role of her idealized mother. In Session 10, I was treated as a peer and confidante on sexual matters in the everyday realm; and, in Session 11, I was made a teacher as well as a confidante on matters of sexuality in the play realm. I had become a source of approved and overt socialization for Helen. Accompanying this role was a shift to discussion and conversation about intimate matters.

Helen's behavior in both the everyday and play realms on this occasion clearly corroborated her awakening interest in sex and her own bodily development. That this was part of her peer-group interest was supported by Jill's stories about the games they played at school.

In the play realm, the girls used familiar scripts for their performances. They used the games "Darlene" and the "The Beautiful Life of the Gods" to suggest the speech activities and guidelines for interpreting and realizing their purposes of action (see Cook-Gumperz, 1977). These games were used as metaphors and as cues for an unending line of data and generalization. Once again, the chief metaphor embodied in "Darlene" was peer hostility and teasing directed toward dumbness or stupidity. Phyllis Carr was once more a symbol of dullness, while Darlene and Julie were symbols of intelligence and talent. In "The Beautiful Life of the Gods," the symbols elaborated the following main themes: celebrating the superordinate strength of female goddesses, especially their success at defeating evil; endearing oneself to an angry father who has rejected his female daughter; and pursuing interest in sexuality and men.

The symbols for characterizing the motivation in these performances were drawn from myths. Helen played Athena, the Goddess of Wisdom and Love, as well as Starbuck, an irresponsible although attractive man. Jill played Thor, the father of the goddesses, and Corona, a Goddess of Beauty. These characters were all resources of appeal in the drama. The resources of enmity were posited but not played by either child. They took the form of a general category of enemies and a specific evil witch, all of whom were defeated in the end, so that the game ended in resolution and harmony.

Conclusion

Both games enacted on videotape in this session may be seen as recipes for perfecting or empowering the self and thus were acts of persuasion for the girls, for me, and the camera. Their rhetoric was concerned with persuading themselves that they talked the other's language, which was done by mutual identification. In addition, they persuaded themselves and their elders, or superego representations, of their worth by identifying their causes with those interests they perceived their elders to have (e.g., defeating evil, being smart, and being strong or adult). The video studio in which these acts of persuasion took place encouraged self-display. Thus, the immediate scene, the children's biographical or personal agenda, as well as the agents to whom the action was addressed all dictated the generating principles that governed Helen's and Jill's behavior on this occasion.

SESSION 13, JULY 23
Conflicting Interests

As the reader will recall, I last saw Helen on June 12. Soon after this, according to plan, she traveled overseas to visit relatives with her father for a period of five weeks. I telephoned her on July 18, shortly after her scheduled return. Helen's first words to me were, "I twisted my foot. I also have an infection," quickly adding, "Are you gonna come?" "Yes," I said, "in a few days' time." Disappointedly, the child said, "That's too long. You said you'll come every three weeks. Isn't it more now?" I explained that a long time had lapsed since our last visit because she had been away for more than three weeks. Sensing her dissatisfaction, though, I said, "Perhaps I could see you on Friday, which is in two days' time. Could you ask your parents if this would be okay?" She rushed off to find her parents and on overhearing the conversation that ensued, I became aware that Friday did not suit the Kings. Helen was very upset as she insisted that she did not wish to go out with her parents but wanted me to come instead. However, the Kings' plan stood firm, and Helen returned dejected and nearly silent to the phone. I tried comforting her and finally said that I would call her mother the next day and speak to her about setting up a more suitable time. When Pamela and I talked, she suggested that it would be best for them if I came on Monday. "Come in the afternoon." I'll tell Helen that this is the time we decided upon." With this, our telephone call ended.

On Monday the 23rd, I visited Helen as planned, arriving at 4:00 P.M. I was met at the door by both the child and her mother. It was a steamy hot day, and we sat briefly in the living room talking about the weather. After awhile, Pamela excused herself and Helen jumped up to join me on the sofa. Her first question to me was, "How long are you gonna stay?" As I hesitated for a second, she added, "Can you baby-sit me? My Mom's going to ask you—not for money or anything—I mean, just—for a few hours while they go out?" I said that I had to leave by 6 P.M. but would be happy to look after her if her parents went out while I was there. Helen seemed satisfied and suggested that we go to her room, where it would be cooler.

Once in her room, she whispered that she had some slime, which she would show me. She was whispering, she explained, because her mother did not even like the mention of the word. Before showing me the slime, however, Helen showed me various mementos of her overseas trip, such as posters, cards, rocks, and some books, as well as a photograph album. Following this, she reached for a container that stood on her shelf and took out the mass of slime that lay in it. She clearly enjoyed this gooey substance as she poured it from hand to hand, giggling while she did so. Having persuaded me to handle the slime and feeling satisfied that I did not recoil from it, she abruptly said, "Come on, let's play something. It's up to you. We can play whatever you like." I did not make a direct suggestion but appeared thoughtful about what we might do. At this, she became a little impatient and said,

"No, come on; I'll be getting in a bad mood if we don't start. I've been in a bad mood for awhile." "Why's that?" I asked, to which she replied, "Well, I'm not now, but, come on, what d'you want to play?"

At this point she resumed her play with the slime and began pouring it from her hands into mine and back again. While doing so she began to wonder aloud about why some grown-ups like me liked slime and others like her mother did not. Rather than solve the issue, she said that she wished her mother would enjoy playing with slime. Then she returned to her earlier question to me about playing: "Come on," she said. "What'll we play? 'Starbuck' or 'The Gods,' or 'Aqua Man' or 'Narnia,' or—or— Come on, what do you want?" I said, "Okay, let's play 'Aqua Man,' because we haven't played that before." To that she said, "Um, how about 'The Gods' or 'Battlestar,' like something that you know?" She then went over to her bookshelf and took out an "Aqua Man" comic so that I could look at it. This gesture was followed by asking whether I knew about C. S. Lewis. On replying that I did, she asked whether I had read *The Last Battle*. When I looked uncertain, she took the entire set of Narnia books and gave them to me to read. It is of interest to note that *The Last Battle* is about the final victory of good over evil, in a grand battle. If you will recall, from the very beginning, Helen had been preoccupied with the question of good and evil and had pledged to outdo evil in so many of her fictional escapades. Of course, I duly took the books, saying that I would have them read by the time I visited her next.

After this, Helen once more returned to seeking my help in initiating a game. At this point, I asked her how she thought the game should proceed. I said, "How does it go? Where shall we start? As the gods, or as the . . ." At this point Helen interrupted to say, "Of course, 'The Gods.'" Then, she began to outline a game by suggesting that Athena or Artemis could first appear but then interrupted herself to ask me whether I would mind if she used the proper words for various sexual organs and functions. When I said that I did not, she proceeded to tell me that she had learned about this stuff in sex education classes at school. She became more animated and told me of a boy named Bernard who "still didn't know the facts of life," concluding from this that he was quite a "dumb kid." "You know, this boy has a crush on Jill. Remember my friend Jill?" I nodded. "Well I have to protect Jill and keep her away from him, because he's so gross," she added. Her rendering of this account was quite histrionic, and she kept on adding that the whole situation was "hysterical." Her role was clearly as mediator and rescuer in this situation between Jill and Bernard.

Soon after this story, Helen returned to asking me about what we should play. We talked about the characters we would be, and I agreed to be Athena. She agreed to this but stressed that she, not I, would be the main god. While we were once again involved in choosing a name for her, Helen interrupted to sketch out a plot and drew my attention to an abrasion on her finger. She wanted to talk about this, and then showed me a cut on her toe, which she said was infected. And then, once more, she moved back into pursuing her wish to play: "Now, let's start playing, Okay! Come on, let's plan."

The story that we planned was very similar to one we had played during Session 11. It told of Athena, who came disguised as a beautiful woman in order to tempt Captain Apollo. Helen emphasized the fact that I, who played Athena, had calculated this meeting, knowing that Apollo, on seeing me, would begin dating me. She added that I knew that this would all occur because I had ascertained it from a reader of the future, who was also a god. Helen suggested that, after we were married, a child (to be played by her) would be born to us. She insisted, however, that I not tell Apollo of my pregnancy. She added that I would come upon him as a light, that we would conceive a child at that moment, and that I was then to go quietly away, leaving Apollo alone. At this point, Helen asked me whether I would rather have Starbuck as a husband, since he was very good at dating. She then warned me, however, that he had had two girlfriends at the same time. In contrast, she said, Apollo's wife had died and since her death he had had no girlfriend. She added that Apollo's sister, who was jealous of Starbuck's girlfriends, had inflicted a smoke rash on him as a punishment. As Helen paused for a moment, I said that I thought it might be fun if Starbuck were my husband, because then we could have Apollo's sister discover that he was double dating, even after his marriage to me. In response to this, however, Helen said, "He wouldn't have a girlfriend then. Don't you remember, you'd be the beautifullest?" She laughed. "You keep on forgetting, you're going to be the beautifullest, not including Aphrodite, of course. Or, you could act Aphrodite and change places, if you like."

Helen then began to posit several alternatives about the details of the plot. She said, "Or you could go before . . . or else, if you like, you wouldn't have to marry him but then go away and then be a light. Which would you rather have? . . . Or, at least pretend to die . . ." To all this, I said, "That's getting very complicated." Helen laughed and continued suggesting further alternatives, saying *sotto voce*, "This is fun." At this point, not quite seeing that this process was itself the play, I was eager to get on with the enactment and said, "We'll take it as the game goes." To this Helen hurriedly added, "We can't. We have to decide beforehand because it's *on* the game that you do it . . . You have to decide now. You have to come just as a light or as a beautiful woman and get married and . . ." Quickly I decided to come to Apollo as a beautiful woman and then return as a light just before we would make love and conceive a child. Helen seemed satisfied and smiled. "Good. Let's turn the tape recorder on" she said. In fact, I had turned the recorder on although Helen was unaware of this.

However, on this occasion, unlike the others, she did not begin to enact the story we had finally outlined. Instead, this planning episode was followed by quite an unrelated conversation. We talked about mosquito bites, her susceptibility to strep throat, the school bus and how awful riding on it was, and her next birthday, which was a couple of months away. She made up a little ditty about her birthday and how it made her happy, especially so because she would begin getting an allowance. While singing this, she began to wiggle her hips and dance. This brief episode was followed by more play with the slime and more talk about the books she was reading. She talked about Ursula Le Guin's *Earthsea Trilogy*, which dealt with a young boy's coming of age, finding himself, and dealing with his shadow, whom he finally overcomes. Fortunately, I knew these books very well and was able to talk to her about them. Our discussion excited her, and she said quite suddenly in the midst of our talk, "Okay, let's act that. I could be a wizard; You be the mother. We'll both do Ged, the boy, and . . . Oh, great!" At this point she began to dance about again and in the process became distracted by a mosquito, which she chased around in an attempt to kill.

The next little while was laced with discussions about a variety of books, such as Richard Adams' *Watership Down* and Tolkien's *The Hobbit* and a discussion about superheroes such as Superman, Batman, and Wonder Woman. Helen mentioned that she knew all the powers of these superheroes, although she "was not so much on them now." She added, "I'm on Apollo and Battlestar Gallactica now." She kept playing with her slime throughout this conversation.

Then, turning to me, Helen asked that I tell her some stories about various adventures that I knew. "You seem, you could tell me stories, and we could turn that into a game, like, er . . . I could listen and question and then we could have a real adventure. So, I could be a little goddess, just born, and I ask you, my mother, to tell me a story, okay?" At this point, our efforts were interrupted by Helen's mother, who came in bringing us cool drinks. This seemed to serve as another distraction, because Helen began talking about the ingredients in the drinks and then invited me into the bathroom, where she said it was cool. She proceeded to fill the bath and said that she wanted to play at being a two-year-old having a bath and splashing about. She promptly undressed and jumped into the water, where she made gurgling noises, talked like a baby, and splashed about. As she stepped out of the bath, she heard her mother outside and warned her not to enter, since she was playing with her slime, adding, "I don't want you to tell me it's parent abuse," and laughed. She asked me to persuade her mother that slime was fine. She said, "Tell her it's beautiful, it looks like a beautiful maiden, like jelly."

I was struck by the enormous lability of Helen's behavior that afternoon. She moved from one topic to another, was quite regressed in her behavior, and did not seem able to settle down to much. No story was developed along the usual lines, although it struck me later that the larger story of this session was about Helen's growing interest in *talking* about matters sexual rather than *playing* at them, although her ambivalence about it all seemed to keep getting in the way. Further, it is possible that the hot and humid summer weather also added to her pattern of initiating various snippets of play in a loosely associative manner and then abandoning them quite quickly.

After spending a few hours in this manner, it was time for me to think about leaving. Although Helen grimaced a little at this, she asked me to come down to the kitchen and explain to her mother that slime was okay. She said, "Since you and I and my Mom are alike, she should like slime too, right?" I did as she asked, although it was to no avail. Her mother's response to my attempts was, "No—it will definitely be parent abuse if I have to tolerate that awful thing. You're lucky that I even let you have it, Helen. So that's the end of that, I hope." We all laughed.

Before I finally left at about 6:20 P.M., Helen asked whether, since I had promised to come every three weeks and had not always done that, I could make up for it by coming every week. Overhearing this plea, Pamela came out of the kitchen to let me know that her daughter would be attending summer day camp and would not be as available as Helen would have me believe. "Once in a while would be fine," she said, adding that after camp they usually went swimming. Helen was noticeably upset by all this. I suggested that Helen and I could perhaps talk on the phone each week and that I would plan on coming over on one or two more occasions before concluding the work I was doing with her. Pamela thought this was a good idea because of Helen's "busy schedule," as she put it, and Helen fell silent. "Don't worry, Helen, we'll work something out," I said and put my arm around her before leaving. Pamela closed the door after me.

Commentary

This was a complicated session in which there were three situations of concern for Helen. First and foremost was her concern with reestablishing contact with me. Second was her compelling preoccupation with the origin of babies, and third were her ambivalent feelings toward her mother, which are characteristic of children this age (see Erikson, 1963). These concerns structured the session and motivated Helen's rhetoric and symbolism. In this section, I will elaborate each of them and illustrate how they dictated the symbolic action of this text.

It had been a long while since Helen and I had spent time alone with one another. Not only had her recent overseas trip interrupted our meetings, but the last time we had met had been in the company of Jill and my friend, Brenda. If we consider Helen's comments to me during the phone conversation that preceded this meeting, as well as what she said to me at the beginning of our session, they can be seen as being concerned with restoring what she perceived to be a lost relationship. She talked of various injuries and illnesses she'd had and of being hurt. She was also eager for me to visit her and to baby-sit her on this occasion.

Unfortunately, my motivation was somewhat different. Although I wished to see Helen, I wanted to do so fairly cautiously, given my plans for terminating the research relationship fairly soon. Our respective stances and levels of enthusiasm were reflected in the way we related to each other throughout the session and partially account for the restless and episodic spirit of the pattern of events that afternoon. Although a great deal was ventured, little was sustained or developed by either of us. However, the child's other major concerns also played into fashioning such a pattern of events.

Helen used a container of slime as the first object for initiating our interactions. Several attitudes were called out by this symbol. Her furtive whispering around it indicated that, although this was a substance she enjoyed, it was disapproved of by her mother. As such, it was part of her world. Helen's enjoyment of the substance and recurrent playing with it throughout the afternoon suggested some collusion against her mother, at least in play, which is also normal for children this age. She also made a bid to persuade me to side with her in this slime play. Finally, it served as a focus for her tendency to regressive behavior. In psychoanalytic terms, slime is usually taken to be symbolic of feces and an interest in it to be characteristic of the anal stage. Her play with the slime was a recurrent feature throughout the session and stood in an interesting relationship to her attempts to story.

Helen initiated leaving the everyday realm and entering the play realm with her comments, "Come on, let's play something. It's up to you. We can play whatever you like." This was characteristic of her style of initiation. It turned out to be somewhat of a paradox, however, because, although Helen suggested that initiating and structuring a story was a matter of my choice, she never allowed it to happen. It was purely a rhetorical offer. Anything ventured by me was either modified or contradicted. When she finally decided on one of the story alternatives, it was one we had played before. She justified it on the grounds of its familiarity, the implication being that I should prepare myself before venturing into new story territory. Accordingly, she gave me the Narnia books to read.

The story she chose concerned the sexual relationship between a man and woman and the conception of a child. All the elements of the plot revealed a concern with sex and the origin of babies. Her story-planning activity was strikingly reminiscent of A. S. Neill's experiences with children of a similar age at his school, Summerhill (Neill, 1960). He found that at the heart of the majority of the children's questions and stories was a veiled curiosity about the issue of their origins and the matter of conception in general. He claimed that, once he had successfully dealt with this basic concern, their endless stream of questions subsided.

When considering Helen's play-realm activity, what was notable was not only its grammar as delineated in the play, but also the constant interruptions of the activity by seemingly unrelated outside issues. We cannot assume, however, that symbolic actions and concerns apparently related only by time are not otherwise connected, especially at some latent level. Indeed, when examining the story-planning attempts and the pattern and nature of the interruptions more carefully, the common thread was Helen's preoccupation with sexual matters, manifested both in her play-realm concerns (the story of Athena and Apollo and Starbuck's activities, for example) as well as in her personal, everyday-realm anecdotes and strips of activity (the story of Bernard and Jill, for example). Her conflicted attitudes toward the topic were represented by an oscillation between persuading herself that she was grown up, knew the facts of life, and was sexually "wise," on the one hand, and being regressed, scared, and injured, on the other. This duality can be deduced by considering her overt sexual concerns alongside her playing with slime, becoming a regressed baby, wishing me to give her a bath, casting herself as a baby needing the protection and teaching of a "good" mother, and being preoccupied with various bodily injuries such as strep throat, mosquito bites, and toe infections.

The tensions generated by such polarities of feeling lent the session a quality of distractedness and prevented the emergence of a fully developed story performance. As in the prior two sessions, there was a thrust to have me generate and elaborate story plots while she played a more passive role as listener to my tales. This was a reversal of the pattern of story performance that had predominated throughout the first two phases of the relationship, but it was akin to her growing interest in my personal and fictive stories, which she had begun manifesting during Session 11.

Conclusion

In the face of my own motives to withdraw from the relationship before too long, along with my sense that the Kings were beginning to be less enthusiastic about the continuation of the study, and the hint that a new and different pattern for negotiating Helen's and my relationship was emerging (one where I was to be a story teller), I left the session with a clear sense that the end of the study was imminent. This decision was mine. Clearly, Helen had no interest in ending the relationship and was as yet very much invested in it. The next session mirrored these opposing agendas and brought the study to a close.

SESSION 14, AUGUST 20
"I Don't Care. It's Up to You"

Our final visit was initiated by my phone call to Helen on August 13th. Soon after hearing my voice, Helen said, "Are you coming today? You promised to come every three weeks." This was said somewhat petulantly, and I felt that Helen was angry and hurt. I tried to soothe her and draw her out into having a talk with me, but she seemed little interested. Her major concern was whether or not I was coming, and of this I reassured her. Since her mother was not at home, I concluded the phone call by promising to call her mother to set up arrangements for the next meeting.

The stress of the last few meetings was very much part of my experience of working with Helen at this time. I felt very strongly that the time had come to terminate the study. Although I knew that I wished to stop working with Helen, I hoped to be able to see her periodically so that I could keep up my relationship with her. I was fond of this little girl, and she had shared a great deal of her very special life with me. All this I planned to discuss with the Kings in my next call to them.

I telephoned them that night to let them know of my decision. I spoke to Pamela, who said that she thought that I should have more than sufficient information for my study. She added that Helen was also very busy with camp, swimming, and new theater classes that would begin soon. As such, she thought that my decision was timely and said that she and Don would speak to Helen about it. Pamela seemed supportive of my seeing Helen once more and then to maintain contact with her on a casual basis. At the end of this phone call, I felt tremendous relief. The end was in sight, but I also knew that it would be hard to predict how things would go between Helen and me on our next meeting. Anything could happen, and it might be difficult.

On the 19th, I called Helen again to make plans to see her the following day. She was fairly quiet on the phone but asked if I knew the game "Connect Four." "No," I said, but quickly added that I'd like her to tell me about it when I saw her the next day. She said nothing in reply and then hung up the phone. Although such phone calls are not unusual in the case of children Helen's age and younger, I felt that there was some difficulty brewing about my decision to end the relationship.

I arrived at about 2:00 P.M. on the 20th, as planned. Don King opened the door and invited me in. We chatted for a few moments, after which he called out to Helen that I had come. Helen came down with a book in her hand, apparently reading as she ambled down the stairs. On reaching the living room, she paid no attention to the adults there but was engrossed in the book, E. B. White's *Charlotte's Web*. The story is about a little girl and her growing attachment to a little pig and then a spider, who finally has to die.

Her father said something to Helen in the language of the home, which I took to be a reprimand for ignoring me. Then, turning to me, he said, "I'll leave you two to it" and left the room, adding that he wished to take Helen swimming at four that afternoon and hoped that we would be done by then. On hearing this, Helen reminded him that she had a cough and did not wish to go. She began coughing in a rather forced manner, and her father responded to this by reaching into the kitchen for the bottle of cough medicine, which he said would cure her. He gave her a dose, winked at me as Helen spluttered over the mixture, and then left.

Turning to Helen, I asked her whether she wished to continue reading her book. She said, "Let me see how long the chapter is," adding, "Would you like me to read to you?" When I said that I did not mind this if it was what she wished to do, she said, "I don't care. It's up to you." In a bid to ease the tension I felt between us, I asked, "Tell me, did you see the film based on the book?" "Yes," she said, and then launched into a discussion of how the film compared with the book. After that, Helen began to read aloud to me. As she did, she stopped periodically to quiz me about the various parts of the book. She asked me questions like, "What comes next?" or "What does *arable* mean?" When she finished the chapter she was reading, she continued on to the next and entitled it, "The Fog." However, since I knew the book well, I felt sure that there was no such chapter and told her so. She retorted, "I tricked you! It's called 'The Miracle.'"[5]

My decision to stick to the reality of the book and insist on the correct title seemed to reveal Helen's hostility and bring it to the surface. After that, we seemed to feel more relaxed with one another. Helen laid her book aside and drew closer to me. "I have a secret to tell you," she said with a smile. She said that she was saving money to buy her father a birthday present but made me promise not to tell anybody about it. She then said, "Come on, let's go upstairs." I felt that the hostility had become diffused and that Helen had made a bid to be more open to me. On reaching her bedroom, Helen said, "Do you have any Nancy Drew books?" "No," I said, to which she replied, "Oh drat! I thought I would borrow some from you. I'm really into them now. They're great." We talked for awhile about the series, and then Helen asked me what I wished to do next.

---

[5]What struck me was Helen's coolness and disappointment on the one hand and yet her symbolic requests that I give her more than I was giving. Using the principle of free association for thinking about some of Helen's responses, it does not seem accidental that she mentioned the game "Connect Four" on the phone and renamed the chapter in *Charlotte's Web*, "The Fog." If we take Helen's responses as projective of what was on her mind, they revealed the way she felt about our relationship and her hopes for it. The child felt (I believe) that something was changing in the relationship and that the ease and dependability of our meetings were at stake. For my part, I was caught between wanting to respond to her but also feeling that she expected more than I could give.

I suspect that Helen was bitterly disappointed in me and experienced it in an intensely personal and self-centered way, as is characteristic for a child of her age. Thus, she could not be expected to have much of a sense of appreciation for my situation. In addition, however, I felt that many of her feelings of anger and disappointment with her caretakers from the past were being added to her responses to me, making her expectations of me wildly impossible to fulfill and yet driven by intense needs and feelings. Thus, by the first stage of our interactions that last afternoon, I was unnerved and uneasy about Helen's anger with me and the demands that were behind the anger.

Only able to respond in a nondirective manner at this stage, I said,
"Well, is there something you'd like to do especially?" Shrugging her
shoulders, she replied, "It's up to you."[6] Feeling confused and frustrated by the situation, I asked Helen whether she was sure she wished
me to stay. In reply, she said that she did not care one way or the other.
"But, you see, it's important that I find this out, so that we can sort
ourselves out," I said. To this the child said, "Now, come on, what d'you
want to do?" Feeling that we were at an impasse, I continued, "You see,
I come because I am interested in you and your stories." Before I could
go on, she snapped, "They aren't my stories." "Well, aren't they ours,
then?" I asked. As she looked at me, I said, "Helen, although the stories
are ours, the book that I am writing is about you and how we make
stories for the recorder. That is the reason for my visits to you,
although we have also grown to be friends and players, which is
something very special to me." At this, Helen became visibly angry,
seemed on the verge of tears, and rebuffed me: "Stop saying this stuff! I
know why you come, but I don't want to hear about it!" Stamping her
foot, she added, "You are making me very mad!" "I can see that you are
mad, but what is making you feel this way?" I asked. "I am angry at you
for talking about all this stuff, so come on now, what'll we do?"

Rather than answer her question, I reassured her that it was all
right if she did not wish to make stories any more, but added that it was
important that I know if that were the case. Emphasizing my agenda, I
said, "You see, I wish to finish the book." Looking mildly interested,
Helen asked, "When are you going to finish it, and what are you gonna
call it?" "I'd like to finish it soon," I said, adding that I was not sure what
to call it. "Do you want me to name it for you?" she asked. When I said
that I would like that, she said, *"Children's Literature* or *Children's Games."*
"Ooh! I like *Children's Games,"* I said. But she said, "I don't. I prefer the
first . . . Because, I mean, the second could mean anything, I mean,
anything—a game like checkers. But *Children's Literature* means that it
has something to do with stories which is the kinda game we play."

---

[6]Throughout this time in her bedroom, I felt that Helen was desperately
looking for me to give her something—a book, a suggestion for a game, some
gesture by which she would be reassured that I was involved with her and
would continue to be so. Looking back on the situation, I wish that I had felt
sufficiently detached and in control to understand what was going on so that I
could have told her that I cared about her, but in a way that was not threaten-
ing to me. Instead, it seems clear to me now, Helen and I were both resonating
to the same feeling of being hurt, confused, and rejected by the other, as the
next series of interactions between us bears out.

Delighted by her response, I said, "That's what I'll call the book. I love it."

A momentary smile crept over Helen's face but soon disappeared as she walked over to her shelf. From it she took a game of "Match Ups" and another called "Connect Four." She laid them on the floor and said, "Let's play." During the game, Helen was intent on winning, as small children quite often are. To this end, however, she made up the rules quite arbitrarily, tended to trick me, and, when I queried the rules, told me that I had a memory like an elephant. She elaborated the last point by saying that the books she read had mentioned that elephants could not remember anything. A little later in the game, she added that I had a memory like a fly. Feeling the child's anger, I felt stressed and after two games decided to stop playing.

After a pause, I said, "You know, Helen, we can continue to be friends. The difference will be that I won't bring my tape recorder with me when seeing you, but if you like we can talk and play stories." Her response to this was, "I don't care, whatever you want. But I still play secret stories." Although I sensed that she was trying to tell me that nothing had changed, that she continued to do the thing in which I had shown so much interest, and that she would be available if only I kept my part of the bargain, I desperately needed to change the conversation. This need was driven by my anxiety but also by a feeling that it might be helpful in the situation. So, I said, "Well, I think we should also think of other things to do, like perhaps going to some films together."

The mention of films sparked Helen's interest. With more enthusiasm than I had witnessed so far that afternoon, she said, "Great! Maybe we could see *The Odd Ball*—or—how about *The Muppets*?" She suggested that I buy a newspaper and check on times and locations for the movies. "Great!" I said, relieved that the impasse had been broken and the mood lifted, at least temporarily. I promised Helen that I would check on a paper that night and call her the next day to set up arrangements for taking her to a movie.

I was ready to leave and told Helen so. She arose from the floor and walked downstairs with me. It was close to 4 P.M. As I called out to her father to let him know that I was leaving, he came out of the kitchen and instructed Helen to say goodbye to me. Rolling her eyes and muttering at her father, she walked quietly with me toward the door. I put my arm around her shoulder and said, "You know, I'm looking forward to seeing you and going to the movies. I'll call you, okay? Perhaps tomorrow." But Helen's response revealed no enthusiasm at that moment: "I don't care. It's up to you," she said, with an air of detachment.

With this heavy feeling between us, I finally said goodbye and walked quickly to my car, wishing only to get away. As I left, I caught sight of Helen walking over to the fence and calling out to a child next door to come play with her.

The next day, I called Helen. Although quiet on the phone, she was eager to have me take her to the movies. We agreed that, subject to her parents' approval, I would pick her up the following Saturday, take her to lunch first at a restaurant of her choice, and then go to the movies. That night, I called the Kings, and they were agreeable to our plans. Don then asked that I send them copies of the scholarly articles that I would write, based on my work with their daughter, to which I agreed. (In fact, a few years after the study was completed, as some of the information about it was published, I sent these articles to the Kings.)

Helen and I went to see *The Odd Ball* and enjoyed our afternoon together. A few weeks later, she invited me to her birthday party, and we continued to see each other periodically thereafter until she moved with her parents to another state.

Commentary

This text marked the final event in Helen's and my research relationship. It was about anger, withdrawal, and loss, and may be understood only in such a context.

On this occasion, unlike the first, each participant's motives ran counter to the other's. Consequently, the actions, which reflected the scene and the motives that each participant had in mind, expressed a range of attitudes from anger to sadness and loss. Unlike the consensus and harmony that operated within the first session, on this occasion there was a sense of ambivalence. I was much more active in defining this situation. The end of the relationship was discussed, but the decision made was not a mutually negotiated agreement. Rather, my claims about termination held sway. Customarily, it is unusual for research subjects to take part in the decision to end the relationship, in contrast to other situations such as friendships or therapeutic relationships. I believe, however, that it would have been more in accord with the general tenor of our relationship to have had its demise better negotiated.

Nevertheless, the decision to terminate the study was not arbitrarily made, but was influenced by several factors. I had fulfilled the needs of my research design, which had been to collect data for about a year. The study had generated a vast amount of information, which needed analysis. More important, after Helen's overseas trip the constellation of events in her life had changed. Her parents were showing a desire that the study should end, and, strikingly, Helen had become more interested in conversation than narrative play. Although these conversations were filled with personal narratives and other kinds of anecdotes, as forms of organizing experience and making meaning they were in contrast to the expressive forms that had predominated earlier. These recent discussions and conversations about dreams, fears, heroes, and other intimacies were a much more direct means of handling experience and were more characteristic of the prepubertal and peer-oriented phase into which Helen was moving.

An examination of the pattern of events at our last session revealed the following. First, the phone call prior to our meeting was actually a preliminary orientation to the session. Helen expressed her anger at being unable to control my movements by criticizing my irregular visits. In turn, being motivated by my own agenda, I was detached rather than supportive and reassuring in the face of the child's frustration. Consequently, when I saw Helen at the planned session, her early behavior played out this sense of detachment and rejection toward me. Our opening conversation was very reminiscent of Helen's early behavior in Session 1. Her engrossment in *Charlotte's Web* and her quizzing me on the text were symbols both of her withdrawal and of her public presentation of self, which was guarded, competent, and controlling. It was part of her known rhetoric for managing the situation. Once more, the quality of the action was matched by the quality of the location, the living room, in which our early interactions had taken place on first being introduced to one another.

Her tone and attitude at the end of this session also reminded me of the face she had presented during my first session with her, when she had portrayed herself as the competent, cool, Bible-reading person. Although I had felt a little helpless then, I also had felt great anticipation. In contrast, on this final occasion, I felt depressed and very sad, and I knew that Helen felt the same way. Her detachment at our parting was a result of her vulnerability and her feeling that her pain was caused by me, whereas on our first meeting it had been a matter of displaying competence and cautious control.

Alongside this strand of behavior, however, ran another set of responses on the child's part. They suggested that she was eager to play, as before, and to continue the relationship. This was reflected in several of her responses: her reply to her father's comment to me about taking her swimming, her shift from being a bossy and competent reader to a sharer of secrets, her decision to move the location of our activity to our familiar sharing place, her talk about her latest reading interests, her assumption that I would share her choice in books and might own the Nancy Drew series, and her wish to borrow my books. All of these indicated a desire to connect with me rather than terminate the relationship.

My response to Helen's behavior was directly linked to my motives and was an overt gesture of disengagement. On this occasion, rather than supporting her cues for engagement, I insisted on holding her accountable for her behavior. My comments were overly directed at impressing her with the logic of the researcher/subject relationship, especially in the face of the intimate and positive sharing we had experienced as co-participants in the research enterprise. Understandably, Helen had no interest in talking about the pragmatic aspect of our relationship, and her comments, "Now come on, stop saying those things. What shall we do?" and "What is it going to be?" were part of her rhetoric for talking play. She cared about the closeness and fun we shared, but, given my agenda, I failed to attend to these signals.

Consequently, as I made it quite clear that this was the end, Helen decided to do something very different. She chose to play a board game, an activity in which we were minimally involved verbally and one in which she was able to control and frustrate me because she played by her own undisclosed rules. After a few unsuccessful attempts at the game, I decided to withdraw from it and conclude our time together.

My way of ending was striking because I continued to insist on bringing my agenda to the fore. I even implied that she may not be interested in story telling and this lack of interest may lead me to stop bringing my tape recorder in future. In fact, although the child had given me cause to believe that she was now more interested in conversations and direct personal narratives, she had in no way articulated this. However, my perceptions and motives were uppermost in my mind at the time. This is an instructive example of how adults, despite their claims to flexibility, are always in a position, by dint of their greater power, to assert their wills over children if they choose to do so. In the face of my implacability, the child made one final bid to persuade me back into her world and its agenda. In response to my suggestion to conclude our afternoon, she said, "I don't care whether you come or not. I still play secret stories." Indeed, she did, although the details of these belong elsewhere.

Conclusion

Given the lack of mutual motivation, joint attention, and cooperative co-construction of meaning, the session was difficult and disharmonious. In Burke's (1969a, 1969b) terms, the grammar, symbolism, and rhetoric in the session operated to encompass the basic situation being negotiated, which was one of disengagement and termination of a meaningful and intimate relationship. It left me feeling sad and distressed and was an encounter I have taken great care not to repeat. It taught me to pay careful attention to endings.

ENDINGS

Like beginnings, endings, too, are fraught with a mixture of emotions. In particular, such situations, whether they be the end of a school year, the end of an important relationship, or the end of a journey or life phase, are often characterized to varying degrees with a sense of loss. At such moments, we have to deal with that which has sustained and nurtured us, and with those on whom we have depended and with whom we have formed attachments. There are questions that swell within us as we face endings, such as, Will we be able to manage without the persons we are losing? Have they abandoned us to feel lonely and left? Will they remember us, and can we give up our demand that they be available to us endlessly? Although our lives are full of endings, the anxieties and pain that accompany such situations are rarely acknowledged and faced. In particular, many of us who work with children as researchers, teachers, or caretakers of one kind or another often fail to prepare both ourselves and our children for the many occasions on which we have to face endings. This was certainly the case with Helen and me.

In retrospect, the endings within the relationship (as, for example, at the conclusion of Session 5 and then again at Session 12 and finally at Session 14) were not well prepared for by me. Such issues were never mentioned by the numerous research studies I had read or courses I had taken, which attempted to introduce me to working with children in a variety of relationships. The final session graphically demonstrated the difficulties experienced by both Helen and me as we struggled with bringing our relationship to a close. In addition, it poignantly highlighted the fact that researchers do not usually negotiate the end of a research relationship with their informants, and this is especially so when those with whom they work are children. In this instance it was clear that, if I had left it to Helen, she would not have terminated our original relationship. As is often the case in child/adult relationships, however, it was my agenda that held sway, thus underlining her powerlessness. This was noticeable most poignantly in the last session of the story of my relationship with Helen.

To date, the myths of the neutral researcher and the much-desired objectified research account have made it both mandatory and possible to ignore the human reality of the research relationship, in all its chaos and with its many foibles. However, some have always known this and others are far less tolerant of the myth of the pristine and ordered research endeavor. The story of the relationship between Helen and me is testimony to the importance of the relationship between researcher and informant and highlights its crucial role in shaping the contours of the behavior that emerged between us, as well as its meaning.

Our deep respect and affection for one another allowed us to move our relationship onto a different level, so that, despite the hardship experienced over the ending of the original relationship, both Helen and I were able to accept a solution that allowed us both to save face. In addition, our casual but friendly and enjoyable outings to lunch, movies, and the theater prepared us to let go finally with a sense of ease, when it was time for us to see each other no more. Like all of life, there was a finality to our relationship, too.

Today, Helen is a teenager and one with whom I have lost touch. I wish to thank her for allowing me access to her secret play life, as she called it, and for helping me understand a wealth of information about play, story, herself, myself, research, and the nature of child/adult relationships. It is a year I shall never forget.

Part III
INTERPRETIVE AND
THEORETICAL POINTS

As a researcher and writer, this study has been for me an excursion of both a scholarly and a personal nature. Constructing an account of what occurred has been a constant challenge. It led me to attempt continuously to fathom the relationship between the observed and observer—between Helen and me—to understand the nature of focused, face-to-face interaction and to discover ways of lending form to the mass of information it yielded on several fronts. As noted in Chapter 2, the conventional modes for presenting social science data, which take as their aim the objectification of data in the service of truth and "reality," were unsatisfactory for this study. The reconstruction of the event at hand, like play itself, refused to be contained by such constraints and called for an account that centered on the subject herself and attempted to blur subject/object distinctions.

Thus, although conducted under the aegis of social science, this study is unlike the usual social science account of children's play. To many it may seem idiosyncratic, too subjective, and more akin to the domain of fiction. As was made clear at the beginning, however, this is not a work of fiction. The world described in these pages is coextensive with the everyday world in which we live, from which the players entered it as a clearly framed realm. It is the telling and presentation of the lived experience, rather, that resembles a story. The participants and their relationship are firmly located in the everyday world, although the documentation and interpretation of the events parallel a narrative mode of fiction.

In choosing this narrative mode of documentation, I sought to advance my goal of understanding the lived character of this play event as it intricately revealed itself in the relationship between the players. Thus, believing that the knowledge gained from fiction is that of revealed understanding, my aim was to present a multi-layered description of the event so that the ideas and happenings could be grasped with a sense of their unruly complexity but yet made sufficiently systematic and coherent by their transformation into narrative time. As such, authentication of the event may be sought and located within the narrative text. In addition, I believe that this temporal view of the event will stand above any conceptual analysis of it and, in interaction with the reader, assume a life of its own.

Once we have gained a sense of the lived character of a social event, then we may more confidently turn to addressing its import as part of a larger and more generalized order of events. Accordingly, having laid bare the narrative details of what occurred when I went to a child as an observer of her play, in this part of the book, I will turn to the interpretive and theoretical points that the study reveals. I begin in Chapter 7 with a summary of Helen's play life, discussing its most striking features, stages, and behavioral components. In Chapter 8, I point out the implications of the study for methodology and for understanding the ecological conditions for children's play, effective child/adult relationships, and the needs and competencies of children in play activities. Chapter 9 reviews the contributions of the study to play theory. Each area of interpretation will be considered separately, although they are by no means discrete. Rather, they are differentiated in order that they can be highlighted. In the final analysis, they must be synthesized by the reader, rather than simply added together, so that a sense of the connections and underlying patterns of communication and meaning in the event at hand can be grasped (see Bateson, 1979).

7 Summarizing Helen's Play Life

Helen's play life was a mass of diffuse yet intricately patterned symbols, structures, and rhetoric. It was colorful, complex, and elusive as it erupted, ebbed, flowed, and spilled over its borders. It challenged the often-used discrete categories used to describe what appears to be a protean phenomenon in the hands of specific players. She did, of course, have a preferred style of play, namely, the use of make-believe, through which she plotted and enacted dramatic story scripts of her own making, but there was much more than that to her play.

CHARACTERISTICS

What is most striking about Helen's play is the tremendous sense of mastery that she had over the medium, her awareness of its use for her own purposes, her tireless involvement in it, and the enormous pleasure that she derived from it. Further, her play was filled with behaviors that have been variously categorized in the literature as motor play, symbolic play, associative play, word play, and the like. These categories are often used to suggest that children are involved in one category of play or another but not all of them. Helen's play, however, included examples of them all and more. Such adult categorizations mean nothing to those who play, whether child or adult. In contrast, what was often of importance to this player, and others I have observed, was the purpose of the play and what was going on within it. The study of Helen's play would argue that it was the excitement and power of the child's personal agenda that underlay and motivated her play with me and her companions. In fact, it makes sense to see the whole play study as a set of changing enactments and narratives. As Bateson (1955, 1956) might have said, the play was, in its substance, a set of metacommunications about her deeper concerns and these metacommunications were produced by a series of interpretive practices that she had carefully learned. Thus, we might argue that the play was a mixture of this individual's carefully nurtured competence and experience, her subjective input and style, and her purposes, all of which are central to understanding its meaning.

Such a perspective of Helen's play is important because the aim in this study is to understand the phenomenon itself in a situated context and to see the behavior as an "interpretation" or framing of events (Goffman, 1974), rather than to find objective indices of the phenomenon that stand on their own. Further, I have avoided the use of analytic categories that predict data, whether the concern be with antecedents or consequences of play, or with objective operational phenomena that would be used to define the presence of play. Rather, my concern is with understanding the player's world, particularly how it is constructed and what it means.

It is possible to delineate several features that characterized Helen's play and that she used for creating and structuring it. She used many culturally influenced scripts and social conventions, drawn from various sources, in relating to the themes in her play. These included biblical, Greek, and Norse myths; television myths of superstars; and stories drawn from her everyday life at home and school. These were the primary bases for her make-believe enactments. Scripts of social constructs are part of the child's growing knowledge of classes of individuals and their relationships, of categories and types of goals, and of the possible actions and sequences of actions that can be employed. Helen's scripts, however, were not simply imitative of these cultural scripts upon which she drew. Instead, she elaborated upon, schematized, and in many instances transformed them into a variety of forms. More important, Helen's play made it clear that these culturally sanctioned resources are not necessarily used by children in pursuit of adult-valued achievements like creativity, language development, and reading, to name a few. Rather, they are used for dealing with a variety of children's own purposes, which are communicational and expressive in intent.

Accordingly, the themes of Helen's scripts included the following:

- The child's origin and identity
- The battle between good and evil
- The testing of her powers and weaknesses
- Her relationships with parents, peers, males and females
- Strong women rescuing men who were weak and abandoned
- The upgrading of her own supposedly inferior status as a girl by performing super feats

- Understanding the polarities of smartness versus dumbness
- Sorting out the differences between good and bad mothering
- Making sense of her own sexuality
- Exploring the power of language to posit worlds and transform situations

These themes were intensely personal and yet contributed to Helen's reality not only as an individual but as a member of the groups to which she belonged.

Her themes were given shape and played with in metaphorical terms drawing on the sources on which her scripts were based; the same is true of the roles, objects, and actions she used in elaborating her scripts. The roles and character types upon which she drew were mythical figures and superheroes who were used to represent a range of positive and negative qualities and a series of relationships to her playing self. The actions included battles, births, rescue operations, domestic duties, family nurturing and socialization practices, courtship, marriage, the carrying out of various quests, and the celebration of victory. Objects included mysterious flying things, superplanes, battleships, spaceships, bows and arrows, miniature animals such as dinosaurs and other archaic creatures, spinning wheels, and flying horses. These roles, actions, and objects were the raw materials of Helen's dramatic play or make-believe and were used to enter the fictive worlds she constructed. As the play sessions in Part II show, there was a constant recycling of old and new themes, characters, and plot events over the course of the fourteen sessions of play that I witnessed.

Helen's play also illustrated that she knew that imaginary events, personages, places, and things can be represented by a variety of selected and condensed verbal and gestural acts that are symbolic of the meaning being communicated. Helen constantly showed her mastery of such overt representation. In fact, this is what is called enactment or acting out, and it is central to the mode of play she used most, that is, dramatic play.

A sense of power and control in the way Helen used speech and action to mediate her imagined worlds was also evident in her play. Although young children—and on some occasions all children—do construct their imaginary worlds alone, because Helen played with me or her friends on the occasions that I observed her, her communication via speech and gesture was critical to the production of her dramas. In fact, although the requirements set out in the planning phase control the specific transformations that can be made and provide an essential scaffold for what occurs in the play, often there is much negotiation, especially at the beginning, about correct or acceptable selection and execution of plans. Helen's case corroborates the view that dramatic play or make-believe must be seen as a form of negotiated action, which is used by the participants to achieve their various purposes.

Further, speech and gesture are also used to signal the various transformations that are made within the play world. For example, Helen spoke in many different voices in differentiating the thirty-odd roles she played over the course of our time together. She also announced these identities or changes in location by moving or gesturing in a manner that was associated with the transformation and that obviously contrasted with her behavior in the nonplay, everyday realm.

Helen was also clearly able to distinguish between the categories of real and pretend. Her meta-awareness about the phenomenon of play was evident as she talked about events and characters that existed only in play worlds, as she explained that the character Wonder Woman on television was played by a person called Linda in the everyday world, and as she at times reassured herself that certain gestures were safe in play, as when she wished to engage in play fighting with me. The implication of this is that Helen, like other children who engage in make-believe, understand that, in the construction of play and other fictitious worlds like story, the order of the everyday world is transformed and all manner of irregularities and reversals might obtain. They know that, by adopting a nonliteral orientation to the world, all manner of imaginery situations may be played into being.

Helen also knew, as do other players, that one may not behave without restraint in these imaginary worlds; there are indeed guidelines and restrictions for behavior in these worlds and an internal consistency to pretending. Helen often answered the questions I asked her about characters and actions in the play by reminding me that the answers were obvious if only I paid attention to the fact that we were gods in mythical realms. Nevertheless, from my point of view, these guidelines often seemed arbitrary, irrational, and far from explicit, but this also is in keeping with the spirit of play and the paradoxical form that it is.

In concluding this discussion of the characteristics of Helen's play, I want to reiterate that it is the excitement and compulsion of a personal agenda that motivates much self-initiated and self-directed play in the lives of children, even those much younger than Helen. In the privacy of a space of their choosing and among friends, the dramatic play of children is an alluring and incredibly complex kind of behavior that is likely to encompass most, if not all, of a child's resources and integrate them into a whole. The value of tapping its momentum and power, in the child's own terms, should be obvious to those of us concerned with facilitating children's communication and their sense of their own power.

STAGES

There were five stages that contoured the individual sessions I spent with Helen, and these also applied to the time she spent playing with her friends in her room. The five stages may be identified as follows: (1) greeting and making acquaintance, (2) sharing and planning, (3) enactment, (4) festival or celebration, and (5) taking leave. The first two stages moved her into the excitement of stage three—the play world—and out of the everyday, while the fourth and fifth led her back to the everyday, often buoyed by the flow that had been generated and experienced by the journey into the heart of her play. The stages may be elaborated as follows.

The first stage is self-explicit. It was a matter of touching base and usually occurred on the way to Helen's room and lasted for a brief while inside the room. Generally, this was followed by Helen's returning her thoughts almost immediately to the day's agenda—the play and her plans for operationalizing it.

The second stage was a time when plots were initiated and developed, accepted or rejected. It was also a time when Helen shared new interests such as her latest television shows, books recently read, or gossip about her peers. All this was grist for the play mill. On occasion, we would also listen to replays of tapes from prior play sessions and look for costumes that might be used in the play. This stage often served as a warm-up to the play. Helen found this time involving, and she often giggled with anticipation at what was to unfold. On occasion, she became so excited in what may also be called our brainstorming stage that, after a few sketchy plot details had been articulated, she was ready to play. She had, it seemed, tacitly filled in for herself the several gaps that still existed in my mind. Further, toward the end of the relationship, there were some sessions in which this talk about the play became the goal of the session for Helen. The sheer excitement generated by the prior experiences that we had had and the intimacy that had developed as a result of the emotional sharing seemed at these moments to be sufficiently fulfilling. More often than not, however, this second stage led directly to the next.

The third stage was a time for the generation of the spontaneous make-believe dramas that had been outlined in the prior stage. During this time, I witnessed a host of gestures and expressive forms which were all part of Helen's play world. Her repertoire was made up of dramatic role play; schematic gestures to stand for various acts like eating, flying, or sleeping; the putting on of up to thirty voices; singing, dancing, and wiggling her hips and body; some physically aggressive moves such as fighting off enemies and having sword fights to prove one's honor; chants and word play; nonsense rhymes, and the use of repetitious routines signifying the passage of time. This was the stage where Helen's play was at its most intense. At times, she was so taken by what was being generated in her play that she would step out of role momentarily to tell me how much fun she was having. It was amazing to watch the child's involvement, abundant energy level, and intense excitement as we played. It was, moreover, quite different from the wishy-washy ideas that we as adults often hold about children's play, where we imagine them to be pottering about imitating the domestic life and other routines they see about them. At some level, of course, play is mimicry, but it is so much more. This third stage often spilled over into the fourth.

What overflowed was the excitement that had just been generated in the playing out of the story. It was caught in what I have called a "spirit of celebration and festival" (Kelly-Byrne, 1982), and it also manifested itself in moments of intimacy, corroborating the tremendous sharing that had indeed gone on during the previous phases. This fourth stage involved a number of behaviors. Sometimes, either immediately following the end of the make-believe play or shortly thereafter, Helen would roll on the floor, clapping. She would sing in an exaggerated voice, making accompanying gestures and frolicking about. The dancing and singing often caricatured adult song-and-dance routines and sexually provocative gestures. The child would lift up her skirt (she often wore one over her long pants, for playing), attempt to engage me in more tests of physical courage such as judo or sword fighting, and do rough-and-tumble play to the accompaniment of much laughter and excited noise. This frenzied activity would at times be punctuated by comments like, "It's so fun!" or "Ooh! I love it."

At other times, Helen would celebrate her play by more quiet behavior, such as insisting on sitting in my lap while listening to a replay of the taped drama and quietly giggling or commenting evaluatively on her performance. On occasion, she also engaged in a range of intimate behaviors with herself—like sniffing her toes—and did so as if I were not there. Having had the opportunity to observe carefully three young children aged five, six, and seven, subsequent to my work with Helen, I had noticed a similar pattern of behavior in them. When involved in excited or engrossing activity of an imaginative nature, like watching a television drama or listening to a story being read, these children seemed lost in private worlds as they touched themselves in private and intimate ways, quite oblivious of my presence. (These studies will be included in a book on play and gender which I am currently writing.) The behavior seemed a corroboration of the pleasure and flow of positive feeling and energy that the play had generated.

The last stage, taking leave, whether it involved getting Helen ready for bed or accompanying her down the stairs, was always done quietly and slowly. Helen was loath to see the sessions end, and her reentry into the everyday world of her family and home was made reticently and with requests to set as early a date as possible for our next meeting. Although I only witnessed two sessions where Helen played with her close friend, Jill, I noticed that, at the end of these, too, she was loath to let Jill go and anxious to anticipate the next meeting for play with her. In all, Helen played hard and loved it. Like all good players, she lived for the excitement and passion that her play life gave her.

BEHAVIORAL COMPONENTS

Helen drew on her best capabilities in order to play the way she did, and brought together several components of behavior which may be described as follows:

- Expressive—her use of singing, dancing, and the taking on of dramatic and grotesque roles
- Instrumental—her use of her play (a) to construct a desired identity and set of relationships for herself and a world that was secret and special, (b) to persuade me to share these worlds with her, and (c) to communicate several symbolic meanings to herself and her partner.
- Symbolic—her use of her personal and inner agenda, including her struggles with her lack of power, good and evil, her sexuality, her peers, and her parents
- Coordinative—her coordination—with, I might add, sense of mastery—of her thoughts and actions in playing out stories that were long and complicated, both verbally and ideationally
- Social developmental—her competent management of the scripts and their planning, direction, enactment, transformation, and evaluation

Helen had learned that the means and goals of her play were always controlled by the players and that she was the arbiter of her own imagination as she engaged in play. She had also learned that play is a special kind of medium for packaging life's contradictions, for ordering confusion, and for destroying and transforming patterns and realities that are disliked; and, moreover, for doing so with a spirit of involvement, happy abandon, madness, and festival. The materials she used in shaping her imaginary worlds were provided by the culture and motivated by her inner conflicts and agenda. She also had a sense of the spirit of play, one that was in keeping with the negative cultural status that play holds in our society. Therefore, her play was often irrational, exuberant, combative, unbridled, and grotesque in its moments of intense passion. But at all times, she knew that her play was at once symbolic of various phenomena and yet real, thus clearly exemplifying the double negative that lies at the heart of this communicative and expressive behavior (Bateson, 1955, 1956a).

Helen understood the ways in which play allows one to deal with gross emotions, with caricatured oversimplifications, and with disorderly outcomes. She had learned that the unspeakable and undoable could indeed be expressed in play because the communication could always be denied as being not literally true. Thus, she knew that the power of the communication lay in its metaphoric thrust. By using the frame of play, Helen was able to operate a mediational system which, by its paradoxical nature, conveyed meanings that everyday uses of language disallow; she was able to link the normative and the non-normative, the tolerable and the intolerable meanings in the culture. Protectively framed as play, these meanings entered the everyday arena as masked phenomena. She generated a fantasy world of super-heroes in which she was the heroine. Undaunted, there she did battle with the giants who stalked her own inner world, perfectly disguised as the archetypal villains and powers of the mythic worlds to which we socialize the young.

Finally, through her dramatic play, she gained sufficient confidence and mastery over these personal struggles to be able to express them directly and acknowledge them as part of her life. In these sessions with Helen lies the evidence that play is a passageway to trust and intimacy, a power that should not be lightly dismissed.

8 Implications Drawn from the Study

As with many research endeavors, the implications of this work were not immediately obvious. Much of what is suggested became clear only as the data was combed over a period of years. What emerged at first was an understanding of the larger gestalt, which then gradually led to the etching of finer and more precise detail. What follows tends to reflect a similar pattern in which the reader is offered implications that are both broad and highly specific.

Many aspects of the study, like methodology, the environment, adult-child interactions, child play, and children's needs and competencies, are highlighted as warranting comment. However, what permeates all these aspects and emerges as being of crucial importance is the relationship between researcher and informant. The relationship emerges and is considered as a locus for understanding the course of events described in the preceding sections. Further, it is seen to facilitate, hinder, and shape the data in several ways. Although always focused in terms of the present case, it has wider implications for childhood culture, education, research, and play studies as the following sections demonstrate.

METHODOLOGY

Some of the more striking aspects of this work are methodological; they pertain to the actual "doing" of the study and its reconstruction for presentation to another. Four features of the study bearing a methodological hue can be singled out as noteworthy.

First, as far as is known, this is the only example in the literature to date of an intensive case study of the play of a "normal" child in a "naturalistic" setting in which the play developments, relationships, and contexts are made explicit. All prior case studies, such as the work of Axline (1964), Erikson (1963), and others, have been presented schematically in terms of these authors' theoretical preconceptions and, in addition, have been treatment oriented. In contrast, the theoretical biases of the present study have required a fuller explication of the play process and a laying out of the details pertaining to each play session, as was done in Part II. Such detail enables one to examine the claims that are being made here or elsewhere about play relationships. It provides carefully contexted examples of play for use by students in their discussions and explorations of play.

Second, it is also perhaps the first work in the literature on children's play to stress that the story must be told in its entirety, trivia and all, so that the reader might get a sense of the life of the relationship and the environment set up in the play event. Thus, in constructing my report of these encounters, I have emphasized my perceptions of feelings, the evidence that there were repeated encounters where "real" exchanges between informant and researcher took place, the fact that I was an active participant, and the problem of reciprocity. My decision to stress these aspects flows, I believe, from my own socialization as a woman, which includes not simply a female identification, but personality and family attributes as well. All of these were brought to the research situation.

Third, it is important to this research that I played the role of an active participant with my subject, thus contributing to an ongoing and strong relationship between us. Cottrell (1942), Wax (1952), and Whyte (1955), among others, have argued that changing from a researcher to a more directly involved participant is not a liability but an asset. Their experience was that it improved their fieldwork. In this study, my direct participation in the event became crucial to shaping and therefore understanding the behavior that unfolded between Helen and me. Although this is not the first time in which an adult has actively engaged with a child as part of a research project—as the work of Smilansky (1968), Rubin (1980), Rubin and Pepler (1980), and countless play therapists including Erikson (1963) suggests—nevertheless, there are differences between these other instances and this study. In the others, the adults have either set out to model play behavior explicitly for their subjects in experimental situations and thereby to influence their ideas and actions (Gardner, 1971; Smilansky, 1968), or they have only participated intermittently (Schaffer, 1977). In this case, as researcher, I was intent on the child setting the tone, pace, and agenda for the activities and interactions. Therefore, rather than modeling or activating plots or actions, as some teachers or researchers would, I was instead reactive to Helen's play and fantasy behavior. The child was at least an equal if not the more powerful participant in the play situation;

it was her world that was valued and brought into play, rather than a world selected and initiated by the researcher.

I am not suggesting that my behavior did not affect Helen or the situation. As noted in an earlier chapter, it undoubtedly did, just as the child's influenced mine, creating a context for reciprocal learning, as the narrative of each play session has demonstrated. As the work of Goffman (1959, 1961) has shown, linguistic, gestural, and other borrowing is inevitable when two people are motivated to relate to each other. In fact, one of the major tenets shaping the study is a belief in the primacy of human relationships as the location for understanding particular talk or storytelling. Play is thus perceived as a relational matter and endemic to the contours and textures that are brought to the relationship. Indeed, the play develops as a result of it.

Fourth, a concern for the researcher's ontology differentiates this study methodologically from prior studies in which adults have interacted with children in play. That is to say, I have attempted to account for my way of being in the world—with its history, beliefs, and biases—and for how "who I am" became an aspect of the situation I was studying.

In a long-term and active relationship such as the present case, discounting the presence of the researcher would make it difficult to understand important shifts in the situation. Agar (1980) argues that many aspects of who a researcher is deserve careful thought and raise problems for all social scientists. He suggests that the problem is not *whether* the researcher is biased but, rather, *what kinds* of biases exist. We need to consider how they enter into our research projects and how their operation can be documented. Agar sees the necessity of dealing with these issues as part of methodology and advocates acknowledging these when drawing conclusions. This aspect of methodology is as yet a great unknown, even in ethnographic work, where it is readily seen as important and has been discussed by some (e.g., Powdermaker, 1967) in reconstituting the narrative of the relationship. Nevertheless, I have made some small attempts to appreciate aspects of myself as being contributing factors in the study.

Dealing with this was complicated. It was difficult to know how such material might be relevantly integrated into methodological and interpretive discussions, but I decided to include in Chapter 3 some of the cultural, professional, and personal influences that, as researcher, I brought to the study. I have also allowed the reader some sense of me as an active participant in all phases of the relationship and its narrative reconstitution.

What I wish to emphasize is that the relationship that developed was not inevitable simply because it was a play relationship, just as an educational relationship between teacher and child does not inevitably lead to successful learning. Rather, it became what it was because of the prime ecological conditions in which it took place. That is to say, it developed because it was of the participants' choosing; because they knew how to play and valued the same modes of play; because they manifested a certain verbal facility and flexibility of spirit; and because both parties brought shared personal biases, communal biases, and reciprocal needs to the situation. In these circumstances, what developed was a relationship of growing trust between a highly imaginative, lonely, and vulnerable little girl and an imaginative, flexible, and intuitive adult, the latter isolated from her native culture and its supports and personally committed to the understanding of childhood—both that of others and her own. That we save others in order to save ourselves is not an unusual notion; however, it is rarely acknowledged and made explicit in the writing of most social scientists, especially those studying childhood. Not surprisingly, feminist anthropological writing has increasingly been calling attention to this notion and to the place of the participating and observing self in research. The present study shares more in common with such work than with the usual accounts of childhood play. (See Cesara, 1982, and Golde, 1986, for similar points of view.)

In short, as far as is known, this study is one of the first accounts of childhood play that advocates and illustrates how researchers may enter into long-term, reciprocal relationships with child informants; which takes the home as the location for fieldwork on play; which puts down as much detail as possible, however chaotic, minute, and incoherent in order to tell as much of the story as possible; and which acknowledges the self and attempts to write descriptively about it as a tool of importance in accomplishing research goals and understanding that occurred in the research situation. It is in keeping with the change that has been taking place in some quarters of the social sciences during the past two decades, which has involved a shift toward greater acceptance of subjectivity and of the intercultural, cultural, and psychic dynamics set up between researcher and informants; and the recognition of researchers as reflective, sensitive human beings who struggle with ambivalent feelings, experience difficulties, and face pitfalls (Golde, 1986; Ruby, 1982).

ENVIRONMENT

The findings of this study support the view that a play space of the child's choosing, used with the cooperation and—in this instance—the participation of an accepting adult, is a setting that facilitates play.

Further, both seclusion and collusion on the part of the players against the outside world—parents, in this case—were essential to the ecological context for the play transformations that took place. This is in keeping with other descriptions of play as a secretive and private phenomenon (e.g., Huizinga, 1958) and the play diaries of many who mention playing in secret and private spaces (e.g., Mergen, 1982). The complexity of the transformations that took place in this case was supported by the private setting, the long-term relationship in which repeated encounters with the same play partner were possible, the history and familiarity that evolved between the players as a consequence, and the relatively lengthy and uninterrupted sessions the players had. Such factors are missing in the majority of play studies undertaken in public settings like nursery schools, playgrounds, laboratory settings, and homes, in which the play is observed as part of the flow of other daily activity and its attendant interruptions from the outside world.

However, psychotherapy with children, as well as the Singers' (Singer, 1973; Singer & Singer, 1981) work on make-believe play, illustrate that the manifestation of play in children, as with other primates (see Fagen, 1980), is associated with a protected and interpersonal setting. Further, a context of felt security and time and space apart from other people and reality situations have been noted to nurture all manner of meaningful interpersonal relations, including play (Betcher, 1981). In addition to these ecological variables, the existence of a protected milieu, in an existential sense, has also been noted to be facilitative of play. This existential location has been variously described as "the potential space" (Winnicott, 1974), a *spielraum* (Erikson, 1963), and a "field of play" (Sadler, 1966). In the present study, I, as researcher, together with the ecological conditions in which the event functioned, worked to set up such a milieu for play.

There are quite profound implications of all this for supporting children's own friendship groups, for providing some secluded areas for play, and for facilitating play as part of close relationships, both between children and between children and adults. Unfortunately, the tendency in our culture to emphasize playground and playgroup play and for tutored play (which is often linked to other valued behavior such as language of mathematics) ignores the possibilities for the rapid and extensive growth that occurred on the part of the child in this highly intensive, participatory study. (See Vygotsky's zone of "proximal development," 1967, 1978.)

The study also supports the claim that children themselves have a clear sense of the ecological conditions most suited to their various play endeavors. Helen clearly had a sense of this, as the narrative suggests. She established her bedroom and at times the bathroom as being her own spaces and ones in which she really came into her own. It was in these places that she usually played, and they were protected from the outside world: her parents, her less special friends, and other visitors. Helen also had a sense of the importance of time in relation to the play activity. For instance, when in doubt about how long I would spend with her, she first verified that there would be sufficient time to play before embarking on our joint story and play activities. Sessions 6 and 8 illustrate this clearly. My subsequent work with a group of three children aged five, six, and seven had also corroborated this point about children's interest and awareness about how much time they have available for play.

In short, not only were time and space important to me, from a methodological point of view, but they were also of concern to the child, as part of her staging. It is therefore reasonable to believe that the innovation and higher levels of ideational transformation apparent in Helen's stories and play were supported by the environmental conditions under which the expressive behavior occurred. This point is of significance to the many adults who control the times and conditions for children's play and often set them arbitrarily and with little sense of what children need in order to engage in play of an involved, intense, and rewarding nature.

Another point of note relates to the paucity of play studies in the home. The study of home- and yard-based fantasies and play of children is one of the most neglected areas of children's folklore, education, and psychology. This is particularly ironic in light of the increasing centrality of the home in the play life of the child as opposed to the playground or the street of earlier times. As far as children are concerned, the important point is perhaps that the home puts a boundary between them and the public world and thus creates the possibility of a domain of secrecy and in some instances safety. Most often, in their homes, they are sheltered and safe from the demands of the outside world, so that their own feelings and desires are interfered with less. In their homes, however, they also run the risk of close parental supervision and scrutiny, thus, their needs for retreat, secrecy, and privacy often become crucial conditions for rewarding play in the home and the adjacent yard. In part, they can secrete themselves in their elaborately decorated bedrooms or garages (you might recall that seven-year-old Helen's bedroom wall was filled with posters of various superheroes), but a great part of their privacy they must achieve by means of their own fantasy play. In their homes, their peers will not scoff at their fantasy play and most often their parents will be hard put to interpret or pay any attention to it. Thus, the home is a significant setting and context for the construction of fantasy and play. If we care to admit it, it is clear from the literature and our own experiences as players that these functions of safety and secrecy have been served for hundreds of years in the homes of those children who had the space and time for play, particularly in families of small size and in conditions of relative noninterference (see Mergen, 1982).

RELATIONSHIPS

The relationship between the players was a crucial part of the context for the play that occurred over the course of the year during which Helen and I played together. As I have noted elsewhere (Kelly-Byrne, 1984b), context is not a difficult notion. We look to context in our efforts to understand the meaning of texts describing human behavior. Without context, such descriptions stand in isolation, as incomplete entities. Context is what molds, frames, and brings them to life. It does not stand outside the linguistic or semantic process of communication. It is part of the ever-shifting linguistic process of reasoning and is very much in the minds of the actors. It is part of the total message from within an ongoing interactive situation; it is created by and is part of the meaning of the event. Context includes premises, evaluations, associations, biographical factors, ecological factors, and intentions and rules about the behavior in which the participants are involved. Therefore, the course of a relationship between players affects and is part of the context, which in turn may alter or modify the shape and meaning of the play. As the narrative has shown, not only did the setting and relationship support Helen's play, but, in turn, her play with me affected our relationship, making it more frank and intimate.

There were several significant features that marked the relationship between Helen and me. As is inevitably the case with adult/child relationships, it was asymmetrical. That is to say, although I did not play the roles that most adults Helen knew usually played, neither was I a child or a peer. It was a judicious partnership within which I played willingly and confidently with Helen, although I rarely abandoned myself to the play world as Helen did. As an adult participant, I was constantly vigilant and reflective in observing the details of the child's play. Thus, even as I was playing the role of a baby or child and engaging in regressed activity as freely as Helen was, I also had a set of controls as a reflective adult.

Further, in the everyday world of caretaking, Helen knew that I was in charge. Although I was respectful of her needs and motivated to understand the world from her point of view, I had the ultimate safety of control and power on my side. In fact, although we as adults wield this power differentially, ultimately, it is our defense. It is important to stress the ways that I was empowered by dint of my adulthood. Although children expect the adults around them to be in control of most day-to-day matters, it is easy for us to abuse this power that is so easily ours. Neither the relationship that was set up between Helen and me nor any others that adults set up in relation to children should be idealized. Rather, we need to be explicit about the nature of the range of relationships that can be initiated between adults and children and attempt to understand the factors that motivate them and contribute to their effectiveness or lack of it. Otherwise, we shall continue to nod liberally about the importance of making good relationships with children, with little sense of what these are like.

Helen was aware of my power as an adult. She tended to defer to it in our everyday relationship, although she was openly frustrated by the lack of control she felt in seeing me as often as she desired. Her view of adulthood posited power as a pivotal point and included access to wisdom, knowledge, beauty, sexuality, and a moral sense. She felt she had little access to any of these aspects of adulthood. Her desired worlds, as created in play, inverted this everyday reality to include herself as a super and godly being, invested with all these qualities and successfully in control of all situations. Her use of play for dealing with her own experience and desire for adulthood thus involved inverting and thereby controlling the relationships she set up in play with a real adult.

As an adult, in playing the way I did, I precipitated a new and desired paradigm for the child. For Helen, this was the appeal of the relationship: Instead of adopting secretive, masked, or caricatured symbolizations of childhood, as adults often do by adopting the role of a clown, a condescending figure, or a saccharin mother type, I was intent on making an authentic relationship with Helen, on her terms and in her play world. It is then interesting to note that she cast me in none of these common roles or any others adults play in setting up stereotypic and static relationships to childhood. In this case, setting up an authentic relationship meant taking Helen and her agenda seriously and playing with her in a way that she initiated. Doing this for extended periods of time, routinely and in a manner that focused on her, made the relationship exciting, special, and irresistible to Helen. Looking at our relationship from her point of view, she played with an adult who legitimized her worlds, who was accepting of her behavior in all its variety, and who gave her the safety to express herself in a manner that most adults in the everyday world generally reject. Thus, in play, she was able to transform some of the asymmetricalities she felt in regard to the adult world with which she had to deal in the everyday realm.

It was not only that I was willing to play with Helen on her own terms that lent her some sense of redressing the imbalance of adult power; in addition, Helen actively sought to deal with my power as a playmate. One of the first moves she made in dealing with me was to limit my power by controlling most of the moves between us. In session 1 she set herself up as a literate, socially competent, and rule-making individual who set the agenda and pace for our meetings. Further, in the play worlds, she limited my power by giving me negative and less powerful roles, for example, a criminal, a bad mother, Satan, a plain old girl, and an abandoned baby. At the same time, she was omniscient and omnipotent as she played the roles of arbiter, producer, director, actor, and co-actor, and often the role of audience as well.

This bid to control situations is usual with young children in their play with others; however, such bids do not remain uncontested by their peers. In fact, the play of children is marked by incessant negotiation and power plays that often end in deadlock. In contrast, in our play, while Helen was power seeking, I was willing to be subservient to most of her whims.

Helen's moves to limit my power and accord it to herself are revealing of the generally powerless condition of children vis-à-vis adults. For instance, Helen's desire for power in play is not so unusual when one considers that, after all, children are in play worlds at least in part because it is to such worlds that we as adults have relegated them. Since children lack all forms of power—physical, sexual, economic, and political—we locate them in worlds in which they can play at such things as part of their socialization but in ways that have no consequences in the everyday world, as is our intention. As adults, we are invested in giving children a currency that is only make-believe, and we thus socialize them early to the forms of play and fantasy. This trivializing of children's worlds, and as such their play, is part of the discontinuity that we maintain between adulthood and childhood. It also points to the ambivalence that characterizes the various relationships we set up to the category of childhood. (Both of these points are discussed further in Chapter 9; also see Kelly-Byrne, 1984a, 1986a.)

To return to Helen's relationship with me, in addition to aggrandizing herself and diminishing me, she sought to make connections with the child in me, thus holding my adulthood in abeyance. In play, she had access to this child as she enacted and celebrated her imaginary worlds. In so doing, Helen penetrated many of the well-established barriers that exist between children and adults and also gave vent to the regressed and perverse aspects of her life that adults usually deny and control. The opportunity that Helen had of relating to an adult in such terms gave her a sense of the nurturing and meaningful ways in which relationships with adults can be made, despite the asymmetricalities that reside in the liaison.

Changes in the Relationship During the Study

The course of the relationship between Helen and me also illustrates how the initial pattern of control and omniscience that Helen asserted changed as the play progressed. These changes were evident in the ways in which the child cast herself, her plots, her concerns, and her play partner. A summary of these changes over the three phases of the relationship follows.

Initially, power was taken to mean the domination of all points of choice (Sessions 1–5). Helen used my willingness in play to relinquish my adult power as her go-ahead for pursuing her own self-assurance, freedom, and competence with respect to wisdom, beauty, and power. These were all facets of her root metaphor and desired identity, but she had little grasp of or certainty about them.

In the second phase of the relationship (Sessions 6–9), Helen sought to relinquish some of this power and venture more of her own everyday feelings about her state and needs. She did this by transforming my prior evil and low-status identity, recreating me as a good mother. In this way, she also allowed herself to be a new subordinate. In fact, as the play sessions progressed, Helen more and more allowed herself to be a baby with me, illustrating Bateson's (1956) point that, in play, we enact the opposite of what we mean in order to mean the opposite of what we enact. Thus, Helen began by enacting power roles to mean the opposite of this—powerlessness—which is the way she felt about herself. This powerlessness was more directly expressed in the second phase, even though it was masked by her drawing her baby character as a superbaby. Further, in the play phases, she also allowed me increasing participation and choice, thereby suggesting her increasing ability to deal with uncertainty in that situation.

Concomitant with her increasing flexibility and openness was her decreasing rigidity in drawing and maintaining distinctions between her presentation of self in play and the reality of who she was in the everyday world. In fact, by the third phase of the relationship, she was able to acknowledge that her play concerns were the same as her everyday concerns. Session 9 marked a point at which Helen's play replicated the substance of her everyday concerns rather than reversing them, as had been the case in the earlier sessions. Further, in the third phase, distinctions between the various stages and activities that made up her play were less rigidly drawn and often blurred. Sessions 11 through 13 were more readily given to discussions and conversation about personal matters than to enacting a play on them. In this final phase, I had been transformed into a confidante of her interest in sexuality and other personal concerns and played a role more akin to a buddy than a mother.

In short, the relationship moved from mainly controlled, closed, and indirect structuring of the child's symbolic motives to a direct dramatization of these, to a more shared plotting and staging, and finally to a more candid and personal discussion and enactment of matters that hitherto had only been symbolized. Personal sharing and intimacy thus increased as the participants shifted their shared, accepted staging and plots into forms that were progressively more frank and directly revealing of inner concerns. This finding has many implications for those who work in classrooms, homes, or elsewhere with children and wish to work successfully with them. The point is that children are cautious. They let down their guard only after the preliminary politics of the situation have been sorted out and they have tested the adults attempting to make authentic relationships with them. Only then, it seems, do we get past official competence to areas of risk taking and venturing into novel forms, personal concerns, and bonding.

In demonstrating such a relationship between Helen and me, it must also be admitted that the relationships within Helen's play world (a microsphere) mirrored in their own way those in the everyday world (the macrosphere). It has already been suggested that, in her allegorical dramatic play, Helen was reproducing while reversing many elements from her relationship with her parents. Indeed, a psychodynamic analysis could be made of her story, in an attempt to reveal the "real," unconscious meanings of the play. Such an analysis no doubt would claim to shed light on the deeper layers of her relationship with her parents; however, it would require firsthand information about the family and their private lives, as well as a considerable degree of specialized training in interpreting the unconscious symbolism in children's play. I feel that any such attempt is ill advised because there are insufficient data and no opportunity to confirm the interpretations. The process would yield little more than hunches and, further, would impinge on the privacy of the family.

I can, however, make the more general point that arises out of an observation of the changes in Helen's play and her relationship with me. This is that Helen's story illustrates the way in which play not only mirrors everyday relationships and thus implies the character of the everyday realm (Williams, 1982), but also, through its own unique relationships (Helen and myself), constitutes a new society, different from the larger and more powerful society of which it is a part. At critical junctures in the lives of the members of this novel microsociety or play partnership, their play can induce significant personal transformations. This is evidenced in the growth Helen experienced as a result of our play. Such changes are generally envisaged and provided for by the larger culture in the form of peer societies, best friends, and other such structures. At their best, these provide close and meaningful relationships which support antithetical structures and help their members deal with all manner of burgeoning interests in children.

My Pattern of Relating to Helen

Now I wish to consider the details and overall characteristics in my pattern of relating to Helen. I believe that several of my personality traits were brought to bear in seeking to build a relationship with this child so that I could understand her play and learn to see and experience the phenomenon of play to some extent the way she did.

I knew that working with children was hard work. Prior experiences of observing the play of children in London nursery schools, kindergartens, and primary schools had left me with few illusions about what the task would minimally require, which was the ability to tolerate confusion, frustration, and even resentment toward some children. This was not always easy, but it was put in relief by the other marvelous facets of life experienced by setting up relationships with children. I like many children. I find most of them able to engage my interest in some way or another, although there are clearly individuals who I find distinctly appealing as well as unappealing. In the latter case, I had had to strive hard to work out my responses and push past them, not always successfully. Helen, however, was one to whom I was drawn, despite her ability to engender some frustration and anger in me. I found myself growing to love her spirit, which was feisty, funny, and so lonely. Thus, I found myself looking forward to being with her, when I did not feel burdened by the tacit demands of the relationship with her parents as well as with her.

Many who work intensively with children have their time tightly structured and bounded. Such is not the case for anthropologists who are in the field twenty-four hours a day and for others who might be participants in an open-ended situation akin to the one I set up with Helen. In such instances, one has to work as a whole person in a highly personal way that is very draining emotionally. When one's informants are children, the situation becomes extremely taxing and psychologically expensive because of the need to project oneself into the child's position and use the child's modes of interaction, which often requires regression (see Mead, in Golde, 1986).

It is difficult to talk knowledgeably about the phenomenon of projecting oneself in to the child's position. The human elements involved in this process are tremendously complex, and there is as yet much to be learned about the mechanics and psychodynamics of the process (see Gardner, 1986). I found that, for me, remaining highly conscious of my own childhood and of memories from it was very useful in helping me to make a relationship with Helen. I was able to offer her details from my childhood—such as when we shared the secret language that my sister and I had used as children—which not only engendered trust but also let her know that I knew about being a little girl. My own childhood often became the touchstone by which I could understand and empathize with much of what Helen did. I also found this to be the case when I worked with children in London and when I worked as a teacher and researcher with young adolescent girls in Australia. In this last case, a sense of my own adolescence was crucial as a comparison for the experiences and observations I had with several groups of thirteen- and fourteen-year-olds. This striving to see and feel the way Helen did in no way meant agreeing with her; it simply meant being able to let her know that I was able to a large extent to stand in her shoes.

Another personal trait that I found was part of my relationship with Helen was the ability to become excited when watching her play and even later when contemplating it and talking about it with other adults. Helen confirmed my sense that children are fun loving and hedonistic, except in instances where they are very sick physically and mentally (see Gardner, 1986). Like other young children I have known, Helen had a zany sense of humor, a wonderful sense of happy abandon, and the ability to caricature and parody aspects of life. I found myself delighting in this revelry and have throughout the body of the story of our relationship referred to this aspect of her expressive behavior as the festival stage of play. My ability to also be a bit of a "ham," make weird noises, speak nonsense languages, fly, and get down on the floor with ease in moments of regression mirrored the child's behavior and contributed to the *folie à deux*.

This ability to become and facilitate a sense of excitement when working with children is also related to another characteristic that marked my pattern of relating to Helen. I often experienced a feeling of "inner warmth" (Gardner, 1986) when with her. The narrative illustrates examples of such moments, but I know that the ability to feel this way works to communicate a spirit of acceptance of the child, which is experienced by the child very positively. Helen clearly knew that I liked her and accepted her, by my openness with her despite the moments of conflict in our relationship.

My patterns of relating were also marked by a strong parental instinct. This may be described as having children invoke feelings of guardianship and caring for them in you. By the very nature of the early baby-sitting arrangement set up between Helen's parents and me, it was inevitable that I would be involved with feeding, touching, and protecting Helen in the fray of everyday caretaking rituals. Although Mead (in Golde, 1986) warns against becoming involved in research relationships modeled after a primary relationship, I believe that it is difficult to avoid this when dealing with young children in a personal relationship. As with all these patterns of relating, it is a matter of knowing where to draw the line and being able to perceive when any given pattern of relating is causing difficulty. My experience with Helen made me conscious that, in a home situation especially, I had to be very careful not to threaten or antagonize her parents by being seen to usurp their roles or by not deferring to them in all matters that pertained to decision making concerning Helen outside the play world.

Further, being able to be flexible and quick on my feet were both characteristics that I relied on. The demands of working with young children call for an ability to be adaptable to the child's needs, often at a moment's notice. It requires the ability to change course in midstream and follow the direction of the child's play or thought. This occurred on several occasions, as Sessions 3 and 5 illustrate. This flexibility was also useful to me when I faced frustration in dealing with Helen's play, which was often archaic, iconic, and schematic in nature. Playing with children or working closely with them forces the adult to deal with a much larger number of possibilities and unknowns in a given situation. As was the case with Helen, children change tack easily, interrupt the flow of events, become restless, and do not tolerate boredom or the promise of future rewards; thus they require a large measure of investment of energy and concentration. It should be clear from this that not everyone who wishes to work with children can do so.

I also found that I needed to be able to feel as comfortable as possible with a sense of failure or with having said or done what I perceived to be the wrong thing. In such close relationships it is impossible not to feel obligation to one's informants and guilt at sensing their displeasure. I worked hard to reassure myself that the relationship was reciprocal in nature and that much of what Helen felt I misunderstood about her was related to her idealization of me and some of her own projected identification. However, this is not to deny that I could have set up a more structured play schedule in terms of time and frequency and also prepared the child better for the long breaks that occurred after Sessions 5 and 11 and eventually for the demise of the play relationship after Session 14. Such preparation would have facilitated the child's acceptance of the reality of the research situation, with its own limitations. It certainly would have helped protect Helen from the feelings of disappointment and loss that she experienced at these times.

These comments, of course, are made with hindsight. The fact of the matter is that the study was undertaken at a particular historical moment when there was little that had been written and was readily available about adult/child research relationships by which I could have been guided. In retrospect, I see that some of this information would have been available to trainees in child psychotherapy, but, at the beginning of my study, there was no way to have known that I would have encountered the obstacles I did. Thus, to have prepared myself by undergoing specialist training in child psychotherapy would have been unlikely, especially as the study was never conceived in such terms.

Training aside, however, I believe that many of the personality and behavior characteristics that I used in my relationship with Helen helped establish the positive and trusting working alliance that we had. This facilitated her play and my participation in her world, thereby allowing me access to it. Indeed, it was also these characteristics that, together with the play they supported, enabled an intimacy between us which brought us closer together.

Conclusion

It is possible to say that the changes in Helen were a result of her play and the course it ran within a supportive and positive relationship with me. It is also possible to draw several conclusions about what I learned about playing with children and about setting up meaningful relationships with them. These points will be enumerated at the end of the chapter. In addition, it must be said that, although the study pertains specifically to play and a relationship set up for this, similarities may be drawn between what occurred between Helen and me and what often occurs in relationships with good teachers, parents, or therapists. To date, little work has been done in our attempts to understand the details of successful relationships with children, although studies like this suggest that it behooves us to pay more attention to the phenomenon as an important variable in research, educational, therapeutic, or parental encounters.

NEEDS AND COMPETENCIES OF YOUNG CHILDREN

The study of Helen and her relationship and play with me supports the following claims about young children's competencies and needs. Adults who acknowledge these will be in a better position to help children to function at their highest levels.

1. Children have their own agendas and modes for operating.
2. They are eager to share these with adults.
3. They are capable of teaching adults their systems, if the adults are open to seeing things from a child's point of view.
4. Children initiate, plan, direct, perform, and evaluate their own activities.
5. They make distinctions among various levels of reality.
6. As such, they are highly competent metacommunicators about creating, managing, and interpreting contexts for an array of their own behavior.
7. They use whatever forms and modes of operating they know of to shape and orchestrate their creations. They initiate, schematize, blur, and transform scripts and genres in the service of their goals.
8. They need the opportunity and freedom to explore and use antithetical structures and material as an important means of gaining a sense of mastery of the conventions and limits in their worlds, as well as of initiating new forms.
9. They need outlines or scaffolding on which they can elaborate their stories, which suggests that they need a familiarity with cultural forms.
10. They need room to break out of and reframe their activities; to be serious and goofy, hardworking and celebratory. Being locked into tight frames can be counterproductive to their best efforts.
11. They need encouragement and support for their storying efforts, as well as a process for meaningful evaluation, of which they are a part.
12. They need continuity of setting, activity, and relationship to experience the comfort, familiarity, and focus that facilitate creative effort.

13. They need support at working in a mode in which they feel comfortable and competent and in which they can experience the gratification of mastery and success.
14. They have their own rhythms and patterns for producing their best performances.
15. They cannot play or perform creatively under emotional stress.
16. They need to be heard in the polymorphous and sometimes perverse voices in which they speak.

The preceding points have important implications when considered alongside the many adult-centered ways in which adults work with children in various settings. The conditions and relationship that Helen set up for her own best performances need to be acknowledged as having significance for those interested in supporting children's best and most powerful efforts at play and expressive performances of various kinds, despite the challenge they may pose to many adults who take their own omniscience and omnipotence for granted.

As a final point, the study raises many implications for those working with children as informants, whether they be researchers or others. The kinds of needs that must be met for children if they are to be given a "fair go" may challenge many of the conditions under which we expect children to give of themselves for the accomplishing of our adult purposes.

PLAYING WITH CHILDREN: A SUMMARY

In this section I want to summarize the points that have been made in this chapter and illustrated throughout the narrative, about the consequences, complications, attitudes, and aptitudes that come into being when adults seek to play with children.

1. Play for all who find themselves engaged in a play relationship leads to trust and a consequent revelation about the self that makes for intimacy. The portrait of this process is one of the major significances of this study.
2. It takes skill and sensitivity to handle carefully a situation in which children give adults their trust and venture to share their thoughts and feelings. This is because children are far more vulnerable and have much less power than their adult counterparts, despite the constant assertions about children's resilience. In all child/adult relationships, the adults may easily call all the shots.

3. In contrast to the adult view of play as trivial when compared to work, children's play is central to their lives. It is the behavior to which adults relegate them and the mediational system that the culture teaches them on many fronts. It is a system which, by its very paradoxical nature, enables children to explore and experience many aspects of the world from a "not-real-but-real" standpoint. Further, it allows them a category of behavior with which to respond to vagaries, confusions, contradictions, raging impulses, and grotesqueries, from a position of relative safety. I must quickly add, though, that such safety is not always guaranteed and that there are several examples of play in which the players get hurt (see Sutton-Smith, 1981b, on this point of cruel play).

4. Children want to be understood by adults and are delighted when given the opportunity to play with adults.

5. Playing in an authentic relationship with an adult offers a child a rare view of the adult, thus going beyond the boundaries typically seen in child/adult interactions where the adult is the all-seeing, all-knowing, omnipresent character. The gesture of playing with a child on the child's terms goes a long way toward fostering a positive relationship between young children and adults.

6. In playing with children, the adult has to be able to get into the child's reality. My first session with Helen vividly illustrates this point and many of the other points in this section.

7. Being able to get into the child's reality successfully makes the adult irresistible to the child. This often brings with it the problem of idealization of the adult and consequent expectations that cannot be met. Thus, it is important to be aware of this trap and not promise more than can be delivered.

8. Playing with children requires a sense of the time necessary for successfully engaging in the behavior. It also requires a sense of the location and circumstances under which children are motivated to play. It is not true that children can play anywhere, anytime, and under any conditions.

9. Adults who play with children also need an understanding of the stages of play to be gone through. Generally, children move from behavior that is more staged to that which is more spontaneous, and from that which is more guarded to that which is more revealing. These stages may occur within any one occasion as well as across time. Within a single session, it was possible to isolate five stages within Helen's play (see Chapter 7).

10. Playing with children requires certain personal attributes that cannot be taught in the classroom. In addition to possessing warmth and a sense of humor, an adult needs to be able to
    - Not take oneself too seriously
    - Access one's own childhood by memory
    - Tolerate and enjoy regressed behavior
    - Tolerate frustration
    - Understand language that is symbolic and arcane, gestures that are schematic, and thoughts that are only half uttered
    - "Shuttle" continuously between our adult reality and that of the child
    - Give up voluntarily the comfortable and well-known ways of dealing with reality and, instead, mentally and emotionally reach back to much earlier and, for the most part, renounced ways of dealing with the everyday world

11. Playing with children can be very hard work and entail a great deal of psychological expense. In addition, when one faces the anxieties of "collecting good data," the experience can become exhausting.

12. Playing with children also can be invigorating and give one a sense of exuberance, allowing many adults the pleasure of rekindling some of the best aspects of their own childhoods.

13. It also allows us access to a limitless creativity and spontaneity of action, which for many is rarely experienced in day-to-day adult life.

14. If we are open to our own feelings, playing with children may at times allow us to perceive some of the deficiencies in our own childhoods, bringing on a momentary sense of remorse for the amount of play and attendant sense of intimacy and love that were missed.

15. Children's play elicits childish feelings in the adult, which may be strongly positive or negative and in either case require a degree of modification. For instance, strongly positive feelings may lead one to become overly close to the child, entertain fantasies of rescuing the child, feel competitive with the child's parents, and become overly identified with the child's point of view in taking a position against other significant adults in the child's world. Strongly negative feelings may cause annoyance, which may lead to fantasies of retaliation or of being manipulated by the child. In turn, these may lead to having one's own self-esteem and perhaps even one's professional identity challenged.

16. Finally, playing with children brings the added danger of being tempted to play psychoanalyst, naïvely interpreting the "real"

meaning of the play, which is often inaccessible to those who do not have careful training in how to do this. This temptation occurs because children's play has long been treated as a projective device and much of the work and research in the area has been strongly linked to psychoanalytic and diagnostic models. Yielding to this temptation often distracts one from making sense of the play event in all its diversity.

It is imperative that those who advocate play, not only researchers but supervisors, teachers, curriculum writers, and various child-care workers, become aware of the phenomenon as it occurs in the everyday world of children and of children and adults, and not as an idealized and abstract notion. Working with children is hard work, and many adults who train others to engage with children would be advised to spend as much time on alerting trainees as to how to work with children in meaningful ways as they spend on the often-emphasized research procedures or learning theories. The self must be understood and utilized as part of one's research tools, and the realization that one cannot be all things to all people must be acknowledged. Each of us is a better or worse researcher or teacher or caretaker in different situations, and a recognition and understanding of this is crucial to setting up favorable relationships with the various communities of children around us.

In conclusion, it may be suggested that (1) a conscious acknowledgment of some of the difficulties of working with children; (2) an awareness of their needs, styles, and agenda; and (3) a clear sense of our adult ineptitudes, needs, Achilles' heels, and myopism may all have significant repercussions for the formation of children's culture at home and in school and other institutional settings. As we as adults consciously open ourselves to who we are in our relationships with children, the greater the promise of respecting the rights and lives of children and of redressing some of the lopsided exchanges and discontinuities between adulthood and childhood.

9 Theoretical Considerations of the Study

This chapter considers four theories of play that are supported by the study, thus informing the interpretive commentary offered throughout. In addition, Burke's theory of dramatistic action derived from the study of literature will be discussed as a frame in which to make sense of the data. These theories will be considered as tools for understanding something of what occurred in the play between Helen and me. Furthermore, a discussion of how the study comments on existing views of child play will be presented, arguing that while the data support some such views, they also question other widely held beliefs about children's play. It will be suggested that many of the gaps in the studies of play to date as well as distortions about play's lived character may be usefully reconsidered if adultcentric, sexist, and nonreflexive biases are acknowledged. The chapter ends in asking that the multiple voices of childhood be heard, acknowledged, and considered in the many practices and beliefs we perpetrate in the cause of productive child rearing and socialization.

PLAY THEORY

Helen's play, as presented in this book, can be discussed in relation to the existing research and theory on play. Because of the detail with which I have described the course of our relationship, it is possible to use the data as a single test of many play propositions to be found in the literature. The theories most pertinent to the study include the following: an interpersonal theory of play and relationships (see Sullivan, 1953b), a communications theory of play (Bateson, 1955, 1956, 1972; Bateson & Ruesch, 1951), a dialectical theory of play (Sutton-Smith, 1976 and 1978), and a psychoanalytic theory of play (Erikson, 1940, 1963; Freud, 1953). Further, although Kenneth Burke's dramastic theory applies to literary expression, it is seen as having relevance to play expression, given that both literature and play are cultural and expressive systems that are framed in relation to the everyday world in similar ways. In particular, what Burke calls rhetoric is the larger part of Bateson's communication theory of play; what Burke calls structure applies to structural theories of play (Bateson, 1972; Sutton-Smith, 1978); and what he calls symbolism applies to Freudian theories of play (Burke, 1965, 1966, 1969a, 1969b).

Interpersonal Theory: Play and Intimacy

The major thesis of this work is that mutual expression through social play leads to increased trust and intimacy in personal relationships and therefore leads to the more direct kinds of human development that such sharing of the self typically allows. In the first place, social play is an act of communication, not just a fantasy structure, and because in the course of such communication personal and private meanings are often shared, authentic relationships can develop.

Within an increasingly shared relationship, the study described in this book presents a tale of advancing intimacy. The data show that, after an initial period of scrutiny and trial, Helen began to share herself increasingly with me. Further, as a result of my acceptance of her sharing of herself, a much greater closeness, trust, risk taking, and intimacy developed. Helen came to treat me as a close friend, a maternal yet peerlike partner in her private worlds; hence comes one of the arguments of this work: That a sharing in play in supportive conditions creates intimacy.

The term *intimacy* derives from the Latin, *intimus*, or "most within." As McMahon (1982) has pointed out, intimacy has primary reference to those mental contents most sacred to the self. He writes, "Intimacy refers to those ideas or feelings, attitudes and beliefs, fears and hopes, and even the very modes of perception and processing of information . . . that are 'most within us'" (p. 295). McMahon notes further that different degrees of intimacy correspond to varying degrees of relatedness at an interpersonal level: "I consider relatedness to be that dimension of interaction that involves the revelation of intimacies" (p. 296).

Following McMahon, the present study regards intimacy as a relatedness between interactants that allows for the sharing of the "inner" self. I have argued that Helen's suggestion to me about "getting to know one another" and her subsequent behavior during our initial encounter implied the desire for a relatedness and sharing with me of those things "most within" her.

The details of this study suggest that play was the form of communication used by Helen to effect a relationship of an intimate order with me. The use of play for such ends by the child is not peculiar to this relationship. For instance, Garvey (1976) also suggests that the use of play to effect interpersonal interaction is characteristic of children's communication patterns. Further, Betcher (1981) writes, "Whatever its motivation, clinical and research observations suggest that the play of children is closely associated with interpersonal interaction and the development of important communication patterns" (p. 16).

In order to emphasize the patterns in Helen's behavior, I will briefly reiterate some relevant details of the study. As you may recall, Helen first used play as the medium for establishing a relationship whereby private concerns would be displayed. However, the play itself, as an act, was both medium and mask in this display. Once the relationship had been established largely through play, then private concerns were gradually displayed in conversation within the everyday realm, rather than through activities in the play realm. In fact, as the narrative suggests, the closer Helen got to transforming the purely social exchanges into the outright personal, the better able she was to display an increasing number of her private concerns not only in play but also more directly in conversation. It should be noted that her private concerns are quite typical of seven-year-olds in our culture. These children's preoccupation with power and mastery, with sexual matters, with the origin of the world and language, with their own origin, and with morality, all of which were Helen's concerns, have been discussed by scholars such as Piaget (1926, 1929, 1932, 1952), Sutton-Smith and Roberts (1964, 1970), Erikson (1963), Hartley and colleagues (Hartley, 1952; Hartley, Frank, & Goldenson, 1952), and Freud (1963). A more recent discussion of the seven-year-old is contained in Ames and Haber (1985).

Returning to Helen's direct display of her private concerns, the point is that, although children do share some of their private concerns with their peers, as Helen's relationship with her friend Jill demonstrates (see Sessions 10 and 12), they do not usually share such secrets with adults. In this case, it is striking that Helen was motivated by her confidence in me to introduce me to her friend and their shared private worlds. This was a gesture of further sharing and testing and marked a point at which Helen no longer needed the safety and distance of playing at her real concerns. At that point, she was able to acknowledge more openly her preoccupation with certain tabooed subjects such as sexual matters. With the transformation of a social and more guarded relationship into one of a more personal order, we arrived at a dedication of one human being to another and a context for intimacy. Within such a context, accountability to the everyday world and a proclivity to conformity diminished (see Turner, 1969, 1974, 1982). This is in no way to suggest that within a context of intimacy participants are free of all rules. On the contrary, as in the play world, participants have their own rules and conventions, which stand in a variety of relationships to the everyday world.

Another trend in Helen's behavior patterns was the fact that, with an increased sharing of her inner self with me, her managerial and strategizing aspects, which were quite evident in her earlier dealings with me, diminished and what emerged in their place was a growing concern with the closeness and flow of the relationship. In this state, Helen was more regressed, played the role of a baby, expressed herself in festivals of song and dance, intimated her affection for me, and in general was much more diffuse and spontaneous in her behavior. Further, actions and interactions that were particularly enjoyed were repeated and became ritualized. This was in contrast to her controlled and often taciturn frontstage behavior, both in public situations and during the early stages of her alliance with me.

Such qualities and developments in Helen's behavior were similar to those described by others in their exploration of intimacy among friends, lovers, and marriage partners (Betcher, 1981; McMahon, 1982). For example, Betcher (1981) claims that "intimate play is a spontaneous, mutual interplay in a dyadic relationship whose context and/or style tends to be idiosyncratic and is personally elaborated by the dyad" (p. 15). He goes on to suggest that such play may "enhance communication," develop bonds through "dyadic ritualization," and also "moderate conflict." He stresses that "its regressive character is adaptive" (p. 15).

Further, ritualized play formats, stereotyped and exaggerated gestures, role playing, silliness, provocativeness, and various other play modes that Helen used to communicate truths and traits of her innermost self have been observed by Erikson (1968, 1977) in the play of intimates. Moreover, the repetitive use of such expressive behavior and the sharing of rites of incorporation such as eating together have the effect of uniting people and creating a special bond, thus differentiating the relationship from others (Betcher, 1981; Levi-Strauss, 1966; Van Gennep, 1960). Helen's efforts at distinguishing her relationship with me, as her adult co-player, from others are evident in her concern for excluding her parents and her friends from our play relationship. This pattern was evident in Sessions 1 and 6 and supports the claim that the play sessions were occasions for intimacy. Not only does play produce intimacy, but, in turn, intimacy seems necessary for the development of the deeper levels of play and sharing.

This reciprocal relationship of play and intimacy can be seen in the work of Turner (1969, 1974, 1982). He was an anthropologist who saw society as inevitably in conflict, where the play world inverts the values that are to be found in the everyday world. (This is a notion that Freud asserted at an individual level.) Turner (1974) claimed that large classes of expressive behavior in several cultural groups symbolize in various antithetical ways some of the tensions generated by the normative culture. He argued that these symbolizations appeared to be ways of decreasing those tensions through the formation of new sets of collectivity or *communitas*, as he called them. Turner's views bear a resemblance to the findings of this study, although methodologically this case is very different from Turner's work. Turner was dealing with community conflicts, whereas Helen was dealing with developmental ones. Nevertheless, in both situations, the play led to greater social bonding.

It is worthwhile to speculate on the role of play and intimacy in the larger world beyond this example. One might argue, for example, following Turner, that one of the major functions of all socially expressive forms, including games and sports, is to increase shared group feelings or a sense of *communitas* (Turner, 1974). What sports audiences or sports players normally get out of their sports is closer relationships to others also involved with those sports. While these new forms of community might be quite superficial in many respects, in contrast to other areas of life they are often more abundant and more exciting. Without wishing to make too extended a claim, I will propose that, as play may create intimacy, so perhaps sports may create community.

A skeptic at this point might raise the query, however, as to whether the changes that occur in sports participants, or those that occurred in Helen, are "real" changes or merely the increasing revelation of things already present but not so obvious prior to this new play opportunity. Do we see merely a "warming-up" phenomenon involving freer expression of what was already there, or do we see new behavior? In the most superficial play relationships, the former is probably true. In deeper relationships developed over longer periods of time and involving more enduring friendships, it seems that novelty is likely. Thus, in Helen's case, the early symbolism of presexual matters appeared to be fundamentally different from the later symbolism (from Session 6) of sexual matters. Given that the later sexual interest was at first very indirectly expressed (Sessions 6-9), there is nothing logically to suggest they could not have been entered into the early play dramas if in fact the child was at that time capable of such expression. I am inclined, therefore, to say that the play relationship itself led to a fundamental transformation of the child's symbolic expression, rather than to say that the child had simply gained greater confidence in revealing what was already present.

Communications Theory: Play as Paradox

As discussed in Chapter 1, Bateson (1955, 1956a; Bateson & Ruesch, 1951) introduced a communication theory of play. He argued that play is a socially situated act which is communicated by the production of paradoxical statements about persons, objects, activities, and situations. The notion of play as paradox is itself a metaphor for conceptualizing play. Paradox is a literary term and draws attention to the "as if" quality within the play behavior. It suggests the apparent contradiction of something being at once real and not real, highlighting the character of play as embodying polarities. Thus, Helen at play was a wonder woman and not a wonder woman, at the same time. In fantasy she was a wonder woman and felt herself to be really so; however, in reality she was an ordinary child and knew this to be the case.

The paradoxical alteration of real and unreal creates a structure that makes play a fitting and appealing medium for negotiating a variety of purposes and communicating multiple meanings of a symbolic and often private nature. The inherent paradox allows the behavior to be taken back by the player if she fails to engage with her audience and execute her purposes. Because the player is not held accountable for her actions in terms of the everyday world, she may safely use this form of communication to venture, test, and further her involvement with another, as Helen did. This enables symbolic selves and worlds to be created and shared with safety, thereby giving rise to deepening levels of relatedness, as evident in this study (see Haley, 1955; Hern, 1969; Milner, 1952; Winnicott, 1971).

The making of choices about what is or is not play is as much part of the conceptual work of play as that which actually goes into the play frame. Thus, as was evident in the sessions described in this book, play is as much the activity of oscillating in and out of the negotiations, or the metacommunications, as it is the dramatic content that these negotiations allow. In other words, the framing and negotiation are part of the meta-language of play and are inseparable from its initiation and continuation. Helen's everyday activity, as well as her story planning and the story enactments that followed on each occasion, were all intrinsic to her play.

Thus, referring again to Bateson (1955), it follows that a theory of play as communication sees such behavior as a cognitive operation requiring a logical act of negation. It is concerned not only with the management of relationships but also the building of "paradigms" (Kuhn, 1970) whereby alternative worlds are envisaged. Regarding management, the theory suggests that play is an orientation for communication, a style for the exchange of propositions between communicators, which in turn illuminates their relationship. Regarding the creation of paradigms, Bateson (1955), in explaining why the individual plays, suggested that the player plays in order to create novel frames and therefore novel thoughts for himself. In creating novel meanings, formulations are made that are clearly alternatives, reversals, or amendments to the everyday. In this study, Helen drew on her rich background of literary and other cultural myths, her own biographical experiences, as well as her adult playmate in order to bring her play worlds into being. By reframing the major issues of her life in play, she brought her dreams into being. It is on such a basis that Vygotsky (1978) saw play as the very process whereby meaning was created. Such a view may be further explained by considering the notion of play as dialectic, which we will now discuss.

Play as Dialectic

Stressing the reversible and bipolar character of the phenomenon, Sutton-Smith (1976) also suggests that play is best understood in terms of thesis and antithesis. Offering a brief structural definition of play, he writes, "Play is a subset of voluntary behaviors involving a selective mechanism which reverses the usual contingencies of power so as to permit the subject a controllable and dialectical simulation of the moderately unmastered arousal and reduction of everyday life." (pp. 5–6). He also writes, "Play is that voluntary action which has a dialectical structure and which potentiates reversible operations" (1978, p. 766).

Such views draw attention to the bipolar and paradoxical character of play but do more than suggest there are contradictions inherent in its structure. Following the theories of Simmel (in Wolf, 1950)—as espoused by Murphy (1971), and Turner (1974), and Babcock (1978)—it is argued that the individual in play may express behaviors that are either representative or inversive of cultural themes, and often are both. Behaviors, ideas, or feelings felt to be inconsistent or contradictory in the everyday world can in play be brought into novel syntheses and reexamined in that domain. In the present case, the powerless Helen brought themes of both power and powerlessness into play: She was both a wonder woman and a plain, ordinary girl. Her rather rigid need to be powerful (an antithesis of her own everyday predicament and a modeling of some of the adult behavior in her everyday world), in due course gave way to an ability to be less powerful and to allow someone else to be powerful, even in the heartland of her own private fantasies. All of this material was masked in the " stories" that were played, but it was also evolved through them, and they constituted the narrative structure central to the play events. It was as if the dialectical structures of the stories were the living clay or material that Helen had to manipulate behaviorally in order to come to terms with the forces so represented. Remembering, as has been said already, that these "structures" do not exist separately from the people who are playing them, it was Helen's and my mutual responsiveness and acceptance of them that allowed such malleability in the stories, so that transformations could occur over time.

This was a ludic dialectic in which power and powerlessness were put together in new syntheses (the stories). But there was also an adaptive dialectic. There was such tension between Helen's everyday and play realms that in the beginning she was almost desperate to keep them separate. Only then could she guard her secrets and keep them inviolable. With the sharing of those secrets with me, someone who also operated in her everyday world, this rigidity between spheres began to decrease, and both areas showed a new flexibility: She played in the kitchen, and she loved me in the play. The adaptive synthesis here was a new relationship between the two realms, so that they flowed in and out of each other more readily. Her everyday play activities became more easily reversible.

The structural argument as applied to this study is, in sum, that the characters of the play stories enabled transformations in Helen's key metaphor, power. Both her power figures and her powerless figures entered into evolving relationships, resulting in new syntheses within the dialectic. But, being supported as it was by her evolving everyday relationship to me, this dialectic acted upon and brought about changes in that everyday relationship itself. Her increasing trust in me as her play partner allowed her to become more flexible in her relationships with me, and this was an adaptive outcome of the play activity and the earlier dialectic between the play realm and the everyday realm.

Psychoanalytic Theory: Play as Abreaction

A psychoanalytic view of play has dominated theoretical interpretations of play since the 1930s and emanates from Freudian sources. In

Beyond the Pleasure Principle Freud (1976) gave several interpretations of play. The most important and most often used suggests that children in their play repeat everything that has made a great impression on them in actual life, thereby lessening or releasing the emotional charge attached to that event. Through this process of abreaction, they in effect make themselves masters of the situation.

To this relatively narrow view, Erikson (1963) added an emphasis on the growth functions play may serve: "I would look at the play act . . . [where] the emphasis, I think, should be on the ego's need to master the various areas of life, and especially those in which the individual finds his self, his body and his social role wanting and trailing" (p. 212). He then adds that the purpose of play is to "hallucinate ego mastering," but he is quick to point out that "'play' is the undisputed master of only a very slim margin of existence" (p. 212). Later in the same work, he writes, "I propose that the child's play is the infantile form of the human ability to deal with experience by creating model situations and to master reality by experiment and planning" (p. 222).

Thus, a psychoanalytic view would argue that play allows the emotional discharge of private concerns and brings about a new mastery in the process. Here, too, is a bipolar view of play. On the one hand, the child plays to master his anxieties and conflicts, the contention being that the suffering of everyday experience is released in play, leading to renewed equilibrium. On the other hand, however, the content of the play is from the child's inner life and is full of wish fulfillment, hallucinatory material, and, in general, symbolic content bearing the highly malleable spirit of the child.

Although my original purposes were to demonstrate something quite different, there is evidence in this study for the view that play does indeed allow the emotional discharge of private concerns and has content that is rich with symbolic material. In play, Helen was able to voice her sense of low esteem as a child among powerful adults in the family, through enacting a reversal of such everyday realities. Further, although there is no explicit evidence on whether or not she gained new mastery through this activity, the clear development of a symbolic cast of characters through several social and psychosexual stages within the play texts would suggest that such mastery had been taking place. In addition, I was struck by the transformation in Helen's behavior in the everyday realm. Although her initial stance involved being in control of all the elements in the situation, including me, she was soon able to relinquish some control. Not only was she able to acknowledge my adulthood vis-à-vis her childhood, but she was able to be regressed and infantile in the everyday realm. A comparison of

Helen's behavior in Session 1 with that of Sessions 2 and 3 reveals such changes and suggests a spirit of growing flexibility in her relationship with me.

Communications/Psychoanalytic Synthesis: Play as Paraguise

The theory of play as *paraguise*, which is a neologism a colleague and I created from the term paradox and disguise, highlights the work of the two greatest play theorists, Bateson and Freud, and their respective theories of paradox and disguise. We suggest that play then may be seen as a paradoxical language of communication and a disguised expression of human feeling, which lends itself to a variety of masks and masquerades. The masks and masquerades may be used to obscure the expressions and communications of play or to "look the other way while looking at ourselves in the only way we can" (Sutton-Smith & Kelly-Byrne, 1984a, p. 197).

The notion of play as paraguise is our recognition that much is to be gained by acknowledging that Bateson not only drew our attention to the logical structures of play and its communicative function but also alerted us to the primary process character and consequent psychodynamic uses of play. Bateson (1972) saw play akin to an ancient kind of language or communication. Based on the fact that animals have no negatives and that negatives such as biting must therefore be illustrated positively by *not really* biting, Bateson formulated his famous notion about animals' play-fighting. He said that each must know that their playful nipping of each other is not real biting, although it stands for biting. By the same token, although as humans we *have* negatives in play, because we are usually dealing with things that are only partially accessible to consciousness and for which there are also no negatives, we must, in play, state positively what we mean negatively by stating the truth in some reverse form.

Thus it was that Helen, anxious about being weak and powerless, stated this truth in play by becoming the powerful character, Wonder Woman. She said the opposite (power) of what she meant (weakness) to mean the opposite (weakness) of what she said (power). Here Bateson follows Freud in the belief that primary process does not deal in negatives. What Sutton-Smith and I have suggested is that Bateson converts the Freudian notion of reaction formation from an individual problem in symptomology to a general communicational truth (Sutton-Smith & Kelly-Byrne, 1984b, p. 42).

If we add the wish fulfillment of the Freudian view to Bateson's theory, then we can account for the fact that, in play, players not only make the play a "nip rather than a bite" but often connote much worse, in their own imaginative way. Thus, in play, Helen not only portrayed her primary caretaker as she was (powerful and controlling) but also played her as Hera, the wicked wife of Zeus, which she was not. To rephrase the Batesonian statement to apply to this extreme: "A nip connotes a bite and even worse than a bite connotes" (Sutton-Smith & Kelly-Byrne, 1984b, p. 42).

On the whole, the present study gives one a profound appreciation of the importance of a synthesis between communicational and psychoanalytic theories of play. We see how Helen took the outer and publicly sanctioned form, play, with all its literary and mass-media symbols and plots, as her medium and mask and subverted these to her private ends and thereby emerged with a new kind of knowledge and power over herself and her worlds. By the end of this study, Helen's own life concerns, which she at first played with and narrated symbolically, were much more directly expressed.

Play as Symbolic and Dramatistic Action

In concluding this section on play, I shall consider the usefulness of Burke's (1966) theory (discussed in Chapter 2) of language as symbolic and dramatistic action used to make sense of the play event. What is most striking about the method of analysis implicit in Burke's perspective is that his three principles—grammar, rhetoric and symbolism—may be used to describe the three faces of play in this event, as I did throughout the play session commentaries in Part II. Not only do these principles subsume the other major theories used to discuss play in this study, but they have also been useful in explaining the structures of participation at an individual level in this play event. In the case of the former claim, it can be seen how a communications theory of play underlines the rhetorical aspects of the phenomenon, how a dialectical view emphasizes its structural aspects, and how a psychoanalytic model deals with its personal and symbolic facets. In supporting the latter claim, the study has argued that in each play session the principles, grammar, rhetoric, and symbolism operated to encompass the basic situation being negotiated; that is, that some calculus of these factors intertwined to lend shape to the participants' interactions.

Conclusions

In the final analysis, all models or metaphors are instruments for understanding the phenomenon at hand and only useful if acknowledged as such. They do not constitute the event itself, but are partial descriptions of it which involve a "seeing as," in Wittgenstein's (1958) sense.

It is my hope that, by presenting this elaborate account of the intertwining of play and fantasy on the road to human understanding, we can free "play" from many of the negative and trivial connotations of its past, and also from some of the idealizations and romanticizations that have developed in this century. Play is a part of the way in which humans communicate their total human nature to each other. Because they are uncertain about themselves, they often must do it in masklike ways; indeed, perhaps they are only able to do it in masklike ways. When these ways are supported by the participation of others, the players join together in mutual acceptance. On occasion, however, the wraps are withdrawn and it becomes possible for the players to understand each other as intimates and truly share in candid and conversational ways their deeper sense of themselves and their worlds, as Helen did with me.

SUPPORTING AND MODIFYING PREVAILING CONCEPTIONS

In the prior section the work of several leading theorists was examined in terms of how their views of play illuminate much that occurred in Helen's play world and in our relationship. In this section, I reverse this perspective and take a look at fourteen ways in which Helen's play both supports and challenges some views of play that have been held to be general truths and lends a different hue to others.

1. Much play research in public settings focuses on staging behaviors as crucial to the behavior. Helen's play, however, shows that, although staging behaviors are necessary and sufficient to accomplish the purposes of the public world, they are insufficient for the personal world and its sharing. The latter world calls for both planned and shared plots (see Session 1).
2. We must modify the notion that management and/or exploration always precede play. As this case shows, among friends (those who have a shared play history), play gestures can provide the initial connection (see Session 3).
3. In the face of those who expect children to play under all manner of conditions, this work suggests that one needs to be in a nonstressed state to contemplate play (see Sessions 11 and 14).
4. In play situations other than solitary play, the ease and intensity of the play are contingent on developments in the relationships. Once

there is a rapport established and a shared library of scripts, play can occur easily and quickly, with little or no negotiation (see Session 5).

5. The study illustrates amply how children and adults define situations for each other, via their use of metacommunicative signals such as imitations, orientations, evaluations, temporal and spatial arrangements, front- and backstage behaviors, and so on (see Sessions 1 and 10).

6. The course of the relationship and its many interactions show that encounters are never just encounters; there is a situation to be managed and particular kinds of people involved whose needs require consideration. Many play studies name the encounters according to their settings (e.g., playgrounds, peer groups, or nursery schools) and ignore the numerous other variables that influence the meaning of what occurs.

7. The study corroborates the finding by many play therapists that, for most children, the fantasy realm is their arena for autonomy, a place where they feel less inclined either to explain their behavior or surrender their authority (Erikson, 1963).

8. Helen's play exemplifies that play is often a struggle to deal with conflicts of experience in terms of a variety of disguises that will protect the player from the dangers perceived in that experience and at the same time permit an intensely motivated assertion of the player's own power to make sense, to synthesize, and to overcome dangers.

9. The study illustrates that play is a mask for other concerns than those overtly suggested by the action.

10. We see that all manner of transformation is clearly possible in play.

11. The child's behavior in and out of play suggests that activity in prior plots as well as in other nonplay realms (e.g., TV or the everyday world) affects behavior not only in later plots but in other realms. Thus, behaviors are not contained within specific realms but overflow into and influence others.

12. The study corroborates Garvey's (1976) point that the use of play to effect interpersonal interaction is characteristic of children's communicational patterns.

13. Helen's play suggests that, although children draw on a common cultural repertoire of scripts in their play, the particular structural organization of the play is related to the particular players and their relationships. Thus, the common library of scripts is peculiarly translated by individual players and their mates.

14. Helen's early play with her peers (Anne and Jill), in contrast to her play with me, corroborates the point made by Garvey (1976) and Schwartzman (1978) that much play among peers is taken up with negotiation. However, contrary to this view, Helen's later play with Jill, after they had progressed past this initial stage, included the sharing of plots and much euphoria.

ROUNDING OUT THE VIEW

Just as the study supports some well-known theoretical positions, it also illuminates some aspects of play in childhood that seem to have been hitherto largely ignored by the literature.

Sutton-Smith and I (1984b) have argued that we have idealized childhood play. This study corroborates such a position and clarifies some ways in which most studies of the play of children fail to acknowledge its most important qualities. In such cases, attention to the phenomenon itself—its spirit and protean character—has been subjugated in the quest to define its structure and understand the stages of mastery and competence gained in relation to play. This asymmetry may be considered in a feminist light. I believe that the failure to place children and relationships at the center of inquiry into play, and to see both as active agents in the construction of experience and knowledge, often personal and unruly, reveals the sexist biases and tacitly male assumptions of traditional views of play. Schwartzman (1978) has pointed out that the emphasis on games in the culture also reflects a dominantly male orientation. Careful, contextualized studies of the play of girls, as well as of boys and girls together, suggest that in many instances the play is highly personal, sometimes dreamlike, and at others active and competitive. In all cases, however, the play is a private affair, where the relationships among the players are paramount. The denial of the presence of the subject as active—a constructor, actor, and knower in the play—and of the subject's motivation to connect with another in the play, is a manifestation of a sociocultural system in which the impersonal and instrumental are valued over the personal in the name of precision and progress. It is a similar concern with precision, ease, and order that drives adults to the sidelines from which to unravel the meanings of children's behavior in play that often results in pallid and incomplete accounts of the give-and-take of play.

A fundamental focus of Helen's play was clearly the character of the interpersonal relationships involved in risking, initiating, and maintaining play. It may be argued that, in contrast, the culture encourages boys to subordinate relationships to a concern for action, skill, and/or victory. As Helen's play shows, however, she was as much concerned with action, skill, and victory as she was with the shaping of relationships in her play. Both collaboration and competition were evident in our sessions. With the exception of the work of Hughes (1983), which illustrates the competitive and nasty nature of the games of little girls alongside the other nice and collaborative qualities usually associated with girls' play, the literature is sadly lacking in describing the multifaceted play lives of girls.

Helen's play also alerts us to how important a sense of power was to Helen. She explored it in connection with her own identity and life relationships. It was a central metaphor and motive for her play. In order to be all-powerful, Helen set up many hierarchical structures in which she sought to control others and in so doing aggrandize herself. This behavior stands in contrast to the view that, in play, girls always set up egalitarian communities and are not concerned with power and hierarchy.

Further, the study draws attention to the display of sexual interest as well as the hedonistic quality of Helen's play. I have observed these qualities in the play of other children as well (Kelly-Byrne, 1984a, 1985, 1986a, 1986b) and find it strange that it has been largely ignored, despite Freud (1963), who alerted us to the sexuality of children a good while ago. Helen's play, as well as that of the five-to-seven-year-olds I am currently observing, suggest that childhood play often is concerned with genitalia; the infringement of taboos pertaining to sexuality and scatology; and curiosity about bodily functions, kissing, and making love; and is filled with excitement generated by touching of genitals, pulling down others' pants, spying on other children using bathrooms, and the like (Kelly-Byrne, 1988). To date, however, as far as I know, there have been no accounts of latency-aged female children's experience of play and sexuality, other than in terms of preadolescent romance with animals, prelatency oedipal romance, and the stereotypes associated with teen romance.

As adults, we must acknowledge that little girls and boys are creators and perpetrators of a rich folklore of sexuality that includes far more than the veiled representations of childhood interest in sexuality that adults generally are willing to concede. We need several other detailed accounts that describe how girls and boys learn about intimacy and bonding with their peers. Helen experienced both bonding and intimacy in play, and this is being corroborated by the behavior of the three children I am currently observing, who share long periods of play together, engage in taboo behavior where they run the risk of being discovered, trespass in forbidden areas, and squirrel away objects usually denied them by their elders, for use in their own play. It appears that such shared activity, all seen as part of these children's play, functions to create a sense of *communitas* among these children.

These are all aspects of children's play that bear testimony to its perverse, immoderate, and unruly aspects; to its sexuality, its competitive spirit, its rough-and-tumble quality, and its passionate, bacchanalian revelry. Yet these facets remain largely unacknowledged by those who advocate for and study children's play with few exceptions (see Sluckin, 1981; Sutton-Smith, 1981a). In particular, such qualities are especially unvoiced in relation to the play of girls. But, as Helen's play suggests, to ignore such elementary aspects of the play of girls is to continue to take a two-worlds approach to the study of gender, separately describing and comparing the subcultures of boys and girls. Such an approach continues the dichotomized, idealized, and stereotypic categories that have bedeviled attempts to define and understand play as gender-specific behavior. Being so far off the mark, it fails to conceptualize gender as part of a system of relationships and differences in which productive interaction involves the active participation of the players (both girls and boys) in the instruction of meaning. When systems, texts, or prescribed experience are firmly in the hands of a homogeneous, dominant class (usually adult and male influenced), then there is no chance to entertain or face the differences and risks inherent in genuine reciprocity.

What we need instead are carefully contexted studies of the play of female children with each other, as well as in close relationships shared with boys, so that we can understand the social relations and meanings generated and communicated in play.

An acknowledgment of the full range of qualities that textured Helen's play, in addition to questioning the pallid, asexual, impersonal, and idealized accounts of childhood play, especially the play of girls, also confronts the distinctions that are assumed to exist between children's and adults' play. Commonly, these realms of behavior are seen to be discontinuous; however, this study suggests that, if we were to look at the play life of children in conditions that were of their own choosing, then features such as sexuality, competitiveness, aggression, secrecy, and intimacy, often associated with adult play, would be seen to characterize much of children's play as well. This suggests a continuity rather than a discontinuity in the uses and spirit of children's and adults' play (Kelly-Byrne, 1984a).

The tendency toward discontinuity and containment in the culture is also evident in the ways in which we make the experience of children conform to rigid categories. Thus, we have not only discrete forms of play but discrete uses of play, as well as other expressive forms that are taken to be categorically separate from play. Such distinctions are tethered to our adult purposes of the socialization and control of children. As the study of Helen's play suggests, however, for young children like her, these genres, so carefully classified by the adult world, are often blurred. Children pay little heed to the ways adults pattern and sequence their thoughts and actions in conformity with adult-oriented "standard" models of these forms. The point is of relevance to educational enterprises of various kinds that require children to organize and evaluate their expressive forms in accordance with adult-conceived models and purposes, thereby disenfranchising the voices and poetic forms of childhood.

It is important that we encourage more studies that explore children's own motivated uses of a variety of cultural forms such as story, drama, and play, so that we can better understand the nature and uses of such forms when in children's hands. We may find that their responses may be far more in keeping with constructs that adults deem innovative than we might care to admit (see Kelly-Byrne, 1986b, for fuller discussion).

Finally, this study is a hymn to the play of childhood. Helen's play unequivocally pays tribute to the excitement of childhood play, to its pleasure, fun, and deeply engrossing spirit. As adults, having trivialized the domain of childhood and its pursuits, we have also trivialized play except as a means by which adult-valued, work-oriented patterns and behaviors are facilitated—whether these be literacy, knowledge of subject areas such as mathematics or history, flexibility, originality, or problem-solving abilities. This attitude has conveniently allowed us to ignore, curtail, constrain, and monitor to death the very qualities of childhood that compel children to risk play away from their elders, even at some cost. Helen's play facilitated meaningful human relationships and symbolized deep and passionate concerns. In the playing out of these concerns via myriad transformations, her play empowered her. The success and power she felt in her play led her into a festival celebration of herself and of the close relationships established, and to a sense of sheer exuberance where she cared little for the constraints of public behavior. It is little wonder that the triviality of play in contrast to the seriousness of work is supported by most adults and their institutions concerned with the socialization of children. It serves these interests to defend against the true spirit of play, which, if encouraged as I did with Helen, would unleash the chaotic and sometimes tabooed aspects of human nature, making a largely adult-controlled and censored childhood problematic.

Our alternative, as adults, is to consider allowing children to manage their own play; to initiate, direct, enact, layer, and transform their concerns and finally close out their play, with all the attendant celebration, whether in wild exuberance or lost in quiet reverie. Then, as was the case with Helen, we open ourselves up to a world of wonderful possibilities and the opportunity to recapture something of our own lost power to transform our experience and our lives.

Epilogue

Helen's story never ends. It is a significant part of my consciousness and informs my thought on many aspects of childhood, in addition to the realm of play and the relationships we as adults set up to it. The power of my experience with Helen has helped me to question continuously much that I read about children and doing research. In a sense, it was somewhat of a trial by fire, in that it constantly challenged the often constraining categories with which I had assumed I could make sense of this data in conventional scholarly ways.

What the study taught me had little to do with undertaking an exercise to confirm scholarly epistemology or satisfy institutional demands. Rather, it asked that I make sense of it on its own terms, where the overarching frame was the story of two human beings who came together with very different motives but who, in the fray of playing together, made a relationship in which they grew to trust and respect one another and to encounter a great deal about their individual selves.

I have sought to convey as much as possible of this to the reader. My efforts to transform experiential time into narrative time in telling the story of Helen and myself were in an attempt not only to lend coherence to the experience but also to take the reader through much of what I underwent during the course of the play sessions with Helen and the relationship that developed.

The study was begun about a decade ago, and yet, years later, I find myself returning to it, to rethink the issues to which it speaks. The dialogues that have ensued about various aspects of the "text" were not only with myself but also with a variety of others who represented different points of view. It is no longer possible to think of this experience without summoning the multiplicity of voices that inhabit my consciousness. But, in the end, they coalesce to represent a voice for which I alone am responsible. The voice reflects my membership in many sociocultural groups, but it is also an intensely personal voice and bears the mark of my own advocacy on behalf of childhood. It urges that we seek to understand our adult investments in childhood and work toward making relationships with children as individuals, in which they are empowered to stake out a place of their own.

References

Adler, A. (1956). The individual psychology of Alfred Adler: A systematic presentation. In H. L. Ansbacher & R. R. Ansbacher (Eds.), *Selections from his writings* (pp. 1009–1037). New York: Basic Books.

Agar, M. H. (1980). *The professional stranger: An informal introduction to ethnography.* New York: Academic Press.

Ames, L. B., & Haber, C. C. (1985). *Your seven-year-old: Life in a minor key.* New York: Delacorte Press.

Axline, V. M. (1964). *Dibs in search of self.* New York: Ballantine Books.

Babcock, B. (Ed.). (1978). *The reversible world.* Ithaca, NY: Cornell University Press.

Baruch, D. W. (1964). *One little boy.* New York: Delta Books.

Bateson, G. (1955, December). A theory of play and fantasy. *Psychiatric Research Reports, 2,* 39–51.

Bateson, G. (1956). The message 'This is play.' In *Group processes: Transactions of the second conference* (pp. 145–246). New York: Josiah Macy Foundation.

Bateson, G. (1972). *Steps to an ecology of mind.* New York: Ballantine Books.

Bateson, G. (1979). *Mind and nature.* New York: Dutton.

Bateson, G., & Ruesch, J. (1951). *Communication: The social matrix of psychiatry.* New York: W. W. Norton.

Bauman, R. (1975). Verbal art as performance. *American Anthropologist, 77,* 290–312.

Berlyne, D. E. (1960). *Conflict arousal and curiosity.* New York: McGraw-Hill.

Betcher, R. W. (1981). Intimate play and marital adaptation. *Psychiatry, 44,* 13–33.

Buhler, C. (1930). *The mental development of children.* New York: Harcourt Brace & World.

Buhler, C. (1935). *From birth to maturity.* London: Routledge & Kegan Paul.

Burke, K. (1941). *The philosophy of literary form.* Berkeley: University of California Press.

Burke, K. (1965). *Permanence and change: An anatomy of purpose.* Indianapolis: Bobbs-Merrill.

Burke, K. (1966). *Language as symbolic action: Essays on life, literature and method.* Berkeley: University of California Press.

Burke, K. (1968). *Counter-statement* (Californian ed.). Berkeley: University of California Press.

Burke, K. (1969a). *A grammar of motives* (Californian ed.). Berkeley: University of California Press.

Burke, K. (1969b). *A rhetoric of motives* (Californian ed.). Berkeley: University of California Press.

Butler, D. (1979). *Cushla and her books*. London: Hodder & Stoughton.

Cesara, M. (1982). *Reflections of a woman anthropologist: No hiding place*. New York: Academic Press.

Cheska, A. (Ed.). (1981). *Play as context*. West Point, NY: Leisure Press.

Cook-Gumperz, J. (1977). *Situated instructions: Language socialization of school age children*. In S. Erving-Tripp & C. Mitchell-Kernan (Eds.), *Child discourse* (pp. 103–121). New York: Academic Press.

Cottrell, L. (1942). The analysis of situational fields in social psychology. *American Sociological Review, 7*, 370–381.

Crago, H., & Crago, M. (1983). *Prelude to literacy*. Carbondale, Southern Illinois University Press.

Csikszentmihayli, M. (1980, April 10). Lecture on author's work on adult leisure pursuits given at the Graduate School of Education, University of Pennsylvania.

Douglas, M. (1966). *Purity and danger*. London: Routledge & Kegan Paul.

Ehrmann, J. (1968). Homo ludens revisited. *Yale French Studies, 41*, 31–57.

Erikson, E. H. (1940). Studies in the interpretation of play: Part I, Clinical observations of play description in young children. *Genetic Psychology Monographs, 22*, 557–671.

Erikson, E. H. (1963). *Childhood and society* (2nd ed.). New York: W. W. Norton.

Erikson, E. H. (1968). *Identity: Youth and crisis*. New York: W. W. Norton.

Erikson, E. H. (1977). *Toys and reasons*. New York: W. W. Norton.

Fagen, R. (1980). *Animal play behavior*. New York: Oxford University Press.

Freud, S. (1953). *The complete psychological works: The interpretation of dreams. Vols. 4 & 5*. J. Strachey (Ed.). London: Hogarth Press. (Original work published in 1900)

Freud, S. (1963). *The sexual enlightenment of children*. New York: Collier.

Freud, S. (1976). *Beyond the pleasure principle*. J. Strachey (Trans.). New York: W. W. Norton. (Original work published in 1920)

Gardner, R. A. (1971). *Therapeutic communication with children: The mutual storytelling technique*. New York: Science House.

Gardner, R. (1986). *The psychotherapeutic techniques of Richard Gardner*. Cresskill, NJ: Creative Therapeutics.

Garvey, C. (1976). *Some properties of social play*. In J. S. Bruner, A. Jolly, K. Sylva (Eds.), *Play: Its role in development and evolution*. London: Penguin Books.

Garvey, C. (1977). *Play*. Cambridge, MA: Harvard University Press.

Garvey, C., & Berndt, R. (1977). *Organization of pretend play. Catalog of Selected Documents in Psychology, 7*, 1589. American Psychological Association.

Geertz, C. (1972). Deep play: Notes on the Balinese cockfight. *Daedalus, 101*, 1–37.

Giffin, H. (1984). The co-ordination of shared meaning in the creation of a shared make-believe reality. In I. Bretherton (Ed.), *Symbolic play: The representation of social understanding* (pp. 73–100). New York: Academic Press.

Goffman, E. (1959). *The presentation of self in everyday life.* New York: Anchor Books.

Goffman, E. (1961). *Encounters.* New York: Penguin Books.

Goffman, E. (1963). *Behavior in public places.* New York: The Free Press.

Goffman, E. (1967). *Interaction ritual.* New York: Anchor Books.

Goffman, E. (1974). *Frame analysis.* Cambridge, MA: Harvard University Press.

Goffman, E. (1981). *Forms of talk.* Philadelphia: University of Pennsylvania Press.

Golde, P. (Ed.) (1986). *Women in the Field.* Berkeley: University of California Press.

Groos, K. (1901). *The play of man.* New York: Appleton.

Haley, J. (1955, December). Paradoxes in play, fantasy and psychotherapy. *Psychiatric Research Reports, 2* 52–58.

Hall, G. S. (1917). *Youth: Its education, regimen and hygiene.* New York: Appleton.

Hartley, R. E. (1952). *Growing through play: Experiences of Teddy and Bud.* New York: Columbia University Press.

Hartley, R. E., Frank, L. K., & Goldenson, R. M. (1952). *Understanding children's play.* New York: Columbia University Press.

Hern, H. (1969). Play as an aesthetic concept. *Humanitas, 5,* 21–28.

Herron, R. E., & Sutton-Smith, B. (1971). *Child's play.* New York: John Wiley.

Hughes, L. (1983). Beyond the rules of the game: Why are Rooie rules nice? In F. Manning (Ed.), *The world of play* (pp. 188–199). West Point, NY: Leisure Press.

Huizinga, J. (1958). *Homo ludens.* Boston: Beacon Press.

Hutt, C. (1979). Exploration and play. In B. Sutton-Smith (Ed.), *Play and learning* (pp. 175–194). New York: Gardner Press.

Hyman, S. E. (1955). *The armed vision.* New York: Vintage Books.

Hymes, D. H. (1964). Introduction: Toward ethnographies of communication. *American Anthropologist* [Special Publication], *66,* 1–4.

Hymes, D. H. (1974a). *Foundations in sociolinguistics.* Philadelphia: University Press.

Hymes, D. H. (1974b). Ways of speaking. In R. Bauman & J. Sherzer (Eds.), *Explorations in the ethnography of speaking* (pp. 433–451). New York: Cambridge University Press.

Hymes, D. H. (1975). Breakthrough into performance. In D. Ben-Amos & K. Goldstein (Eds.), *Folklore: Performance and communication* (pp. 11–74). The Hague, The Netherlands: Mouton.

Hymes, D. H. (1980). *Language in education: Ethnolinguistic essays.* Washington, DC: Center for Applied Linguistics.

Hymes, D. H. (1981). *"In vain I tried to tell you." Essays in Native American ethnopoetics.* Philadelphia: University of Pennsylvania Press.

Kelly, D. (1977). *Play and drama: Some theoretical considerations.* Unpublished master's dissertation, University of London, Institute of Education.

Kelly-Byrne, D. (1982). *A narrative of play and intimacy.* Unpublished doctoral dissertation, University of Pennsylvania.

Kelly-Byrne, D. (1984a). Continuity and discontinuity in play conditioning: The adult-child connection. In B. Sutton-Smith & D. Kelly-Byrne (Eds.), *The masks of play* (pp. 171–180). New York: Leisure Press.

Kelly-Byrne, D. (1984b). Making a relationship: A context for fabling. In F. Kessel & A. Goncu (Eds.), *Dialogue and imaginative play*. New Directions for Child Development (pp. 37–51). San Francisco: Jossey-Bass.

Kelly-Byrne, D. (1985, September 3–5). *Child culture, girls' play and ambivalence*. Paper presented to the International Symposium on Youth Culture: The Third Rainbow Week, Toulouse, France.

Kelly-Byrne, D. (1986a, May 12–15). *The childhood stockmarket: Hidden and ambivalent investments*. Keynote address to the Australian and New Zealand Conference on The First Years of School: Today's Challenges, Sydney, Australia.

Kelly-Byrne, D. (1986b, July 2–5). *Children and literature: First steps*. Keynote address to the Australian Reading Association Conference, Perth.

Kelly-Byrne, D. (1988, April 21–24). *The rhetoric of control: Asexual and innocent portraits of children*. Paper presented to the Meeting of the California Folklore Society and the Association for the Study of Play, Berkeley, California.

Kelly-Byrne, D., & Sutton-Smith, B. (1983). Narrative as social science: A case study. *The Quarterly Newsletter of the Laboratory of Comparative Human Cognition, 5,* 4.

Knapp, M., & Knapp, H. (1976). *One potato, two potato*. New York: W. W. Norton.

Kuhn, T. S. (1970). *The structure of scientific revolutions* (2nd ed.). Chicago: University of Chicago Press.

Lancy, D., & Tindale, B. (Eds.). (1976). *The anthropological study of play: Problems and prospects*. West Point, NY: Leisure Press.

Levi-Strauss, C. (1966). *The savage mind*. Chicago: University of Chicago Press.

Lieberman, J. N. (1977). *Playfulness: Its relationship to imagination and creativity*. New York: Academic Press.

Lofland, J. (1971). *Analyzing social settings*. Belmont, CA: Wadsworth.

Loy, J. (Ed.). (1982). *The paradoxes of play*. West Point, NY: Leisure Press.

Luthi, M. (1976). *Once upon a time: On the nature of fairy tales*. Bloomington: Indiana University Press.

Manning, F. (Ed.). (1983). *The world of play*. West Point, NY: Leisure Press.

McMahon, J. H. (1982). Intimacy among friends and lovers. In M. Fisher & G. Stricker (Eds.), *Intimacy* (pp. 293–304). New York: Plenum.

Mead, M. (1986). Fieldwork in Pacific islands, 1925–1967. In F. Golde (Ed.), *Women in the field* (pp. 293–331). Berkeley & Los Angeles: University of California Press.

Mergen, D. (1982). *Play and playthings: A reference guide*. Westport, CT: Greenwood Press.

Milner, M. (1952). Aspects of symbolism in comprehension of the not self. *International Journal of Psycho-Analysis, 33,* 181–195.

Moreno, J. L. (1972). *Psychodrama* (Vol. 1). New York: Beacon House.

Murphy, R. F. (1971). *The dialectics of social life*. New York: Basic Books.

Mussen, P. (Ed.). (1983). *Handbook of child development*. (Vol. 4). New York: John Wiley.

Nash, D., & Wintrob, R. (1972). The emergence of self-consciousness in ethnography. *Current Anthropology, 13,* 527–552.

Neill, A. S. (1960). *Summerhill*. New York: Hart.

Opie, I., & Opie, P. (1959). *The lore of language and school children*. New York: Oxford University Press.

Pelto, P. J., & Pelto, G. H. (1978). *Anthropology research: The structure of inquiry*. New York: Cambridge University Press.

Piaget, J. (1926). *Judgement and reasoning in the child*. M. Worden (Trans.). New York: Harcourt, Brace & World.

Piaget, J. (1929). *The child's conception of the world*. J. Tomlinson & A. Tomlinson (Trans.). New York: Harcourt, Brace & World.

Piaget, J. (1932). *The moral judgement of the child*. M. Gabain (Trans.). New York: Harcourt, Brace & World.

Piaget, J. (1952). *Play, dreams and imitation in childhood*. G. Gattegno, F. M. Hodgson (Trans.). New York: W. W. Norton.

Powdermaker, H. (1967). *Stranger and friend*. New York: W. W. Norton.

Rubin, K. H. (1980). Fantasy play: Its role in the development of social skills and social-cognition. In K. H. Rubin (Ed.), *New Directions for Child Development, 9*, 69–84. San Francisco: Jossey-Bass.

Rubin, K. H., Fein, G., & Vandenberg, B. (1983). Children's play. In E. M. Hetherington (Ed.), *Handbook of child psychology* (Vol. 4, pp. 694–774). New York: John Wiley.

Rubin, K. H., & Pepler, D. J. (1980). The relationship of child's play to social-cognitive growth and development. In H. Foot, J. Smith, & T. Chapman (Eds.), *Friendship and social relations in children* (pp. 209–233). London: John Wiley.

Ruby, J. (Ed.). (1982). *A crack in the mirror: Reflective perspectives in anthropology*. Philadelphia: University of Pennsylvania Press.

Sadler, W., Jr. (1966). Play: A basic human structure involving love and freedom. *Review of Existential Psychology and Psychiatry, 6*, 237–245.

Schafer, R. (1981). Narration in the psychoanalytic dialogue. In W. J. Mitchell (Ed.), *On narrative* (pp. 25–50). Chicago: University of Chicago Press.

Schaffer, H. R. (1977). *Studies in mother-infant interaction*. London: Academic Press.

Schechner, R. (1977). *Essays in performance theory, 1970–1976*. New York: Drama Book Specialists.

Schutz, A. (1964). Common sense and scientific interpretation of human action. In A. Brodersen (Ed.), *Collected Papers II: Studies in social theory*. The Hague, The Netherlands: Martinus Nijhoff.

Schutz, A. (1967). *Phenomenology of the social world*. F. Lehnert (Trans.). Evanston, IL: Northwestern University Press.

Schutz, A. (1976). *On phenomenology and social relations*. Chicago: University of Chicago Press.

Schwartzman, H. B. (1973). *An ethnographic study of make-believe in a nursery school*. Unpublished doctoral dissertation, University of Chicago.

Schwartzman, H. B. (1976). Children's play: A sideways glance at make-believe. In D. F. Lancy & B. A. Tindale (Eds.), *The anthropological study of play: Problems and prospects* (pp. 198–205). New York: Leisure Press.

Schwartzman, H. B. (1978). *Transformations: The anthropology of children's play*. New York: Plenum Press.

Schwartzman, H. B. (Ed.). (1980). *Play and culture*. West Point, NY: Leisure Press.

Scollon, R., & Scollon, S. (1981). *Narrative, literacy and interethnic communication*. Norwood, NJ: Ablex.

Shultz, T. R. (1979). Play as arousal modulation. In B. Sutton-Smith (Ed.), *Play and learning* (pp. 7–22). New York: Gardner Press.

Simmel, G. (1977). *The problems of the philosophy of history: An epistemological essay*. (G. Oakes, Trans.). New York: Free Press.

Singer, J. L. (1973). *The child's world of make-believe*. New York: Academic Press.

Singer, J. L., & Singer, D. (1981). *Partners in play*. New York: Random House.

Sluckin, A. (1981). *Growing up in the playground*. Boston: Routledge & Kegan Paul.

Smilansky, S. (1968). *The effects of sociodramatic play on disadvantaged pre-school children*. New York: John Wiley.

Spariosu, M. (1982). Literature and play: History, principles, method. In M. Spariosu (Ed.), *Literature, mimesis and play* (pp. 65–106). Tubingen, West Germany: Gunter Narr Verlag.

Spencer, H. (1873). *The principles of psychology* (Vol. 2). New York: D. Appleton.

Sullivan, H. S. (1970). *The psychiatric interview*. New York: W. W. Norton.

Sutton-Smith, B. (1971). Boundaries. In R. E. Herron & B. Sutton-Smith (Eds.), *Child's play* (pp. 103–106). New York: John Wiley.

Sutton-Smith, B. (1974). Toward an anthropology of play. *Newsletter of the Association for the Anthropological Study of Play, 1*, 8–15.

Sutton-Smith, B. (1975). Play as adaptive potentiation. *Sportwissenchaft, 3*, 103–118.

Sutton-Smith, B. (1976). *The dialectics of play*. Schorndoff, West Germany: Verlag Hoffman.

Sutton-Smith, B. (1978). The dialectics of play. In S. Landry & W. Oban (Eds.), *Physical activity and human well-being* (Vol. 2, pp. 759–767). Miami, FL: Symposia Specialists.

Sutton-Smith, B. (1979). Play as metaperformance. In B. Sutton-Smith (Ed.), *Play and learning* (pp. 295–322). New York: Gardner Press.

Sutton-Smith, B. (1981a). *The folkstories of children*. Philadelphia: University of Pennsylvania Press.

Sutton-Smith, B. (1981b). *A history of children's play*. Philadelphia: The University of Pennsylvania Press.

Sutton-Smith, B. (1983). One hundred years of change in play research. *Newsletter of the Association for the Anthropological Study of Play, 9*(2), 13–15.

Sutton-Smith, B. (1985). *Toys as culture*. New York: Gardner Press.

Sutton-Smith, B. (1986). The spirit of play. In G. Fein & M. Rivkin (Eds.), *The young child at play* (pp. 3–13). Reviews of Research, Volume 4. Washington, DC: National Association for the Education of Young Children.

Sutton-Smith, B., & Kelly-Byrne, D. (Eds.). (1984a). *The masks of play*. New York: Leisure Press.

Sutton-Smith, B., & Kelly-Byrne, D. (Eds.). (1984b). The idealization of play. In P. K. Smith (Ed.), *Play in animals and humans* (pp. 305–321). Berkshire, England: Van Nostrand.

Sutton-Smith, B., & Roberts, J. M. (1964). Rubrics of competitive behavior. *Journal of Genetic Psychology, 105,* 13–37.

Sutton-Smith, B., & Roberts, J. M. (1970). The cross-cultural and psychological study of games. In G. Lucshen (Ed.), *The cross-cultural analysis of games* (pp. 100–108). Champaign, IL: Stipes.

Turner, V. (1969). *The ritual process: Structure and anti-structure.* Chicago: Aldine.

Turner, V. (1974). *Dramas, fields and metaphors.* Ithaca, NY: Cornell University Press.

Turner, V. (1982). *Celebration, studies in festivity and ritual.* Washington, DC: Smithsonian Institute Press.

Van Gennep, A. (1960). *The rites of passage.* M. Zedom & G. Caffe (Trans.). Chicago: University of Chicago Press.

Vygotsky, L. S. (1967). Play and its role in the mental development of the child. *Soviet Psychology, 5,* 6–18.

Vygotsky, L. S. (1978). *Mind in society.* Cambridge, MA: Harvard University Press.

Wax, R. (1952). Field methods and techniques: Reciprocity as a field technique. *Human Organization, 11*(3), 34–47.

White, D. (1954). *Books before five.* New York: Oxford University Press.

Whyte, W. F. (1955). *Street corner society: The social structure of an Italian slum.* Chicago: University of Chicago Press.

Williams, R. (1982). *Towards 2000.* London: Chatto & Windus: Hogarth.

Winnicott, D. W. (1971). *Playing and reality.* Harmondsworth, England: Penguin Books.

Wittgenstein, L. (1958). *Philosophical investigations* (2nd ed.). Oxford, England: Basil Blackwell.

Wolf, K. H. (1950). *The sociology of George Simmel.* New York: Free Press.

Wolfson, N. (1979). Speech events and natural speech: Some implications for sociolinguistic methodology. *Language and Society, 5,* 189–202.

Bibliography

Bateson, G. (1956). Towards a theory of schizophrenia. *Behavioral Science, 1*, 251–264.

Benedict, R. (1959). *Patterns of culture*. Boston: Houghton Mifflin. (Original work published 1934)

Berger, P. L., & Luckman, T. (1966). *The social construction of reality*. Garden City, NY: Doubleday.

Birdwhistell, R. L. (1970). *Kinesics and context*. Philadelphia: University of Pennsylvania Press.

Britton, J. (1970). *Language and learning*. Harmondsworth, England: Penguin Books.

Cassirer, E. (1961). *The logic of the humanities*. New Haven, CT: Yale University Press.

Chatman, S. (1978). *Books, story and discourse*. Ithaca, NY: Cornell University Press.

Cottrell, L., & Gallagher, R. (1941). *Developments in social psychology (1930–1940)*. New York: Beacon House.

Covenay, P. (1967). *The image of childhood*. Baltimore, MD: Penguin Books.

Derrida, J. (1976). *Of grammatology*. Baltimore, MD: Johns Hopkins University Press.

Devereaux, G. (1967). *From anxiety to method in the behavioral sciences*. New York: Humanities Press.

Dewey, J. (1916). *Democracy and education: An introduction to the philosophy of education*. New York: Macmillan.

Dixon, J. (1975). *Growth through English* (3rd ed.). Reading, England: Cox and Wyman.

Doyle, A. B., Connolly, J., & Rivest, L. P. (1980). The effect of playmate familiarity on the social interactions of young children. *Child Development, 51* 217–223.

Dundes, A. (1965). *The study of folklore*. Englewood Cliffs, NJ: Prentice-Hall.

Erikson, E. H. (1943). Clinical studies in childhood play. In R. G. Barker, J. S. Kounin, & H. F. Wright (Eds.), *Child behavior and development* (pp. 411–428). New York: McGraw-Hill.

Fabian, J. (1971). Language, history and anthropology. *Philosophy of the Social Sciences, 1*(1), 19–47.

Fein, G. G. (1981). Pretend play in childhood: An integrative review. *Child Development, 52*, 1095–1118.

Fein, G. G., & Apfel, N. (1979). The development of play: Style, structure and situation. *Genetic Psychology Monographs, 99*, 231–250.

Freud, S. (1909). *The Complete Psychological Works of Sigmund Freud: Vol. 10. Analysis of a phobia in a five-year-old boy* (standard ed.). London: Hogarth Press.

Freud, A. (1964). *The psychoanalytical treatment of children.* New York: Schocken Books. (Original work published in 1946)

Goffman, E. (1971). *Relations in public.* New York: Harper & Row.

Griffin, M. S. (1978). *A study of structure in films made by children.* Unpublished master's thesis, Annenberg School of Communications, University of Pennsylvania.

Griffiths, R. (1949). *A study of imagination in early childhood and its function in mental development.* London: Routledge & Kegan Paul.

Hardy, B. (1975). *Tellers and listeners.* London: Athlone Press.

Heath, S. (1983). *Ways with words: Language, life and work in communities and classroom.* London: Cambridge University Press.

Isaacs, S. (1933). *Social development in young children: A study of beginnings.* London: Routledge & Kegan Paul.

Isaacs, S. (1935). *Intellectual growth in children.* London: Routledge & Kegan Paul.

Jacobson, R. (1971). Studies in child language and aphasia. A. R. Keiler (Trans.). The Hague, The Netherlands: Mouton.

Kaplan, B. (1980). *Basking in Burke.* Unpublished manuscript.

Kelly-Byrne, D. (1983). A narrative of play and intimacy. In F. Manning (Ed.), *The world of play* (pp. 160–169). New York: Leisure Press.

Kirshenblatt-Gimblett, B. (1976). *Speech play.* Philadelphia: University of Pennsylvania Press.

Klein, M. (1955). The psychoanalytic play technique. *American Journal of Orthopsychiatry, 25*, 223–237.

Kristeva, J. (1980). *Desire in language: A semiotic approach to literature and art.* New York: Columbia University Press.

Levinson, E. (1974). Changing concepts of intimacy in psychoanalytic practice. *Contemporary Psychoanalysis, 10*, 351–369.

Levi-Strauss, C. (1967). *Structural anthropology.* Garden City, NY: Anchor Books.

Lowenfeld, M. (1967). *Play in childhood.* New York: John Wiley. (Original work published in 1935)

Matthews, W. S. (1978, March). Interruptions of fantasy play: A manner of breaking frame. Paper presented at the annual meeting of the Eastern Psychological Association, Washington, DC.

McDermott, J. J. (Ed.). (1977). *The writings of William James.* Chicago: University of Chicago Press.

Mead, G. H. (1934). *Mind, self and society.* Chicago: University of Chicago Press.

Mead, M. (1930). *Growing up in New Guinea.* New York: Dell.

Mead, M. (1949). *Coming of age in Samoa.* New York: Mentor Books.

Mead, M., & Wolfenstein, M. (1955). *Childhood in contemporary cultures*. Chicago: University of Chicago Press.

Medvedev, P. N., & Bakhtin, M. (1978). *The formal method in literary scholarship*. Albert J. Wehrle (Trans.). Baltimore: Johns Hopkins University Press.

Michaels, S. (1981). Sharing time: Children's narrative styles and differential access to literacy. *Language in Society, 10*(3), 423–442.

Miller, S. (1968). *The psychology of play*. Harmondsworth, England: Penguin Books.

Moffet, J. (1968). *Teaching the universe of discourse*. Boston: Houghton Mifflin.

Moreno, J. L. (1973). *The theatre of spontaneity*. New York: Beacon House.

Mueller, E., & DeStefano, C. (1973). *Sources of toddlers' peer interaction in a playgroup setting*. Unpublished paper, Boston University.

Mueller, E., & Vandell, D. (1979). Infant-infant interaction. In J. D. Osofsky (Ed.), *The handbook of infant development* (pp. 591–622). New York: John Wiley.

Natanson, M. (Ed.). (1963). *Philosophy and the social sciences*. New York: Random House.

Opie, I., & Opie, P. (1969). *Children's games in street and playground*. Oxford, England: Clavendow Press.

Perry, H. S. (1982). *Psychiatrist of America: The life of Harry Stack Sullivan*. Cambridge, MA: Belknap Press.

Piaget, J. (1926). *The language and thought of the child*. M. Gab (Trans.). London: Routledge & Kegan Paul.

Piaget, J. (1954). *The construction of reality in the child*. M. Cook (Trans.). New York: Basic Books.

Rorty, R. (1979). *Philosophy and the mirror of nature*. Princeton, NJ: Princeton University Press.

Sacks, H. (1967). Fall quarter transcribed lecture notes given at the University of California at Irvin, Department of Anthropology.

Sacks, H. (1971, April). Transcribed lecture notes given at the University of California at Irvin, Department of Anthropology.

Sacks, H. (1972). On the analyzability of stories by children. In J. Gumperz & D. Hymes (Eds.), *Directions in sociolinguistics* (pp. 325–345). New York: Holt, Rinehart and Winston.

Schutz, A. (1954). Concept and theory formation in the social sciences. *The Journal of Philosophy, 51*(9): 257–274.

Schutz, A. (1962). *Collected papers, Vol. 1: The problem of social reality*. The Hague, The Netherlands: Martinus Nijhoff.

Sullivan, H. S. (1953a). *Conceptions of modern psychology*. New York: W. W. Norton.

Sullivan, H. S. (1953b). *The interpersonal theory of psychiatry*. New York: W. W. Norton.

Sutton-Smith, B. (1979, June 2). *Piaget, play and cognition revisited*. Paper presented at the annual meeting of the Jean Piaget Society, Philadelphia.

Sutton-Smith, B., & Heath, S. B. (1981). Paradigms of pretense. *Quarterly Newsletter of the Laboratory of Comparative Human Cognition, 3*(3), 41–45.

Sutton-Smith, B., & Kelly-Byrne, D. (1983). The phenomenon of bipolarity in play theories. In T. D. Yawkey & A. D. Pellegrini (Eds.), *Child's play: Developmental and applied* (pp. 29–47). Hillsdale, NJ: Lawrence Erlbaum Associates.

Thorne, B. (1986). Girls and boys together . . . but mostly apart: Gender arrangements in elementary schools. In W. Hartrup & Z. Rubin (Eds.), *Relationships and development*. Hillsdale, NJ: Lawrence Erlbaum Associates.

Vandenberg, B. (1978). Play and development: An ethological perspective. *American Psychologist, 88,* 724–738.

Volosinov, V. N. (1973). Marxism and the philosophy of language. L. Matejka & I. R. Titunik (Trans). New York & London: Seminar Press.

Wax, M. L. (1977). On fieldworkers and those exposed to fieldwork. *Human Organization, 36,* 321–328.

Wax, R. (1983). The ambiguities of fieldwork. In R. Emerson (Ed.), *Contemporary field research*. Boston: Little, Brown.

Weir, R. (1962). *Language in the crib.* The Hague, The Netherlands: Mouton.

Wolfenstein, M. (1958). *Children's humor.* Glencoe, IL: Free Press.

Young, K. (1978). Indirection in storytelling. *Western Folklore, 1,* 44–55.

Index

About the Author

Diana Kelly-Byrne received her Ph.D. in education from the University of Pennsylvania in 1982. While there, for many years she directed a program called Child Culture, Literature and Imagination, in the Graduate School of Education. At present, she is a full-time research fellow at the Centre for Studies in Literary Education in the School of Humanities, at Deakin University, Victoria, Australia. She is currently coordinating a new project entitled, "Gender Frames in Literary Learning."

She has studied and taught in Australia, Britain, and the United States. Her publications include *The Masks of Play*, which she co-edited with Brian Sutton-Smith, and several professional articles in the areas of children's literature, folklore, play, socialization, and adult/child interaction.